Connecticut &
Rhode Island

Anna Mundow
Photography by James Marshall

D1412383

COMPASS AMERICAN GUIDES
An imprint of Fodor's Travel Publications

Compass American Guides: Connecticut & Rhode Island

Editors: Daniel Mangin, Chris Culwell, Kristin Moehlmann
Designers: Tina Malaney, Siobhan O'Hare
Compass Editorial Director: Daniel Mangin
Photo Editor: Jolie Novak
Archival Research: Melanie Marin
Map Design: Mark Stroud, Moon Street Cartography
Editorial Production: David Downing

First Edition
ISBN 0–676–90492–0
ISSN 1541–2857

Compass American Guides, 1745 Broadway, New York, NY 10019

PRINTED IN SINGAPORE
10 9 8 7 6 5 4 3 2 1

For my parents

C O N T E N T S

Literary Extracts and Essays

Sidebars

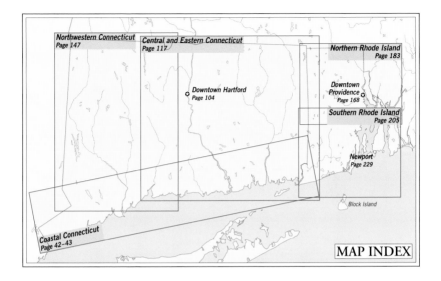

Northwestern Connecticut
Page 147

Central and Eastern Connecticut
Page 117

Northern Rhode Island
Page 183

Downtown Hartford
Page 104

Downtown Providence
Page 168

Southern Rhode Island
Page 205

Newport
Page 229

Block Island

Coastal Connecticut
Page 42–43

MAP INDEX

Maps

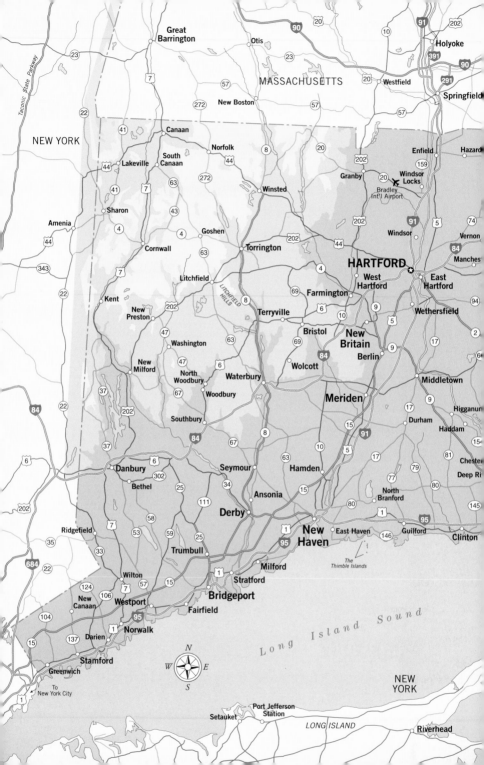

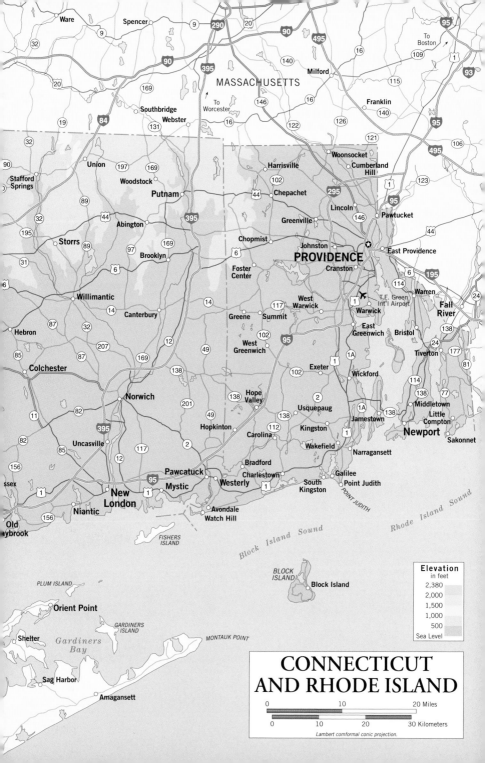

CONNECTICUT
AND RHODE ISLAND

Elevation
in feet
2,380
2,000
1,500
1,000
500
Sea Level

0   10   20 Miles
0   10   20   30 Kilometers
Lambert comformal conic projection.

Ware
Spencer
9
290
20
95
To Boston
109
1
32
9
90
93
MASSACHUSETTS
140
Milford
16
115
495
Southbridge
395
146
Franklin
140
95
19
84
Webster
131
To Worcester
16
122
126
121
106
32
90
Union
197
169
Harrisville
Woonsocket
Cumberland Hill
1
123
Stafford Springs
Woodstock
102
295
95
20
Putnam
44
Chepachet
Lincoln
Pawtucket
89
395
Greenville
146
44
32
44
Abington
Greenwich
6
195
195
Storrs
89
97
Brooklyn
Chopmist
Johnston
PROVIDENCE
East Providence
31
6
6
Foster Center
Cranston
114
Warren
6
Willimantic
14
West Warwick
T.F. Green Int'l Airport
Fall River
Hebron
87
32
Canterbury
14
Greene
117
Summit
Warwick
24
85
207
12
102
East Greenwich
Bristol
138
Colchester
87
169
49
West Greenwich
95
102
Exeter
Wickford
24
Tiverton
177
81
11
82
Norwich
201
138
Hope Valley
2
1A
114
Middletown
77
82
49
Usquepaug
1A
138
Little Compton
156
Uncasville
117
Hopkinton
138
Kingston
Jamestown
Newport
Sakonnet
1
85
12
2
Carolina
112
Wakefield
Narragansett
Pawcatuck
95
Bradford
Charlestown
Galilee
Essex
1
New London
Mystic
Westerly
1
South Kingston
Point Judith
Old Saybrook
156
Niantic
Avondale
Watch Hill
POINT JUDITH
FISHERS ISLAND
Block Island Sound
Rhode Island Sound
PLUM ISLAND
BLOCK ISLAND
Block Island
Orient Point
GARDINERS ISLAND
MONTAUK POINT
Shelter
Gardiners Bay
Sag Harbor
Amagansett

■ CONNECTICUT FACTS

The Constitution State
Capital: Hartford
State motto: *Qui Transtulit Sustinet* (He who transplanted still sustains)
State bird: American robin
State flower: Mountain laurel
State tree: Charter oak
Entered Union: January 9, 1788 (fifth state to do so)

■ POPULATION (2000 U.S. CENSUS)
State: 3,405,565
Largest cities by population:
Bridgeport (141,686)
Hartford (139,739)
New Haven (130,474)

■ GEOGRAPHY AND CLIMATE
Area: 5,554 square miles (48th in U.S.)
Highest point: Mount Frissell, 2,380 feet above sea level
Lowest point: Connecticut River, sea level
Lowest recorded temperature: minus 32 degrees, February 16, 1943, Falls Village
Highest recorded temperature: 106 degrees, July 15, 1995, Danbury

■ INTERESTING FACTS
- In 1729, Yale University granted the first medical diploma in the United States.
- The oldest newspaper in the United States, the *Hartford Courant*, was established in 1764.
- The first telephone book in the United States was published in Hartford in 1878.
- All steel products manufactured in the state must be made from at least 25 percent recycled steel.
- In 2000, Connecticut had 3,900 farms and nearly four million chickens.

■ Rhode Island Facts

The Ocean State
Captital: Providence
State motto: Hope
State bird: Rhode Island Red hen
State flower: Violet
State tree: Red maple
Entered Union: May 29, 1790 (13th state to do so)

■ Population (2000 U.S. Census)
State: 1,048,319
Largest cities by population:
Providence (173,618)
Warwick (85,808)
Cranston (79,269)

■ Geography and Climate
Area: 1,214 square miles (50th in the United States)
Highest point: Jerimoth Hill, 812 feet above sea level
Lowest point: Atlantic Ocean, sea level
Lowest recorded temperature: minus 25 degrees, February 6, 1996, Greene
Highest recorded temperature: 104 degrees, August 2, 1975, Providence

■ Interesting Facts
- In 1732, Anne Franklin became the first female newspaper publisher in the United States.
- Rhode Island declared independence from Great Britain on May 4, 1776, the first American colony to do so.
- The first African-American army unit was established here in 1778.
- St. Mary's, Rhode Island's oldest Roman Catholic parish, was founded in 1828. Jacqueline Bouvier married John F. Kennedy at St. Mary's Church in 1953.
- In 2002, the state with the highest per-capita spending on lottery tickets was Rhode Island ($932). The national average: $157.

LANDSCAPE & HISTORY

New England is both the threshold and the edge of the North American continent. Approach the region from the east and you arrive on the nation's doorstep, from the west and you soon run out of land. Either way, you notice a sudden change in scale. After the broad sweep of the Atlantic or the numbing expanse of the heartland, this compact corner of the Northeast seems improbably small, too modest a patch to have generated so much of the nation's history and culture.

■ RIVER VALLEYS, PLEATED COASTLINES

Connecticut and Rhode Island combined would fit into one corner of neighboring New York State. What these small regions lack in size, however, they make up for in complexity. The pleated coastline of Rhode Island's Narragansett Bay, for example, doubles back on itself every few miles like the creation of a demented fret worker intent on fitting in just one more cove, one more inlet, before the tide turns. The course of the Connecticut River, running through the center of Connecticut, is straightforward by comparison, but its valleys and tributaries perform their own impressive contortions, swallowing up time and schedules in their undulating switchbacks.

With its often jagged seashore and its dreamy interior, this region of southern New England is a subversive place that slackens your pace and undermines first impressions. From the summit of Connecticut's Talcott Mountain or a peak in the Litchfield Hills, you see mature forest in every direction, though you are looking at land that was mostly open pasture a hundred years ago. The trees that dominate the landscape today gradually reclaimed fields abandoned by disillusioned farmers. In an area known for its human achievement and endurance, even the vegetation is a study in persistence.

■ GEOLOGICAL DRAMA

The setting for so much of the nation's historical drama was itself shaped by ancient cataclysms. Eight million years ago, molten rock expelled from the Earth's core formed the Appalachian Mountains, which extend from northern Maine

Rocks spike the southern New England shoreline; the 1856 Beavertail Light replaced the first of several lighthouses built along the Rhode Island coast.

West Rock at New Haven *(1849), by Frederic Church.*
(New Britain Museum of American Art)

south to Georgia. The geological drama that produced New England's landscape occurred around the same time, and the region's most distinctive landmarks are some of the continent's most ancient formations. Connecticut's massive Metacomet Ridge consists of lava deposits that were produced by an eruption that began 200 million years ago. Totoket Mountain, near New Haven, and Talcott Mountain, west of Hartford, have similar origins; volcanic eruptions long ago created a range of mountains east of the fault line in the Connecticut lowlands.

Cycles of erosion and accretion followed. The most significant occurred in the twilight of the last ice age, about 11,000 years ago, when the glacier covering New England retreated, strewing boulders, gouging ponds, and further shaping the terrain. The ice sheet even favored tiny Rhode Island with altitude, in the form of demure Badger Mountain, which kept its head 700 feet above sea level when the glacial meltdown raised the surrounding ocean. There are more dramatic peaks to the north—Mount Washington in New Hampshire, to name one—but they are young upstarts compared with their southern cousins.

Historical Time Line

1524 Giovanni da Verrazano visits Narragansett Bay.

1614 The Dutch explorer Adriaen Block visits what is now Block Island.

1620 The year the Pilgrims arrive in Massachusetts, 16 separate tribes inhabit Connecticut, and at least six live in Rhode Island.

1636 New Englanders, many of them from Connecticut, attack the Pequot Indians, largely exterminating them. Roger Williams founds Providence, Rhode Island's first settlement.

1639 The Fundamental Orders, the basic law of Connecticut, are adopted. Quakers settle in Newport.

1658 Sephardic Jews arrive in Newport.

1662 Connecticut receives its royal charter.

1663 Rhode Island receives its royal charter.

1676 King Philip's War ends when colonists defeat an alliance of native peoples near present-day Kingston, Rhode Island.

1701 Yale University is founded in Killingworth, Connecticut.

1717 Yale University settles permanently in New Haven.

1764 Brown University is established in Providence.

1774 Rhode Island abolishes slavery. Tapping Reeve establishes the first law school, in Litchfield, Connecticut.

1790 Samuel Slater builds the first water-powered cotton mill, in Pawtucket.

1806 Connecticut's Noah Webster publishes America's first major dictionary.

1810 Hartford Insurance Company is established.

1836 Samuel Colt invents the first revolver and makes manufacturing history by establishing rudimentary production-line procedures.

1839 Enslaved Mende Africans seize control of the ship *Amistad* and are tried as fugitives in Connecticut. After a lengthy trial they are acquitted.

1842 The Wadsworth Atheneum, now the nation's oldest public art museum, is founded.

1848 Connecticut abolishes slavery.

1861 Yale University awards the first PhD in North America.

1871 Mark Twain moves to Hartford.

1873 Julia and Abby Smith of Glastonbury, Connecticut, refuse to pay taxes, saying the denial of suffrage is taxation without representation.

1900 Connecticut adopts the first speed limits, 12 mph in rural areas, 8 mph in cities.

1902 Workers in a Danbury, Connecticut, hat factory go on strike when its owner refuses to recognize their union. The owner sues and wins damages years later.

1943 General Assembly establishes Interracial Commission, the nation's first civil rights agency.

1954 The first nuclear submarine, the USS *Nautilus,* is launched in Groton, Connecticut.

1955 Hurricanes Connie and Diane pass over Southern New England, wreaking more than $350 million worth of damage in cities and towns around Litchfield and Hartford.

1961 The directors of a Planned Parenthood Center are arrested for violating a Connecticut law against providing advice and materials on birth control. The U.S. Supreme Court rules against the state in 1965.

1974 Ella Grasso of Connecticut becomes the first U.S. woman to win election as governor without succeeding her husband.

1982 Stamford native Robert Jarvik invents the first artificial heart.

1985 Hurricane Gloria disrupts schools and businesses and leaves 300,000 people without electricity.

1992 Connecticut legalizes casino gambling.

1997 Release of Steven Spielberg's *Amistad,* parts of it shot in Connecticut and Rhode Island, sparks new interest in the 1839 event.

2002 Westport, Connecticut, homemaking guru Martha Stewart becomes embroiled in ImClone insider-trading stock scandal.

■ WATER AND ROCK

Even the most insulated visitor, cocooned in an automobile, cannot help noticing that Connecticut and Rhode Island are chiefly places of water and rock. Whatever your route, you will find yourself tracing the arc of the ocean, or the meanderings of a river or stream. The region has hundreds of miles of coastline and is bisected by two major waterways, the Connecticut and Housatonic Rivers.

The other key player here, rock, is at its most benevolent in Connecticut's Litchfield Hills, which rise near the border with New York State. These are tasteful rather than grandiose protuberances, substantial enough to give the region beauty and backbone, and gradual enough to inspire affection rather than awe.

Sailors and farmers alike, however, will vouch for the malevolence of New England rock. At its most treacherous, it spikes the coastline and surrounding ocean and has been lethal to shipping, particularly during New England's 19th-century maritime heyday. Inland, rock presents a different challenge. Each spring, in all but the most fertile river valleys, ground frost propels a fresh crop of stones and mini-boulders to the surface—a reminder that ice can still rearrange things.

This small, defiant place is an oddity on the continent. Here the American dictum that bigger is better never took hold. Instead, a more subtle theory is demonstrated: that the landscape shaped the people who shaped history.

■ FIRST PEOPLE

The first people to discover New England came not by sea but overland, descendants of hunters who had crossed from Asia to Alaska in a series of migrations beginning thousands of years ago. These groups merged, evolved, multiplied, and broke apart into subgroups, eventually making their way from the Pacific coast to the Atlantic seaboard. Archaeological evidence indicates that the early tribal groups that established themselves in New England were nomadic hunters and fishermen who used basic stone implements but had not yet developed pottery or more refined tools, such as axes.

By the end of the 15th century, perhaps as many as 100,000 people had established settlements east of the Hudson River, where they introduced pottery making and agriculture. Encounters between Europeans and native people increased over the next centuries. In 1578, for example, records show that roughly 400 vessels from France, Portugal, England, and Spain were fishing and whaling off

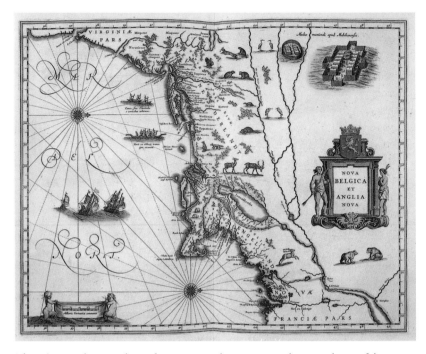

This 1635 Dutch map is drawn from an unusual perspective: with west at the top of the map, and north to the right. (John Carter Brown Library, Brown University)

New England, and that most of the crews were trading with the natives. Charting the New England coast in 1615, Capt. John Smith reported "large fields of corn and great troops of well-proportioned people."

At their peak, tribes belonging to the Algonquian language group covered an area that spanned from the Florida coast to the Canadian Maritimes and west to the Mississippi. In 1620, there were at least 16 separate tribes in Connecticut, and at least six in Rhode Island. Today's place names commemorate some of them— the Massachusetts, Narragansetts, Penobscots, and Pocumtucs, for example. Others like the Mohicans, Abenakis, Pequots, and Nipmucs, were immortalized by James Fenimore Cooper, the 19th-century novelist whose genre Mark Twain derisively termed "the broken twig school of realism."

■ WAMPANOAG LAND

The Pilgrims who landed on New England's shores in December 1620 stepped onto the territory of the Wampanoag, the collective name of the indigenous people of southeastern Massachusetts and eastern Rhode Island. The Europeans had little reason to anticipate serious opposition. In his 1616 "Description of New England"—surely the region's first tourist brochure—Capt. John Smith had downplayed native hostility to English encroachment, preferring to dwell on the bountiful seas and invigorating climate.

As it turned out, the settlers encountered little resistance. For one thing, the Wampanoags the Pilgrims encountered were people severely weakened by a plague in 1616 and 1617. By 1631, the dominant Massachusett tribe would number only about 500. And even at their healthiest, the New England tribes had never centralized their power, as had the Iroquois in New York; recurring intertribal warfare would have made a unified defense against the settlers impossible.

But weakness was not the only reason for the relative lack of hostility to the early settlers. Goodwill, misplaced trust, and a desire to enlist the aid of the newcomers and use it against their native enemies also played a part. In 1631, for example, Chief Wanginnacut of the Podunks approached the English at Boston and Plymouth, urging them to settle in Connecticut as his allies against the Pequots. Invitations such as this were preludes to tragedy.

■ NARRAGANSETTS AND PEQUOTS

Not all indigenous people were cooperative. Most notably, the formidable Pequots in eastern Connecticut remained unfriendly, launching sporadic raids on frontier settlements. The English response was predictable. In 1636, residents of the Connecticut cities of Hartford, Wethersfield, and Windsor, in conjunction with Bostonians—and all of them aided by the Mohicans—mounted an attack on the Pequots and largely exterminated them. (The survivors were sold to the Bermudans, who complained that as slaves the Pequots were "sullen and treachorous.")

The brutal Pequot War—the minister Cotton Mather described the fearful sight of Indians "frying in the fire and the streams of blood quenching the same"—and the relentless expansion of settlements across New England ended the honeymoon between the English and Native Americans. Historians Richard Slotkin and James K. Folsom note that the Pequot War "had showed the Indians that 'the English way of war had no limit or scruple or mercy' and that English weapons were greatly superior to those of the natives." When John Eliot came to preach to the Podunks in 1657, having translated the Bible into their language, it is hardly surprising that he was told, "No, you have taken away our lands, and now you wish to make us a race of slaves."

Even some colonists were outraged by European imperialism. "Why lay such stress upon your patent from King James?" Rhode Island's founder, Roger Williams, had remonstrated during the 1630s. Speaking of Massasoit, the Wampanoag leader, he wrote, "James has no more right to give away or sell Massasoit's lands and cut and carve his country than Massasoit has to sell King James' kingdom or to send Indians to colonize Warwickshire."

■ KING PHILIP'S WAR

Williams protested, but Metacom, a son of Massasoit who had succeeded his father as the Wampanoag leader, or sachem, prepared for war. Metacom, also known by the English name Philip, believed that only a simultaneous attack by all the tribes of the North Atlantic seaboard would end the encroachment that threatened to eradicate the native population. To that end, Philip built alliances and planned a concerted offensive. What turned out to be an exceedingly savage war was precipitated in June 1675, when an Indian leaked Philip's plans to the governor at Plymouth and was subsequently killed. After several Wampanoags were convicted of the murder and executed, Philip attacked Swansea, Massachusetts, in retaliation. Philip, victorious in several major battles, appeared unstoppable until he traveled to Rhode Island to enlist the Narragansetts' support. In a swamp outside present-day Kingston, he and the entire Narragansett nation were encircled and defeated by the colonists.

■ COMMONWEALTH OF THE ELECT

Throughout most of the 17th century, England was more interested in bypassing than settling the American continent. Visions of the fabled Northwest Passage to the golden Orient drew English explorers who doubtless regarded the rocky New England coast as a poor consolation prize. Giovanni Caboto (known as John Cabot) did, however, claim the territory in 1497 for his patron, King Henry VII of England. The Florentine navigator Giovanni da Verrazano visited Narragansett Bay in 1524; Bartholomew Gosnold, commanding the *Concord*, explored the coast

WAR'S LEGACY

Among the handful of seminal events that shaped the American mind and continent, King Philip's War is perhaps the least studied and most forgotten. In essence, the war cleared southern New England's native population from the land, and with it a way of life that had evolved over a millennium. The Wampanoag, Narragansett, Nipmuc, and other native peoples were slaughtered, sold into slavery, or placed in widely scattered communities throughout New England after the war. In its aftermath, the English established themselves as the dominant peoples—and in many New England towns, the only peoples—allowing for the uninterrupted growth of England's northern colonies right up to the American Revolution. As important, King Philip's War became the brutal model for how the United States would come to deal with its native population. Later names like Tippecanoe, Black Hawk's War, the Trail of Tears, the Salt Creek Massacre, the Red River War, and Wounded Knee all took place under the long, violent shadow of King Philip's War.

—Eric B. Schultz and Michael J. Tougias, *King Philip's War*, 1999

from Maine to Rhode Island in 1602; and the Dutchman Adriaen Block visited Block Island in 1614. But Capt. John Smith, exploring the area in 1614, was the first to call this area New England and to advertise its charms.

As a sales pitch, Smith's colorful "Description of New England" was not immediately successful. Most English adventurers preferred the well-established Virginia colony, which promised instant tobacco fortunes. "I am not so simple to think," Smith wrote in his description, "that ever any other motive than wealth, will ever erect there a Commonweale; or draw companie from their ease and humours at home, to stay in New England." In this prediction, however, Smith was mistaken. The settlement of New England was, above all, a religious act, begun when the *Mayflower* set sail from Plymouth, England, in August 1620. The *Mayflower's* passengers were not fortune hunters but religious separatists who had rejected English Protestantism, which they considered decadent. These settlers, the Pilgrims, established the colony of Plymouth, based on God's ordinance as revealed in the Bible. We identify them today as Puritans, a term they would have regarded as an insult—the Puritans were far more authoritarian about their interpretation of morality and the Bible than were the Pilgrims.

By 1629, English settlers of all religious persuasions (and some of none) had established fishing and trading stations along much of the coast. That same year the Massachusetts Bay Company, a solidly Puritan enterprise, was formed as a joint-stock corporation, with its office in London, its colonial base at Salem, and 41-year-old John Winthrop at its head. Boston developed into the vigorous center of the Massachusetts Bay Colony, with Connecticut and Rhode Island soon to become its thriving satellites.

■ LEARNING AND PIETY

The 17th-century historian Thomas Fuller wrote of the Puritan experience that "Knowledge caused piety, and piety bred industry." To follow God's law, citizens had to be able to read the Bible. This central idea of vanquishing Satan with education produced the country's first college, Harvard, founded in 1636, and one of the most literate populations in history. Toward the end of the 17th century, the literacy rate in New England is estimated to have been between 89 and 95 percent for men and about 62 percent for women.

The belief that literacy was everyone's duty—and right—set the stage for democracy, though the political transformation developed slowly. Winthrop and his associates replaced English aristocracy not with democracy but with theocracy. A secret ballot was permitted in 1635, but in the early years only church members or "visible saints" were eligible to elect the governor, deputy governor, and assistants who ran the colony.

The practice was hardly egalitarian, but it did challenge previous notions of social status. Though a rich man rejected by a congregation could not vote, the most indigent church member could elect his rulers. In 1636, a row over taxation ushered in representative government in Massachusetts Bay, when freemen demanded representation in the legislating body of the Great and General Court. In the next century "no taxation without representation" became the clarion cry of the American colonists.

A portrait of Ninigret, chief of Rhode Island's Niantic Indians, relatives of the Narragansett tribe. He was made chief of the Narragansetts by the English for aiding them in 1675 during King Philip's War. Ninigret refused to become a Christian, instead telling the missionaries to "go and make the English good first." (Museum of Art, Rhode Island School of Design)

Roger Williams and the Narragansett Indians (Library of Congress)

■ RELIGIOUS DISSENTERS

Protests over fiscal matters were one thing, but theological dissent was another. Depending on their brazenness, those who expressed "new and dangerous opinions" in the colony could be banished, beaten, or hanged. As the Puritans saw it, the execution of heretics was as necessary as the "divine slaughter" of whole tribes in the Pequot War of 1637 and King Philip's War of 1675. Both the heretics and the native peoples who refused to adhere to the Puritans' beliefs were after all, impediments to God's work.

The dissenters who fled or were banished quickly staked out their own territory. "Forced worship stinks in God's nostrils," Roger Williams declared before fleeing Salem in 1636 to establish the remarkably tolerant settlement of Providence, the first in what would be the colony of Rhode Island. The new colonists insisted on the separation of church and state.

That same year, another Puritan clergyman, the Rev. Thomas Hooker, left Massachusetts with his congregation to establish a more open community at Hartford, Connecticut. Their disagreement with the Massachusetts Bay authorities, less a question of religion than of politics, concerned the restriction of the vote to church members only. In Hooker's view, the foundation of authority was the consent of the people, who had the right to choose their public magistrates and to place limits on judicial power. As set forth in a famous sermon delivered in 1638, Hooker's views inspired the Fundamental Orders, a basic law for Connecticut adopted in 1639 and said to be the first written constitution in the colonies.

Anne Hutchinson, a midwife, also ran afoul of the Puritan hierarchy. Hutchison and her husband, William, were antinomians, people who believed, as did the Quakers, that it was possible to know God without the benefit of a minister. In meetings with other women of Massachusetts, she preached that "laws, commands, rules, and edicts are for those who have not the light which makes plain the pathway. He who has God's grace in his heart cannot go astray." Two years after Roger Williams founded Providence, Hutchinson, who one follower said "Preaches better Gospell than any of your black-coates that have been at the Ninneversity," left Massachusetts with her husband. They and William Coddington established the Rhode Island community of Portsmouth, on Aquidneck Island. In 1639, Coddington moved farther south on the island to settle Newport, and the town soon became a haven for Quakers and Sephardic Jews, who first came from Holland in 1658.

■ TRADE AND REVOLUTION

Connecticut and Rhode Island received royal charters in 1662 and 1663 respectively, permitting the colonists to administer their political and financial affairs. Rhode Island's settlers were protected by a clause in that colony's charter stating "that all and every person . . . may from tyme to tyme and at all tymes hereafter freelye and fullye enjoye his and their own judgements and consciences in matters of religious concernments."

Only a characteristic mixture of bluff and ingenuity would help Connecticut retain its legal status, however. Sir Edmund Andros, appointed royal governor of New England by King James, arrived in Hartford in 1687 demanding the return of the colony's charter as a prelude to the resumption of more direct royal control over the colonies. The document was placed before Andros one autumn afternoon, but a lengthy wrangle about his jurisdiction ensued. At sunset, candles were lit, and then mysteriously extinguished. In the confusion, the charter was snatched from the table and hidden in the hollow of a venerable tree that became known as the Charter Oak. The charter remained hidden until 1715, but the colony's rights had long since been restored by the British rulers William and Mary, who acceded to the throne in 1689 following the overthrow of King James.

As the 17th century drew to a close, economics (a euphemism, perhaps, for greed) gradually replaced theology as the region's motivating force. A new merchant class established itself, chiefly on the booming West Indies trade. With fair winds and the right connections, a merchant's fortune could be made on one voyage. In the infamous "Triangle Trade" for example, New England products—chief among them rum—were exchanged for slaves on Africa's west coast. Those slaves were then sold or traded in the West Indies for molasses and sugar, vital ingredients in rum distillation. New England traders also sold maritime supplies and fish to West Indian slave plantations. The Rhode Island ports of Bristol and Newport reaped huge profits from the Caribbean slave trade. Even smaller towns like Guilford, Connecticut, and Little Compton, Rhode Island, prospered from shipbuilding and fishing. And in the 19th century, whaling centers such as New London profited from the demand for lighting and lubricating oils.

■ INTELLECTUAL GROWTH, PERSONAL CONFIDENCE

Connecticut and Rhode Island, like the rest of New England, were also growing intellectually. Yale University was established in 1701 in Killingworth, Connecticut, and had moved to New Haven by 1717, and Brown University was founded in 1764 at Providence. Both schools began as religious institutions. The highly literate populace also demanded a selection of newspapers and periodicals. The *Connecticut Courant,* launched in 1764, later changed its name to the *Hartford Courant* and remains the oldest continuously operating newspaper in the country.

Gradually a homegrown culture replaced the transplanted English variety. The combination of deeply rooted defiance and newfound confidence proved to be an incendiary one when colonists began to oppose the increasingly extortionate levies imposed by the British monarchy.

■ REVOLUTIONARY WAR

Direct taxes levied between 1764 and 1772—the Sugar Act, Currency Act, and Stamp Act among them—sparked widespread boycotts and mob violence. The British responded in 1774 with a series of punitive measures known as the

Intolerable Acts, which struck at the heart of self-government and prompted the American colonists to convene the First Continental Congress, from September 5 to October 26, 1774, to consider united resistance. Events soon overtook policy, however. By 1775, when Rhode Island's mariners began attacking English ships, piracy had become patriotism. The first such incident took place in Newport, where impressed sailors burned a Crown vessel. By the time the Second Continental Congress assembled on May 10, 1775, the Massachusetts "Minutemen" had faced the British in April at Lexington and Concord, and both sides had experienced their first fatalities.

Rhode Island, the first colony to declare independence—on May 4, 1776—provoked the British to occupy the region. Connecticut's contributions to the Revolutionary War were also critical. Almost 32,000 Connecticut men joined the Continental Army. Israel Putnam of Pomfret was the ranking officer in the field at the Battle of Bunker Hill, and the Vermont patriot Ethan Allen, born in Connecticut's Litchfield County, was credited with capturing Fort Ticonderoga in New York with his Green Mountain Boys—a strategic victory early in the war. Benedict Arnold, of Norwich, was one of the heroes of this battle, though later he became the nation's most infamous traitor.

Though certain religious laws were liberalized, the new state of Connecticut nevertheless retained its insular conservatism and resisted change. There were, for example, no banks in the state until 1792, and slavery remained legal until 1848 (Rhode Island had abolished slavery in 1784, though existing slaves were not freed). Emerging intact from the conflict, Hartford prospered as a shipping and trading center until the War of 1812, between the United States and Great Britain, precipitated a maritime depression and shifted the emphasis to manufacturing.

■ REPUBLIC OF INDUSTRY AND VIRTUE

Connecticut and Rhode Island—in common with the rest of coastal New England—had always depended on the ocean for their good fortune rather than on the comparatively poor land. When Connecticut began to sell off fertile land in the Connecticut Western Reserve—land in present-day northeastern Ohio that Connecticut had received in 1786 in exchange for abandoning its claim to territory farther west—many New Englanders abandoned these rocky states for good.

Home industries had been supplying local markets since the mid-17th century, and the 18th century had seen the emergence of the Yankee peddler, a traveling vendor who originally sold tin goods and, later, sundries such as buttons, combs, kettles, and clocks. He invariably returned home with crude sketches of new items requested by his customers. The peddlers' orders were translated into patterns and these items were then manufactured by hand, keeping numerous riverside workshops humming.

In the 19th century, the region's wealth would again be generated by water, this time by the rivers. Samuel Slater transformed American textile manufacturing when he built the first water-powered cotton mill, beside the Blackstone River in Pawtucket, Rhode Island, in 1790. A home craft industry became one of mass production, and southern New England's industrial revolution had begun. In 1807, the mill town of Slatersville, Rhode Island, was founded, and soon riverbanks across southern New England were dotted with communities built around the factory rather than the meetinghouse. Even after the the high-pressure steam engine was introduced in 1803, about 90 percent of New England manufacturing remained water powered.

The French cultural observer Alexis de Tocqueville discovered on his fabled trip through America between 1831 and early 1832 that one-third of U.S. senators and one-quarter of U.S. congressmen had been born in Connecticut, and that the state had produced the clock peddler, the teacher, and the politician—"the first to give you the time, the second to tell you what to do with it, and the third to make your laws and civilization," he wrote. He neglected Connecticut's other key player, the insurance man—although the Hartford Fire Insurance Company had been founded in 1810 and by the time of de Tocqueville's visit was among several insurance firms operating out of Hartford. The fortunes made from insurance and manufacturing, along with the influx of immigrant labor, transformed an agricultural state into a sophisticated multiracial society that rivaled Boston and New York as a literary and artistic center.

■ CONFIDENT, PRACTICAL IDEALISTS

The industrial age that defined New England was not universally celebrated. "This invasion of Nature by Trade with its Money, its Credit, its Steam, its Railroad, threatens to upset the balance of man," wrote Ralph Waldo Emerson in 1836, when the Transcendental Club first assembled in his Concord, Massachusetts, home. Inspired by Goethe, Wordsworth, and other Romantic poets, and regarding nature as man's spiritual savior, transcendentalists like Henry David Thoreau in his Walden cabin lamented the inevitable victory of commercialism.

This 1793 structure, which still survives, replaced Samuel Slater's original water-powered mill. (Library of Congress)

But the society from which the transcendentalists seceded was buoyantly confident, secure in its position as the nation's cultural nexus and immune to the idealists' subversive judgments. To the rest of the world, after all, New England in the mid-19th century represented not just industrial and commercial ingenuity but also literary and intellectual vitality.

In 1806, Connecticut's Noah Webster published *A Compendious Dictionary of the English Language,* America's first major dictionary. The nation's first public art museum, the Wadsworth Atheneum, was founded in 1842 in Hartford, where a few decades later Mark Twain became a literary celebrity. Harriet Beecher Stowe, the author of *Uncle Tom's Cabin,* was a member of the prominent Connecticut family, the Beechers.

Like transcendentalism, labor unrest barely ruffled the new commercial aristocracy. A strike by female weavers in Pawtucket, Rhode Island, in 1824, was the first instance of female participation in an organized labor action in the United States, but the group's chief demand—free public education—was ignored. It wasn't until almost two decades later, in 1840, that a law was passed requiring every child under the age of 12 to attend school for at least 12 months before starting work.

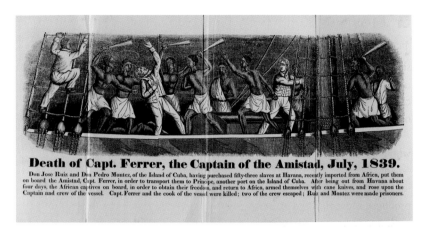

Death of Capt. Ferrer, the Captain of the Amistad, July, 1839.

Don Jose Ruiz and Don Pedro Montez, of the Island of Cuba, having purchased fifty-three slaves at Havana, recently imported from Africa, put them on board the Amistad, Capt. Ferrer, in order to transport them to Principe, another port on the Island of Cuba. After being out from Havana about four days, the African captives on board, in order to obtain their freedom, and return to Africa, armed themselves with cane knives, and rose upon the Captain and crew of the vessel. Capt. Ferrer and the cook of the vessel were killed; two of the crew escaped; Ruiz and Montez were made prisoners.

This illustration from an 1840 book about the Amistad *uprising depicts the killing of the slave ship's captain by captives seeking to return to Africa. (Library of Congress)*

As the 19th century wore on, the issue of slavery became even harder to overlook than the inequities of factory labor. The first Africans had arrived as slaves in the 17th century. Though in the 17th and 18th centuries its citizenry had participated in the slave trade, New England became the birthplace of abolitionism. By 1850, when the federal Fugitive Slave Act became law, making it a crime to knowingly harbor a slave, abolitionists in Connecticut and Rhode Island grew ever more determined to end slavery. Hartford and Farmington in particular were important stations on the Underground Railroad, aiding escapees from the South. In 1839, Farmington had also provided refuge for enslaved Africans who had seized control of the Spanish slave ship *Amistad*. The slaves were subsequently tried in the Connecticut courts and freed.

When the Civil War finally broke out, Hartford's banks loaned Connecticut's governor half a million dollars to equip a regiment; the state ultimately contributed more than 55,000 men in 30 regiments, and sustained 20,000 casualties. The leaders of Rhode Island also heeded the call to arms, assembling an infantry regiment within five days of President Abraham Lincoln's request for troops. Rhode Island's Battery B fought in every major engagement of the Army of the Potomac, including Antietam and Gettysburg. Nearly 24,000 Rhode Islanders participated in the war; 1,685 of them died during the conflict.

■ MOVING INTO MODERN TIMES

The Civil War propelled New England into the modern age. In 1865, fishing was still a viable occupation, but whaling was not: following the discovery of petroleum in Pennsylvania, just prior to the war, the demand for whale oil as a fuel or lubricant decreased precipitously. The number of manufacturers in the region, on the other hand, rose from 5,128 in 1870 to almost 10,000 in 1900.

Profits from large-scale manufacturing created an affluent middle class for whom Emerson's transcendental vision was as irrelevant as John Winthrop's theology of self-denial and rigid authority. The new age needed engineers and mechanics, and colleges and trade schools throughout Connecticut and Rhode Island produced some of the country's finest.

Rhode Island became one of the largest textile-producing states and one of its leading jewelry manufacturers. By 1910, when the population had grown to more than 500,000, Rhode Island had evolved into an established summer destination, not only for the new rich but also for the growing middle class. By the mid-1930s, Rhode Island was the most highly industrialized state in the country, with more than half of its inhabitants engaged in manufacturing.

But even as their economies flourished, for both Rhode Island and Connecticut, the warning signs of decline began to appear in the early 20th century, as manufacturing moved elsewhere, particularly to Southern states. Despite the booms created by World Wars I and II, the region never regained its primacy as an industrial center. In the 1950s and 1960s, many factories relocated, were swallowed by conglomerates, or simply closed.

In the 1980s, however, computer research, development, and manufacturing, along with the biotechnology and defense industries, revitalized Connecticut in particular. The richest state in the country, Connecticut now has a post-industrial economy, with three out of four workers engaged in financial, government, retail, tourism, or other service jobs. The adaptability of both Connecticut and Rhode Island, and their institutions of higher learning and coastlines—visits to which are now a significant source of tourist income—remain among the two states' most profitable assets.

❧ *Connecticut & Rhode Island Notables* ❧

Anne Hutchinson (1591–1643)
Preacher ❧ b. Alford, Lincolnshire, England

"She was a woman of haughty and fierce carriage, a nimble wit and active spirit, a very voluble tongue, more bold than a man." This was the view of Gov. John Winthrop when he expelled Anne Hutchinson from the Massachusetts Bay Colony in 1638 for expressing—worse still, preaching—her unorthodox religious views. Winthrop's assessment appears to have been correct. Already the mother of 14 children when she arrived in New England with her husband, Will, in 1634, Hutchinson soon began to hold religious meetings in her home. Espousing her belief in a "Covenant of Grace" that declared faith alone sufficient to achieve salvation, Hutchinson became a notorious voice of dissent in the theocratic colony and was formally accused of antinomianism, the belief that the Gospel frees Christians from required obedience to any law.

Following her expulsion from Massachusetts, Hutchinson, her family, and followers settled on Aquidneck Island, in Rhode Island, where they enjoyed comparative religious freedom. She later moved to East Chester, New York, where she and five of her children were killed in 1643 in a Mohawk raid.

Newport Gardner (Circa 1746–1826)
Teacher, religious leader ❧ b. West Africa

Newport Gardner, then known as Occramar Mirycoo, arrived in Newport on a slave ship from Africa in 1760 and became the property of Caleb Gardner, a Newport slave merchant. Within four years, Newport Gardner had learned French and English and converted to Christianity. Befriended by Samuel Hopkins, the abolitionist pastor of the First Congregational Church, he taught, wrote, published music and instructed African children at the school of the African Benevolent Society, which he helped establish.

Although not freed by Caleb Gardner until 1792, Newport Gardner was employed as a teacher and blacksmith after the Revolutionary War and became the first president of the African Union Society, the first black cultural society in the nation. Gardner also founded the Union Congregational Church, Newport's first African church, and with his wife, Limas, raised 13 children in a house on Pope Street he bought in 1807. Attracted by the African Colonization movement, Gardner returned to Africa with his sons and some followers in 1826. Settling in Liberia, newly established by freed black slaves from America, he and many of his group quickly succumbed to an indigenous illness.

❧ Connecticut & Rhode Island Notables ❧

Nathan Hale (1755–1776)
Teacher ❧ b. Coventry, Connecticut

Nathan Hale, the sixth of 12 children, chose teaching over Christian ministry and in 1774 accepted an appointment at the Union Grammar School in New London, Connecticut. An establishment founded to educate the sons of local gentlemen, the school allowed Hale an early revolutionary act. Between five and seven in the morning he taught a class of 20 "young ladies" who worked in the town's brothels.

Commissioned as a lieutenant in the Seventh Connecticut Regiment, Hale fought in Boston before his regiment was moved to New York, where Gen. George Washington badly needed information about British war plans. A French officer declined the spying mission, allegedly saying "I am willing to be shot but not to be hung." Hale accepted and crossed to Long Island in citizen's clothes. One week later he was captured, betrayed by the notes he was carrying. On the morning of September 22, 1776, he was hanged from an apple tree on Gen. William Howe's orders. Refused a Bible, he wrote letters to his mother and a fellow officer before making the famous declaration, "I only regret that I have but one life to give for my country."

A statue of Nathan Hale, outside his homestead.

✍ Connecticut & Rhode Island Notables ✍

Eli Whitney (1765–1825)
Inventor ✍ b. Westboro, Massachusetts

Fascinated by machines since childhood, Eli Whitney became a blacksmith and invented a nail-making machine, but was for years denied admission to Yale, an institution that did not recognize the "useful arts." Whitney finally entered Yale, graduating at age 27 and becoming a teacher in North Carolina. In 1793, he was befriended by Catherine Greene, the widow of the Revolutionary War general, Nathanael. During a visit to her plantation, Whitney was inspired to invent the cotton gin. At that time, the manual task of separating a single "point" of cotton lint from the surrounding seeds was an arduous task. Legend insists that within days of his arrival, Whitney had built a machine that accelerated the process and ultimately revived not only the languishing cotton industry but also the slave trade on which it relied.

A patent for the machine was granted in 1794, but by then Whitney's design had been illegally copied, and years of legal wrangling had left him penniless. Returning north to start over, he settled in New Haven in 1804 and persuaded the U.S. government to give him an order for 10,000 rifles. To fill it, he invented the milling machine and introduced the use of interchangeable parts as a way to facilitate mass production, in the process transforming American manufacturing. The kids-oriented **Eli Whitney Museum** (915 Whitney Avenue; Hamden, CT; 203-777-1833) occupies the site of Whitney's mill.

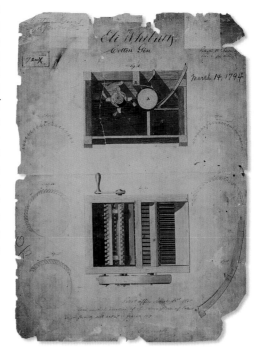

A 1794 patent drawing of Whitney's cotton gin. (National Archives and Records Administration)

❧ *Connecticut & Rhode Island Notables* ❧

William Ellery Channing (1780–1842)
Founder of Unitarian Church ❧ b. Newport, Rhode Island

A nephew of the slave merchant Caleb Gardner, Channing was born into a Newport family that was at odds over slavery. Enlightened by his encounters with Newport's Africans and with abolitionists such as Samuel Hopkins, Channing became one of the cause's leading polemicists in the pre–Civil War years. In *Slavery,* published in 1835, he wrote that "men's worst crimes have sprung from the desire of being masters, of bending others to their yoke."

Channing had graduated from Harvard in 1798 and worked as a tutor in Richmond, Virginia, before being appointed to the pastorate of the Federal Street Church in 1803. His writings and sermons led to the founding of Unitarian Universalism, a Christian religious association that considers God to be unipersonal, salvation to be granted to the entire human race, and reason and conscience to be the criteria for belief and practice.

Oliver Hazard Perry (1785–1819)
Naval commander ❧ b. South Kingston, Rhode Island

Appointed a midshipman in the U.S. Navy in 1799, Perry first sailed on the *General Greene,* a ship commanded by his father. Having distinguished himself in the naval war against France and against the Barbary pirates, the young seaman was made a permanent lieutenant in 1807 and by 1811 was commanding a gunboat flotilla from his Newport headquarters. As war with the British approached, Perry was granted command of naval operations in Lake Erie, and at noon on September 10, 1813, the rival fleets met. Perry sailed directly at the British, and when his vessel, the *Lawrence,* was shot to pieces he abandoned ship and took command of her sister brig, the *Niagara.* By midafternoon the British were defeated, and Perry quickly became a national hero.

During the remainder of the war he participated in the recovery of Detroit and the battle of the Thames. From 1814 to 1817 he commanded the *Java* in the Mediterranean, and in 1819 he was sent on a diplomatic mission to Venezuela. On the return voyage he contracted the yellow fever that finally defeated him.

✐ Connecticut & Rhode Island Notables ✐

Prudence Crandall (1803–1890)
Teacher ✐ b. Hopkinton, Rhode Island

In October 1995, Connecticut's State Assembly named Prudence Crandall "State Heroine," a gesture that might have prompted an ironic smile from this demure but steely Quaker. Educated at the Society of Friends School in Plainfield, Connecticut, Crandall went on to establish a successful school for girls in Canterbury. It was successful, that is, until Crandall accepted an African-American pupil in 1833. When local parents began withdrawing their daughters from Crandall's school, she established the first academy for African-American girls in New England. Soon students were coming from as far away as Boston and Philadelphia.

In response, Connecticut introduced a vagrancy law that specified 10 lashes for any African-American attending the school, and in 1834 made it illegal to provide free education to African-Americans. Refusing to comply, Crandall was imprisoned. She was released following a successful appeal, but when this news reached Canterbury, a mob attacked the school, threatening Crandall and the children. Fearing further violence, she closed it and moved to Illinois, where she married a Baptist clergyman and continued to teach.

Edward Mitchell Bannister (1828–1901)
Painter ✐ b. St Andrew's, New Brunswick, Canada

The son of a black Barbadian and a white Canadian, Bannister studied at the Lowell Institute in Boston, producing landscapes and portraits as well as religious and genre paintings. In 1876, he and his wife, Christina, moved to Providence, and Bannister's landscapes began to show not only the influence of the Barbizon style but also the spirited and ecstatic response to nature that characterized his mature work.

The Bannisters summered in Newport, where the artist enjoyed sailing his catboat around the harbor he so frequently painted. A cofounder of the Providence Art Club, Bannister exhibited at the National Academy of Design in 1879. One of the earliest and most influential of Rhode Island landscape painters, he was also the first African-American artist to win national and eventually worldwide recognition. He died in Providence.

∾ *Connecticut & Rhode Island Notables* ∾

Alva Erskine Vanderbilt Belmont (1853–1933)
Socialite and suffragist ∾ b. Mobile, Alabama

Born into an old Southern family, Alva Erskine Smith married William Kissam Vanderbilt, the owner of the New York Central Railroad, in 1875. Determined to make a splash in New York society, Alva entertained lavishly at the couple's $3 million mansion on Fifth Avenue, scoring her biggest victory in 1883, when Caroline Astor, then the reigning queen of haute New York, was forced to call on Alva to ensure that young Carrie Astor would be invited to the Vanderbilt's masquerade ball.

Marble House, the Vanderbilt's Newport palace, completed in 1892 for $9 million ($7 million of it for its namesake marble), was similarly employed to lure titled European bachelors. In 1895, Alva's daughter, Consuelo, married the Ninth Duke of Marlborough.

Earlier in 1895, Alva had divorced Vanderbilt. In 1896 she married Oliver Hazard Perry Belmont, a descendant of the naval hero, and moved across Bellevue Avenue to Belcourt Castle, Belmont's French-style château. Following Belmont's death in 1908, Alva embraced the suffragist cause, opening her houses and her purse, founding the Political Equality League, becoming president of the National Woman's Party in 1921 and one of the first women elected to the American Institute of Architects.

✍ Connecticut & Rhode Island Notables ✍

Charles Ives (1874–1954)

Composer ✍ b. Danbury, Connecticut

At the age of five, Charles Ives delighted his bandmaster father by banging out the drum parts of band pieces on the family piano, with his fists. The adult Ives would continue to play the piano with his fists and even required a board to play his *Concord Sonata*. An insurance executive by day—he and a partner founded one of America's largest agencies—he is arguably the most original and significant American composer of the late 19th and early 20th centuries.

Inspired by transcendental philosophy and fascinated with bitonal forms, polyrhythms, and quotation, Ives was, above all, idealistic and democratic in his vision. Writes Jan Swafford in *Charles Ives: A Life with Music,* "The result . . . is like nothing ever imagined before him . . . at once unique and as familiar as a tune whistled in childhood; music that can conjure up the pandemonium of a small town Fourth of July or the quiet of a New England church."

Although visited by ill-health and depression, Ives composed at an astonishing rate, particularly between 1908 and 1917, before stopping altogether in 1927.

❧ Connecticut & Rhode Island Notables ❧

Wallace Stevens (1879–1955)
Poet ❧ b. Reading, Pennsylvania

A graduate of Harvard University and New York Law School, Stevens was admitted to the bar in 1904 and took a job with the Hartford Accident and Indemnity Company. Each weekday morning and evening he walked the 2 miles between his home at 118 Westerly Terrace and the office on Asylum Avenue, on the way composing poems that would eventually enter the American literary canon. Four appeared in 1914 in a wartime edition of *Poetry* magazine. His first book of poems, *Harmonium,* was published in 1923, revealing the influence of the English Romantics and French Symbolists but also a uniquely whimsical, exotic style. Widespread recognition came in 1954 with the publication of the *Collected Poems.* Today Stevens's best-known works include *Ideas of Order* (1936), *The Man With the Blue Guitar* (1937), and *Notes Towards a Supreme Fiction* (1942).

Howard Phillips Lovecraft (1890–1937)
Writer ❧ b. Providence, Rhode Island

Raised by his mother and aunts in Providence following his father's death, H.P. Lovecraft was as frequently visited by despair and nervous collapse as he was by the nightmarish, often Gothic visions that inspired his macabre stories. Reciting poetry at age two, reading *The Arabian Nights* at age five, and obsessed with science, chemistry, and astronomy by age eight, Lovecraft first wrote astronomy columns for local newspapers.

In 1914, he joined the United Amateur Press Association, an association of writers who published their own magazines, and produced numerous essays and poems. In 1924 came the publication of the short story "The Shunned House," set in a still-extant house at 135 Benefit Street in Providence. Returning to the city in 1926 after a short sojourn (and marriage) in Brooklyn, New York, Lovecraft flourished creatively until he was diagnosed with cancer of the intestine in 1936. *The Outsider and Others,* a collection of Lovecraft's fiction, came out in 1939, the first book published by Arkham House Publishers, the now-legendary fantasy and horror press.

COASTAL CONNECTICUT

The entire Connecticut coast bustled with sea-related activity three centuries ago, and in many historic towns the seafaring spirit lives on. The coastline, which faces south, not east, at this point, can roughly be divided into two sections. The pull of New York City can be felt more strongly west of New Haven, which is a train ride of a little less than two hours from Manhattan. In Mystic Seaport and other towns east of New Haven, history prevails over contemporary urban concerns.

The area from Greenwich to New Haven, including the neighboring uplands between Danbury and Waterbury, has to a large extent been mercilessly developed. Only state parks, wildlife refuges, and increasingly rare patches of farmland supply the breathing space that the Litchfield Hills, for instance, so generously provide to Connecticut's northwestern corner. Even the back roads in this busy place too often confront drivers with views of spanking new 30-room mansions squatting on bare one-acre building lots. One bright spot: the verdant Merritt Parkway (Route 15), which travels inland and more or less parallel to I-95 between Greenwich and Milford.

The small coastal fishing villages farther east were largely spared the industrialization that transformed New Haven, New London, and numerous inland towns, and here the seafaring mentality endures, especially in Mystic Seaport and Stonington. If after a few days of wandering the coast you find yourself staring at the sea for hours on end, a skill the locals have had years to refine, don't be concerned. There is always the coastal run to New Haven, with its flood tide of New York traffic to snap you back into competitive shape.

■ HISTORY

In 1635, John Winthrop Jr., the son of the first Massachusetts governor, was commissioned as "first governor of the river Connecticut." Winthrop led a group of English settlers who erected a fort at Saybrook, but New Haven, founded in 1638, was the region's first substantial English settlement. New Haven had a generous harbor that attracted minister John Davenport, merchant Theophilus Eaton, and about 500 followers. The brutal conflict of the preceding year had removed any Native American threat, and smaller settlements quickly flourished along the coast, with the colonists later spreading throughout the Connecticut

An 1876 aerial view of New London, looking west. (Mystic Seaport)

River and Thames River Valleys. This pattern of development was to become familiar throughout New England.

Subsistence farming, fishing, and craftwork developed into profitable agriculture, shipbuilding, whaling, trade, and manufacturing in the 18th century, and the coast's industrial base made it pivotal to the fight for American independence. Besides supplying the Continental Army with men and provisions during the Revolution, the coast also witnessed Connecticut's only significant Revolutionary War battle, in 1781, when its traitorous native son, Benedict Arnold, led an attack on New London and Groton. The area also developed a naval manufacturing industry, starting in 1775—when, fueled by revolutionary zeal, Saybrook inventor David Bushnell designed the first submarine. (Two centuries later, in 1954, Groton launched the world's first nuclear-powered submarine.)

In the early 19th century, profits from trade with the West Indies and China financed architectural splendor in even the smallest ports, and the subsequent industrial revolution turned Norwich, New Haven, New London, and other towns

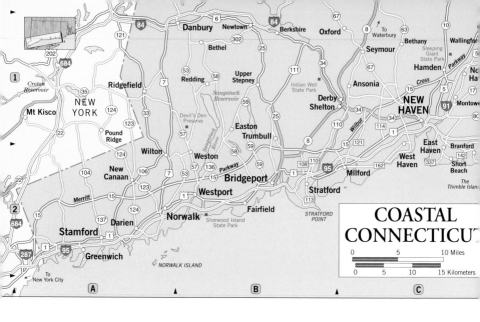

into centers of not only manufacturing, but also invention. The region's products included rifles, pianos, bicycles, cigars, combs, cotton, and paper. All the creative energy here did not revolve around industry or combat, however. Yale was founded in Killingworth in 1701, moving briefly to Saybrook before settling in New Haven, and Wesleyan University was founded in Middletown in 1831. New York painters discovered their neighbor's picturesque charms in the late 1800s, and artists' colonies like Old Lyme have been admiring themselves on canvas ever since.

■ GREENWICH   *map page 42–43, A-2*

The air in Greenwich, one of the nation's wealthiest suburbs, seems almost money-scented. The garish strip along U.S. 1 as it approaches the town center includes not only the ubiquitous fast-food, hardware, and other chain stores but also Mercedes-Benz, Audi, and Porsche dealerships. The "golden arches" of McDonald's are more discreet here, the women more perfectly groomed than nearly anywhere else on the East Coast. Greenwich men in their prime are generally absent during daylight hours, a detail that has changed little since the late 19th century, when trains carried bankers and brokers into New York City. As in times past, money is sometimes used a tool to keep outsiders at bay. After a court ruling in 2001 opened the town beach to all Connecticut residents instead of only Greenwich locals—as had been the situation for years—the citizenry responded by instituting a hefty fee to park at the beach.

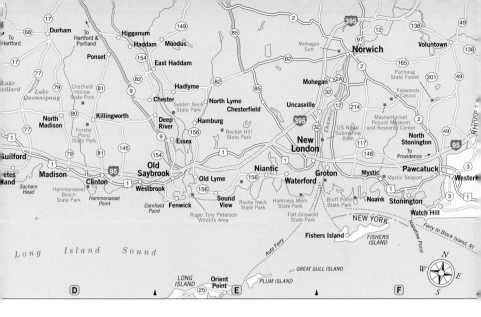

If old money built Greenwich, new money finances its continuing—though carefully controlled—growth, a fact embodied in the newly expanded Greenwich Library. The original 19th-century building in the center of town is now dwarfed by a computer-filled addition any university would crave.

Greenwich was a bargain in 1640, when Capt. Daniel Patrick and Robert Feaks, agents of the New Haven Colony, bought the land from the Native Americans for 25 English coats. After the purchase, New Amsterdam (subsequently New York City) and Connecticut tussled briefly over the boundary. During the Revolutionary War, homes were plundered and burned by British and Hessian soldiers under Gen. William Tryon, an assault that Gen. Israel Putnam and his 150 militiamen failed to repel.

Greenwich has attracted its share of writers over the years. Ring Lardner and Willa Cather lived here. Thomas Flanagan, the Irish writer and author of *The Irish Novelists 1800–1850,* and later Truman Capote attended Greenwich High School. And Clare Boothe, the playwright, journalist, and member of Connecticut's congressional delegation, married Henry R. Luce, the publisher of *Life* and *Time* magazines, in the First Congregational Church here. The surrounding suburbs have provided the setting for novels and short stories by Sloan Wilson, John Cheever, and Richard Yates.

Photogenic red brick buildings that were drugstores, hardware stores, and luncheonettes in their 1930s heyday line the center of Greenwich along U.S. 1, also called East Putnam Avenue and the Post Road. Now the buildings contain stores

A HIGHWAY TO TREASURE

Driving from the interior of Connecticut or from New York State on an early October day is a journey into green and golden light as you trade the harshness of I-95 for the leafy grace of a highway treasure, the famous Merritt Parkway. A beautifully landscaped four-lane highway on which trucks are banned, the parkway invites you to ease out of defensive driving and adjust your breathing.

Completed in 1938 and now a National Scenic Byway, the Merritt is noteworthy not only for its colonnade of pine, hemlock, cedar, maple, oak, dogwood, beech, birch, locust, and tulip trees, but also for its 69 bridges, each designed by George Dunkelberger and collectively an exemplar of 1930s engineering and ornamentation. Think of it as a drive-through art deco gallery.

Dunkelberger worked with the contours of the land, so the bridges on flatter ground have more horizontal lines while those on more dramatic terrain are more vertical. All are remarkable. A soaring arch carries Guinea Road over the Parkway in Stamford, and art deco reliefs decorate the abutments of the Long Ridge Road overpass and the New Canaan Avenue Bridge. Others are clad in finely wrought steel or trimmed with iron railings, like balconies overlooking a Parisian boulevard.

Not everybody adored the Merritt. Writing in 1949 for the Museum of Modern Art in New York City, the critic Elizabeth Mock cited the Riverbank Road Bridge as an example of the "elaborate foolishness of the pseudo-modern Connecticut underpass . . . whose vulgar ornament is peculiar to our times and easy of achievement in this docile material." The opinionated Ms. Mock would still find plenty of "elaborate foolishness" in some of the newer construction along the Connecticut coast, but with the passage of time the Merritt's ornamentation has, if anything, become classier since its debut.

selling antiques, designer clothing and housewares, and gourmet kitchen and food supplies. Anglophilia vies with Francophilia in a genteel merchandising battle. The banner in one store window reads "New Shipment in from England," words that would have meant something very different in 1779, when redcoats chased General Putnam as he dashed for reinforcements. Closing in, the British horsemen forced him to make a daring leap down a steep ravine, heralded now as the Horseneck Escape. Putnam, Washington's second in command, later met with Comte de Rochambeau and other dignitaries at the Knapp Tavern.

It's always time to shop in Greenwich.

Drawing, ca. 1836, of General Putnam's headquarters in the town of Redding, northeast of Greenwich. (Connecticut Historical Society)

The tavern, now known as **Putnam Cottage,** is set back from East Putnam Avenue, just outside Greenwich's commercial district. The red house, which dates from the 1690s, has undergone several restorations. A one-room farmhouse that was gradually expanded, the tavern was licensed in 1734 to provide "entertainment and strong drink." The scalloped shingles on the front, wide-plank floors, handsome beams, massive central chimney, and stark furnishings provide a tasteful contrast to the excesses of present-day Greenwich and recall a less complacent past. The effect is shattered as soon as you rejoin the traffic on U.S. 1, where huge SUVs advance in tight formation. *243 East Putnam Avenue; 203-869-9697.*

Putnam Avenue proceeds to the comparatively modest hamlet of **Cos Cob,** which was named after a Native American chief—an ironic touch, considering the bloody local history. Not far from here, at what was then the village of Petuquapen, Dutch and English settlers united to annihilate the Siwanoy tribe, which had resisted encroachment on its hunting grounds.

Turn right off Putnam Avenue onto Strickland Road to see a neighborhood of 18th- and early-19th-century houses whose restrained facades seem almost to becalm the surrounding air and silence the traffic noise. But the tranquility is short-lived. Strickland Road emerges abruptly onto Long Island Sound, where rows of fiberglass boats make the estuary look like a parking lot. Traffic roars over-head on I-95 like an enraged monster, while a blue heron holds its pose in the shal-lows below, like a steely old dame facing down a charging rhinoceros.

Following the sign to the **Bush-Holley Historic Site,** you may overshoot your mark and end up at the railway station. Proximity to New York City and ease of transport by steam train to what was then a glorious retreat made Bush-Holley the home of Connecticut's first art colony. From 1884 to 1920, Josephine Holley and her daughter, Constant, ran a boardinghouse for artists and writers, among them Childe Hassam, John Henry Twatchman, J. Alden Weir, Theodore Robinson, and other leading American impressionists, as well as the novelist Willa Cather. "There is a lot to do," Constant Holley MacRae wrote to her mother in 1902, "but just keep their bellies full and their tongues wagging and you're alright. Everyone is happy and thinks he is having a good time."

John Twatchman certainly did, complaining on his return to New York, "In the morning I shall wake up and—no—not walk out onto the upper porch to see what the day is like—but look down into the air shaft and in the street see the ugly holes of the subway on 4th Avenue."

"Strong drink" was on the bill of fare when Putnam Cottage was known as Knapp Tavern.

The Bush-Holley House and its still-glorious upper porch.

The house, built circa 1730, was sold by Constant Holley MacCrae, who had married artist Elmer McCrae, to the Greenwich Historical Society in 1957. Researchers drew on the extensive family archive of correspondence and illustrations to restore the rooms and surrounding grounds. The upper porch is still glorious. Standing there on a mild autumn afternoon following a tour of the house, you can erase I-95 if you squint hard enough. Then you can easily imagine the scenes that inspired the artists who took classes on this rickety wooden deck: Cos Cob harbor, with its shipyards, fishing boats, and perhaps a schooner in from New York; and the village square, shaded by huge elms, the entire scene suspended in opalescent light.

"The Hassams are settled in the big room downstairs," Constant wrote to a friend. "Mrs. Hassam says they always sleep together in cold weather, so they just have the big bed." A tour of the house not only communicates the practicality and unerring taste of its owners and their visitors, it also displays its treasures where they belong. Once you cross the threshold you are literally in the picture. Childe Hassam's *Clarissa,* a portrait of the MacRaes's daughter seated in the hallway, hangs in that same hallway; you enter through the same half-door depicted in Hassam's Clarissa etching. The etchings, by the way, are a revelation: study them carefully before you become completely overwhelmed by the paintings—by Hassam, MacRae, Walter A. Fitch, George Edward Hall, Daniel Putnam Brinley, and others—that hang in the hall, dining room, and north bedroom. Much of the furniture belonged to the Holleys.

In the visitors center is a low-key interactive exhibition that, among other things, allows participants to listen to sounds of the area from 100 years ago and plan the seating and menu for an artists' dinner. *39 Strickland Road (I-95, Exit 4); 203-869-6899.*

Inspired by a photograph of Childe Hassam, Charles Ebert, Walter Fitch, and an African-American child shucking oysters at the kitchen door, you may decide to forage for some yourself. Retrace your steps toward Greenwich and turn left onto Greenwich Avenue, where restaurants and cafes resuscitate flagging shoppers and tourists. The price tag for lunch or dinner follows a general rule: the higher up the avenue (toward Greenwich center), the higher the bill; less expensive though not necessarily inferior restaurants do business toward the bottom of the hill. To sample steaks and other American tavern-style food, try **Ginger Man** (64 Greenwich Avenue; 203-861-6400), which has a lively bar. If you're lucky, a celebrity regular like TV star Regis Philbin or movie director Ron Howard might drop by.

The nearby **Bruce Museum** is an institution dedicated to art, science, and environmental history. The museum mounts 12 exhibitions a year, ranging from contemporary art to ethnographic artifacts. The museum's collection includes works by American impressionists (not always on display), and among the permanent exhibits are woodland dioramas, a mineral gallery, and other natural-science wonders. *1 Museum Drive, off Greenwich Avenue (I-95, Exit 3); 203-869-0376.*

West of the Bruce Museum, the private enclave of **Belle Haven** is worth a detour if you can talk your way past the gatehouse to ogle the vast estates dating from the late 18th century to the 1930s. From Greenwich Avenue, follow Railroad Avenue west and turn left on Field Point Road.

If ogling is not enough, stay at the **Homestead Inn,** a mansion built in 1799 and an inn since 1859, by which time Italianate and Gothic architectural flourishes had been added. Chef Thomas Henklemann and his wife bought the house in 1977, and their inn radiates luxury without straying into pretension. The 19 rooms—sorry, chambers—are furnished with Frette linens (not chintz) and rose petals (not potpourri), and the restaurant menu sets an unfair standard for any traveler who is not proceeding directly to Paris or Vienna. *20 Field Point Road; 203-869-7500.*

To prolong your immersion in excess, follow Mason Street (just east of Greenwich Avenue) to North Street. Stately homes line North Street the way ranch houses line a suburban development: Tudor piles, French hunting lodges, Italian palazzi, Federal mansions. Most sit amid acres of manicured parkland or formal gardens. Others hide behind formidable stone walls erected with uniform skill and efficiency by 19th-century Italian stonemasons. A highway ramp or a shopping mall here would be a gigantic faux pas. On North Street, the purring of luxury automobile engines and what Joni Mitchell called "the hissing of summer lawns" prevails.

■ STAMFORD AND DARIEN *map page 42–43, A-2*

Traveling east from Greenwich on U.S. 1 or I-95, you reach Stamford. The first friction clutches, steam-powered wagons, and cylinder locks were Stamford inventions. Exhibits at the **Stamford Historical Society** (1508 High Ridge Road; 203-329-1183) chronicle these and other town accomplishments.

In 2002, the society's Tom Zoubek, who has a PhD in archaeology from Yale University, started an archaeological dig outside the original kitchen of the 1699 **Hoyt-Barnum House,** a restored blacksmith's dwelling the organization maintains. Zoubek found small animal bones, along with clam and scallop shells—evidence of what was once considered poor people's food. His discoveries are incorporated into new exhibitions at the house, which can be visited by appointment only, and at the historical society. The findings supplement those of an amateur dig conducted in the late 1960s, which turned up glass, pottery, clay pipe stems, buttons, pearlware and ceramic bowls, cups, and platters. The excavation will continue throughout the spring and summer over the next few years, and volunteers will be welcomed and trained. *713 Bedford Street; 203-329-1183.*

More about Stamford's past is revealed at the **Museum and Nature Center,** a 118-acre park that demonstrates every imaginable form of 19th-century agriculture and devotes seven galleries to Native American cultures, fine art, Americana, and natural history. *39 Scofieldtown Road; 203-322-1646.*

On a bright spring day, the rhododendrons and wildflowers at the 63-acre **Bartlett Arboretum** seem almost ablaze. Originally half its present size, the site held the residence of Dr. Francis A. Bartlett, a specialist in rhododendrons who also operated a training school and a research laboratory for his F. A. Bartlett Tree Expert Company. The Spring Plant Sale and Garden Fair in May is a great place to buy rare heirloom plants and pick up gardening tips and tools. *151 Brookdale Road, off High Ridge Road (Merritt Parkway, Exit 35); 203-322-6971.*

Farther east along U.S. 1 in Darien, the restored 1736 **Bates-Scofield Homestead** also evokes early Connecticut life. The classic saltbox-style house contains 18th- and early-19th-century regional furniture; planted in the garden are culinary, medicinal, and strewing herbs that would have been found area gardens of the period. *45 Old Kings Highway North; 203-655-9233.*

■ NEW CANAAN *map page 42–43, A-2*

Between Stamford and Darien, along Route 106 and north of the Merritt Parkway, the rocky slopes and forested valleys of the uplands attracted land-hungry settlers in the 17th century, witnessed bloody skirmishes during the Revolutionary War, and later attracted writers and artists seeking rustic rejuvenation. New Canaan has its share of newly minted architectural trophies, enormous mansions, many built with high-tech fortunes, that seem out of place among their more elegant 18th- and 19th-century neighbors. Best to start, though, with a corrective dose of history.

The several-building campus of the **New Canaan Historical Society** (33 Oenoke Ridge; 203-966-1776) includes the **Hanford-Silliman House,** which returns you to a time when a tavern's clay pipes were rented, tobacco twists were purchased by the inch, and checkers and dolls were fashioned out of corn husks. Built around 1764, the saltbox house remained in the Silliman family until the 1920s; it contains exceptional mid-18th-century furniture and an enchanting doll collection. You can also explore the **Rock School,** a 1799 one-room schoolhouse; the tool museum and re-created printing office, with a Smith Hoe Acorn hand

The St. Marks Strawberry Festival is held on Mother's Day weekend.

SALTBOX HOUSES

An architectural variation on early colonial houses, a "saltbox" house takes its name from the slanted-top box used to store salt in the American colonies. The Bates-Scofield Homestead in Darien and the Thomas Griswold House in Guilford are fine examples of this type of construction. Built out of wood, with clapboard siding, these humble frame houses usually had two stories in front, one story in back, and a pitched roof that was short and steep in front but sloping long and low in the back. The saltbox shape was produced when the owner added a one-story section across the rear of a one-and-a-half or two-story structure. A dozen or more people often crowded into colonial homes, creating the need for practical ways to expand living space. The rear, lean-to addition was often divided into three rooms: a central kitchen with fireplace and oven, a room reserved for childbirth and nursing the ill, and a pantry.

Initially conceived as a shortcut strategy for house enlargement, the saltbox eventually became an accepted building form, particularly in New England after 1680. A prominent center chimney or a pair of end chimneys also defined the saltbox style. Other common features included a center front entrance with a transom above, and double-hung windows of four panes over four, or six over six. A tribute to its simplicity and versatility, builders to this day construct houses in the saltbox style.

press; the first town hall, which houses the costume museum and library; and the **Cody Drug Store** (1845), which the morbidly inclined will find endlessly amusing.

Also here is **John Rogers Studio and Museum,** built in 1878. "The Slave Auction is beginning to go like hotcakes," wrote Rogers, one of the nation's most famous sculptors of the late 19th century, to his aunt in 1860 about the sales of plaster copies of his sculpture. "I have had calls from Dr. Cheever and several of the noted abolitionists." The museum chronicles the career of this immensely successful artist, who was born in Salem, Massachusetts, but spent much of his life in New Canaan. With its sympathetic—even romantic—depiction of African-American slaves, the Rogers statuary collection also charts the currents of popular sentiment in a nation on the brink of civil war.

The staff at the Historical Society can direct you on a walking tour of the town's historic district, once known as God's Acre. Among the district's 18th- and 19th-century residences are the **Fitch-Bergmann House,** a school at which, in 1794, one pupil recalled that the hogs that rooted in God's Acre "got in and ate my dinner . . . and my basket." Inquire also about the Depression-era WPA art in the town's civic buildings and schools.

For a glimpse of mansions new and old, follow Oenoke Ridge as it winds away from the historical society building. Alongside excesses from previous eras, 21st-century palaces are being constructed on foundations big enough to support a shopping mall. Most of these architectural parvenus can be easily dismissed, though, when you visit the 18th-century **Roger Sherman Inn,** which modestly conceals superb furnishings and a fine restaurant behind its white-clapboard facade. *195 Oenoke Ridge; 203-966-4541.*

■ NORWALK *map page 42–43, A/B-2*

From New Canaan, you can follow Route 123 south to Norwalk, a tough city that makes the immaculately groomed region from Greenwich to New Canaan seem like a mirage. Once a thriving industrial metropolis that covered both sides of the Norwalk River's harbor, Norwalk has declined since the days when its factories produced Dobbs hats, Norwalk tires, Binner corsets, and Church expansion bolts. The thundering mills and foundries are derelict or have been demolished, but the city seems perky rather than defeated, most noticeably along the rejuvenated waterfront of South Norwalk, or SoNo.

Here the most exotic residents don't mind if you stare; even the great white shark couldn't care less. Nor, frankly, could the river otters, harbor seals, or other inhabitants of the **Maritime Aquarium.** Occupying a huge 19th-century foundry building, this cornerstone of South Norwalk's redevelopment is a welcome reminder that local waters can be as fascinating as any coral reef. Seal feeding time is, of course, a crowd pleaser, along with whatever is playing in the IMAX theater. But the Aquarium's finest achievement is its imaginative depiction of Long Island Sound's underwater world.

In a tank labeled *Boulders off Penfield Reef Lighthouse,* the male oyster toadfish regularly torments his fellow tank dwellers with grunts that can reach 110 decibels, while the meek, distinctly homely lumpfish clings stoically to the nearest rock. *A Wreck off Horton Point Lighthouse* attracts cod and Atlantic wolffish. A dark corridor decorated with ominous fin-shaped shadows leads to the aquarium's star attraction, sharks. In the *Open Ocean* tank, sharks glide by so close to your face that you

stare into what Herman Melville, in his poem "The Maldive Shark," called that "saw-pit of mouth . . . the port of serrated teeth." Try in vain to ignite an expression in those glassy eyes, and you are the one who ends up mesmerized. Relieve the tension with a visit to Bell, the river otter who works ceaselessly on her water ballet, or look in on the aquarium's darting little coral fish and the profoundly unthreatening turtle nesting area. As they hurry to the aquarium's IMAX theater, most visitors ignore the evocative photographs of old Norwalk that line the corridor. They depict the Norwalk Iron Works building with urchin children or a stooped foundry worker in the foreground, the Norwalk Lock Company, the R&G Corset Company, and the schooner *Edward Young* moored at the dock. *10 North Water Street; 203-852-0700.*

The ferry departing regularly from Hope Dock beside the Maritime Aquarium is no schooner, but it shuttles back and forth daily from Memorial Day through September to the **Sheffield Island Lighthouse,** a four-story beacon dating from 1868 on a 3-acre island ideal for picnicking. *132 Water Street; 203-838-9444.*

Revived by your ocean voyage, visit the **Lockwood-Mathews Mansion Museum,** one of the few U.S. houses built in the French Second Empire style. Designed by Detlef Lienau for the investment banker LeGrand Lockwood, the mansion was built during the late 1860s at a cost of $1.2 million, two decades before the biggest palaces in Newport, Rhode Island, were built. The 62-room residence prefigured the Gilded Age not only in its grandiosity but also in the workmanship of the elaborately hand-painted walls, inlaid woodwork, and sky-lit rotunda. The Herter Brothers and other prominent New York cabinetmakers produced furniture, windows, and wainscoting that matched LeGrand Lockwood's ambitious vision. (Aficionados of the Herter Brothers have been known to travel great distances to view the house's exquisite examples of Herter craftsmanship.)

Originally set amid 30 acres of parkland, the house, flanked by a parking lot and a plain municipal building, sits within honking distance of the highway, looking rather forlorn. Concerned citizens saved it three times from demolition, and the ongoing restoration permits views of the skeleton and musculature of the ambitious structure as well as the original architectural and decorative flourishes.

On September 24, 1869, only months after the Lockwoods had moved into Elmenworth, as the estate was then called, the price of gold-mining stocks plummeted. Lockwood & Co., along with many other brokerage houses, collapsed, and

Norwalk is less prosperous than in days past, but the SoNo waterfront area is one bright spot.

LeGrand had to sell off many of his holdings. The railroad baron Cornelius Vanderbilt wound up controlling the mortgage on the house. A photograph taken that year of LeGrand, two of his children, and his sister-in-law, suggests a dour Micawber who must have realized by then that financial recovery was impossible. Four years later, Lockwood died of pneumonia, leaving behind a house that must have begun to feel like a mausoleum. *295 West Avenue, off U.S. 7 (I-95, Exit 15); 203-838-9799.*

If Lockwood's demise strikes you as a little too gloomy, repair to nearby **City Hall** to view the outstanding WPA murals and paintings by Alexander J. Rummler and Arthur G. Hull. Guided tours are sometimes conducted, but you are free to wander the spacious floors and contemplate gems like Rummler's *Mopping for Starfish, Apple Harvest,* or *Danbury Fair. 125 East Avenue; 203-854-7900.*

Alternatively, while away some time at **Sherwood Island State Park** and **Earthplace, the Nature Discovery Center** (10 Woodside Lane; 203-227-7253), which provide the simpler pleasures of a solitary beach walk or a woodland ramble through 62 acres with animal exhibits and an aquarium.

The 62-room Lockwood-Mathews Mansion in Norwalk cost more than a million dollars to build in the 1860s.

■ **WILTON** *map page 42–43, A/B-2*

Drive a short distance north on U.S. 7 from Norwalk and you will reach Wilton, a handsome suburban town that is marvelous to explore on bicycle. Follow any back road that captures your fancy for fine views and peeks at Victorian and colonial-era estates. (For information about cycling around the state, see "Getting There and Around" in the PRACTICAL INFORMATION chapter.)

The rooms in the **Wilton Heritage Museum,** inside the 1757 Raymond-Fitch House are furnished in styles from the mid-18th to the early 19th century. The dining room and chamber provide clues about the social and economic developments during that time, including the evolving nature of women's work in a nascent consumer society. The kitchen, with its huge fireplace and oven, contains an exceptional display of Norwalk redware and stoneware. The museum's other collections include dolls, toys, and textiles. *224 Danbury Road (Route 33); 203-762-7257.*

The nearby **Beth-Sturges Blackmar House** dates from 1735. From here, walk down the street to Lambert Corners to see a collection of historic buildings, most of them relocated from their original sites. The **David Lambert House** (150 Danbury Road), Wilton's oldest extant house, dates from 1726. The town's first railroad station sits on the house's grounds, as do the first general store, a one-room schoolhouse, a gambrel-roof barn, and other buildings.

A pretty bicycle ride follows Route 33 north through Wilton toward Ridgefield. About 2 miles outside Wilton, look for a right turn onto Nob Hill Road, an inviting country byway. Two miles of dreamy pedaling brings you to Whipstick Road, where you can turn left, then left again at Antler Road, finally arriving at the 146-acre **Woodcock Nature Center,** the perfect place for a contemplative rest or a brisk walk. Boardwalks allow you to walk through the fragile wetlands. The nature store and the interpretive exhibits at the center headquarters encourage you to learn and shop at the same time. If you're coming to the center by car, head north 4 miles on Route 33 from Wilton Town Center. Make a right onto Millstone Road and a left on Deer Run Road. *56 Deer Run Road; 203-762-7280.*

The **Devil's Den Preserve,** a patchwork of woodlands, wetlands, and rock ledges between Weston and Redding, measures 1,720 acres. Humans share its 20-mile trail system with bobcats, coyotes, and other wild inhabitants. No bicycles are allowed here, but two-wheel adventurers can head to the southwestern shore of the Saugatuck Reservoir, off Route 53. *Route 57 (Exit 42 off Merritt Parkway) to Route 53, west on Godfrey Road and north on Pent Road; 203-226-4991.*

■ **WESTPORT** *map page 42–43, B-2*

Route 58 off the Merritt Parkway leads to Westport, another wealthy enclave with a long theatrical and literary pedigree. In 1920, F. Scott Fitzgerald lived on Compo Road for a year with his new bride, Zelda, and the exclusive neighborhood credits itself as being the inspiration for the West Egg setting of *The Great Gatsby.* Legendary actors perform during the summer at the acclaimed Westport Playhouse. Paul Newman and Joanne Woodward are permanent residents of the town, but the leading celebrity may be Martha Stewart, who dictates national taste from her immaculate compound on Turkey Hill Road, where even the wildlife is probably color-coordinated.

The bridge carrying the Boston Post Road (U.S. 1) over the Saugatuck River has been widened to include a promenade, and the once-declining wharf district is filled with cafes and boutiques. Serious shopping, though, takes place on Main Street, which resembles an upscale mall and can make the unprepared visitor feel distinctly shabby.

To get a feel for what Westport was and is, visit the **Wheeler House,** the head-quarters of the Westport Historical Society. "The guardians of Westport's past," as the members like to refer to themselves, mount high-quality exhibits about the town and its current and former celebrity residents, who include Paul Newman and Joanne Woodward, Marlo Thomas and Phil Donahue, Robert Redford, and Christopher Plummer. In addition to the Wheeler House, built in 1795 and remodeled in the Italianate style in the 1860s, the society has an octagonal cobbled barn with a walk-around diorama depicting Westport in 1900. *25 Avery Place, off Main Street; 203-222-1424.*

Construct your own celebrity fantasy by reserving one of the 15 suites at the **Inn at National Hall,** each one of them fantastic in the literal sense of the word. Built in 1873, the massive red brick Georgian building overlooks the Saugatuck River, a waterway that facilitated a vigorous 17th-century smuggling trade and later a thriving fleet of "pedlar ships." At National Hall, even the elevator puts you in your place by concealing its buttons in a whimsical trompe l'oeil wall covering. The rates, which start at more than $300, are also humbling, though the decor lives up to the price tag. The rooms and suites vary wildly in style, from the

Classy collectibles and the occasional kitschy item can be found in stores all over Westport.

Turkistan Suite to the Henny Penny Suite, from the equestrian to the colonial. This may sound a bit much, but the workmanship is impressive and the intention is so obviously playful that the overall effect is delightful. Laugh out loud at the excesses of the India Room, and the porter will smile discreetly instead of being offended, gratified that sir or madam appreciates the whimsy. *2 Post Road West; 203-221-1351 or 800-628-4255.*

If the menu at Miramar, the Inn at National Hall's restaurant, seems a little rich, and if Westport's newest establishments strike you as working too hard on their ambiance, wade into a plate of oysters or steamers at the rickety **Mansion Clam House** (541 Riverside Avenue, at Green Farms Road; 203-454-7979). Or reassure yourself with a visit to the **Sherwood Diner** (901 Post Road East; 203-226-5535), open 24 hours a day. When the waitress asks if you're "new in town," you'll feel like a film noir character and briefly smolder over your coffee before ruining the effect by ordering a cheese blintz or the divine pudding. (Film noir characters don't eat.)

You can add variety by taking a solitary walk on stony beaches. **Sherwood Island State Park** (follow the signs opposite the Sherwood Diner on the Post Road) is one of state's best public beaches, but on an early spring or late autumn

A warm autumn evening at Compo Beach brings out the strollers.

afternoon, you will have it to yourself. Don't be alarmed by loud buzzing overhead as you return to your car. The members of the Squires County Model Airplane Club have been perfecting their aerial gymnastics here for decades, and they love to show off. *Sherwood Connector off the Post Road East (I-95, Exit 18).*

Leaving Sherwood Island State Park, follow Green Farms Road heading west past the wealthy enclaves on that road and perpendicular Beachside Avenue, to Compo Road South and Compo Beach Road. Lined with houses only a notch below the ones off Green Farms Road, **Compo Beach** encourages social promenading, not solitary hikes. Toned bodies in black Lycra predominate, but the view of Long Island Sound is restful. Parking is open to Westport and Weston residents only, but large flocks of South American monk parakeets—exotic escapees thought to have arrived in the 1960s—nest and perch throughout the neighborhood, defying any official to examine their permits.

The Pequot Indians were treated less tolerantly than the parakeets have been. At the end of the Pequot War, the Pequot survivors of a combined English and Mohegan attack on West Mystic were surrounded near the present-day border between Westport and Fairfield; the final slaughter came in July 1637. The battle site is commemorated on U.S. 1 in **Southport** with a granite monument.

■ FAIRFIELD *map page 42–43, B-2*

The Old Post Road follows the original Indian trail around which Fairfield was laid out. The town was destroyed in 1779 when the commander of the British forces, Gen. William Tryon, raided the area, and more than a hundred Revolutionary soldiers are interred in the **Old Burying Ground** (430 Beach Road). Fairfield recovered admirably, though, developing into a prosperous farming, whaling, and shipping center.

At the **Fairfield Historical Society** (636 Old Post Road, at Beach Road; 203-259-1598), you can pick up brochures with walking tours of some of the town's nearly 200 houses from the 18th and 19th centuries. Inland relics include the 18th-century **Ogden House** (1520 Bronson Road, off the Post Road), a farmhouse that survived the 1779 British attack. The house's opening each spring coincides with the town's well-attended dogwood festival. Exhibits at the **Connecticut Audubon Birdcraft Museum** (314 Unquowa Road; 203-259-0416), opened in 1914, explain the area's natural history.

■ BRIDGEPORT *map page 42–43, B-2*

The contrast between the wealth of towns like Greenwich and Westport and the poverty of Bridgeport could not be starker. The city's long decline makes the following description from the 1938 Federal Writers' Project *Guide to Connecticut* all the more poignant: "Bridgeport does not depend upon any class of manufactured goods for its prosperity. Probably no city in the United States includes more diversified industries. . . . Today almost five hundred manufacturing firms, many with a large export trade, produce ammunition and firearms, automatic machinery, nuts, bolts and screws, brass products, brake linings, corsets, chains, electrical and pharmaceutical supplies, hardware, marine cables and engines. . . ."

The list continues for paragraphs. When it was written, Bridgeport was a city with a socialist mayor and a predominantly immigrant population employed in turning out every product imaginable. Local engineer Igor Sikorsky developed the helicopter here, and at the beginning of World War II the city became an aeronautical center. From the 1950s through the 1990s, though, Bridgeport's industries either failed or moved south, and Connecticut's largest city became one of the nation's poorest. Atrocious planning decisions in the late 1950s doomed entire blocks of historic buildings to make way for concrete monstrosities and highway construction. Bridgeport's greatest mansion, the Harral-Wheeler House, bequeathed to the city in 1958 by the last Wheeler heir for "educational and park purposes," was bulldozed to make way for a grotesque civic center.

The Wheeler fortune was made from sewing. Founded in 1851 in Watertown, New York, and moved to Bridgeport in 1856, the Wheeler and Wilson Manufacturing Company, later the Singer Manufacturing Company, produced a sewing machine invented by Allen B. Wilson in 1847. Wilson's innovations included the rotary hook-and-bobbin combination.

At the beginning of the 21st century, Bridgeport remains a struggling postindustrial metropolis, its streetscapes fractured by confusing highway ramps. But in the past few years, there have been attempts at rejuvenation, primarily in the downtown area surrounding the Barnum Museum and in the Blackrock Cove neighborhood south of the city. In 2001, after a long absence, the Ringling Brothers Barnum and Bailey Circus paraded down Main Street again, past the Barnum Museum, to trumpet an elephant salute at City Hall—a good omen, perhaps, for a city that badly needs one.

The Easton Congregational Church.

HUSTLER EXTRAORDINAIRE

Showman Phineas T. Barnum based a career on a simple philosophy: "The bigger the humbug, the better people will like it." Born in nearby Bethel, Connecticut, in 1810, Barnum was 15 when his father died, leaving Phineas to support his mother and five sisters and brothers. A few years later, he became publisher of a Danbury weekly newspaper, the *Herald of Freedom*. During his tenure at the paper he was sued three times for libel but never convicted.

Barnum's first big humbug was exhibiting Joice Heth as George Washington's 161-year-old nurse (she died in 1836 at age 70). In 1841, Barnum purchased John Scudder's American Museum in New York City, and turned the five-story marble building into a theater for beauty contests, freak shows, and other outrageous events. P.T., as the showman became known, achieved worldwide fame with Gen. Tom Thumb, the 25-inch-high Charles Stratton, who was presented to Abraham Lincoln, Queen Victoria, and various European monarchs.

In an effort to upgrade his public image, Barnum imported the Swedish soprano Jenny Lind, and, without first seeing her or hearing her sing, dubbed her the "Swedish Nightingale" as part of a huge publicity campaign. After her nine-month concert tour in the United States, Jenny Lind was a household name and Barnum was an even richer man.

Meanwhile, Barnum served two terms in the Connecticut legislature and was elected mayor of Bridgeport. An extraordinary hustler on the town's behalf, he fought union discrimination against African-Americans, improved railroad service, expanded Bridgeport's harbor, and developed municipal parks. But Barnum will forever be remembered for his outrageous humbugs, which were so big that people the world over liked them.

Tom Thumb was one of Barnum's most lucrative acts. (Library of Congress)

A fanciful Romanesque building houses the equally fanciful Barnum Museum.

The **Barnum Museum** chronicles the fantastic life and "inventions" of Phineas T. Barnum—showman, huckster, visionary—but also pays tribute to Bridgeport's industrial history with an exhibit of locally made products that is sure to induce nostalgia in older visitors. Whether you find "The Greatest Show on Earth" exhibits equally pleasurable will depend on how easily you reach your "inner child," who should be released as soon as you enter the museum. The replica of the grotesque "Feejee Mermaid" (the original was made by combining an orangutan's torso with the lower section and tale of a fish), the two-headed calf, and other wonders conjure up a Barnum who was not only a lifelong hustler but also a perennial schoolboy, the type who is happiest when he is displaying his crushed insect collection to a horrified aunt. The hodgepodge of artifacts includes an Egyptian mummy, a hand-carved miniature five-ring circus with half a million figures, and clown paraphernalia. An oddly touching evocation of an era when freaks appeared not on television but in traveling shows, the exhibits make even the most skeptical visitor's jaw drop, just as Barnum intended. *820 Main Street; 203-331-1104.*

Barnum donated **Seaside Park** to the city in 1865, and a statue of him here gazes out toward Long Island Sound. The glorious 325-acre expanse of lawns, parkland, monuments, and sculptures was originally laid out by Frederick Law Olmsted and Calvert Vaux, the designers of New York City's Central Park. The statue of Elias Howe recalls not only the inventor but also the soldier. During the Civil War, Howe recruited a volunteer infantry regiment, the 17th Connecticut, and the newly minted soldier, by then earning thousands of dollars in royalties from his sewing machine, slept on a bed of straw on this promontory. *From the Barnum Museum, head south on Broad Street.*

From Fairfield Avenue, which intersects Broad Street north of Seaside Park, you can follow the signs to the marshy coves of **St. Mary's by the Sea,** where egrets stand sentinel on tidal flats and graceful mansions withstand the passing gaze of visitors grateful to have found respite from the traffic by wandering into this affluent section of town. Fairfield Avenue provides another rewarding detour, to **Captain's Cove** in Black Rock Harbor, where you may see the HMS *Rose,* a reconstruction of a 1757 ship that participated in the Revolutionary War, or the 1936 lightship *Nantucket,* which once stood guard at the treacherous Shoals of Nantucket.

The promenade at St. Mary's by the Sea.

■ **STRATFORD** *map page 42–43, B-2*

Stratford seems like an eastern extension of Bridgeport, but a closer examination reveals a coastal suburb that retains its distinctive heritage. Settled in 1639 and named after Stratford-upon-Avon in England, the town was home to the Stratford Shakespeare Festival during the last half of the 20th century. The festival has been suspended for the past few years, but its backers hope to revive the event.

The Academy Hill neighborhood is ideal for strolling. In the late 1630s, this area was known as Watch Hill because English settlers manned a blockhouse here to keep an eye out for Dutch or Indian attacks. In 1750 or so, the **Captain David Judson House** was built. A noteworthy example of Georgian architecture, it contains exhibits that provide insight into the life style of Connecticut's 18th-century affluent. The outstanding collection of Chinese porcelain, the beautiful paneling, and the period Stratford furniture contrast starkly with the slave quarters in the basement. The small museum behind the house has exhibits about area history. *967 Academy Hill; 203-378-0630.*

Whimsy holds sway at the **Boothe Memorial Park and Museum,** the 32-acre former homestead of the Boothe family, which flourished here from 1663 to 1949. A three-story pagoda-like structure made out of redwood and glass bricks catches the eye immediately, but equally intriguing are the miniature windmill and lighthouse—all built because the Boothes felt like having them built. Among the several other outdoor exhibits is a cabin-like Merritt Parkway tollbooth, moved here after the state stopped collecting tolls on the parkway in the late 1980s. The park grounds are open year-round, but, as with the Judson house, the museum's hours are limited, so it's best to call ahead. *134 Main Street Putney (just south of Merritt Parkway, Exit 53); 203-381-2046.*

■ **NEW HAVEN** *map page 42–43, C-1/2*

New Haven and the surrounding territory were bought from the Quinnipiac tribe for the sum of 23 coats "of English trucking cloathe," 12 spoons, 24 knives, 12 hatchets, and assorted hoes, when John Davenport and Theophilus Eaton settled here in 1638. To appreciate the bargain, take the Lighthouse Point Park exit off I-95 on the city's outskirts to the **Lighthouse Point Park,** a preserve that commands spectacular views of the bay, harbor, and city.

(following pages) The New Haven Green is the center square of America's first planned city.

A vintage postcard depicts the Green and its greenery. (Library of Congress)

Two forts here—**Black Rock Fort,** dating from the Revolutionary War, and **Fort Nathan Hale,** dating from the Civil War—are reminders of New Haven's turbulent history (for information about both forts, call 203-946-8790). Three thousand British troops invaded the city in 1779, hoping to lure George Washington out of New York. They quickly retreated, having burned Black Rock Fort and the nearby **Pardee Morris House** (325 Lighthouse Road; 203-562-4183), rebuilt between 1780 and 1820 and now the city's best-preserved 18th-century dwelling.

■ YALE UNIVERSITY AREA

Swooping off I-95 to Yale University, you feel as if you have gone underwater. The traffic's roar is suddenly muffled and the light is greenish, leaf-filtered. The true "haven" in New Haven, Yale's campus borders the 18-acre New Haven Green and seems hermetically sealed off from the surrounding, somewhat grim metropolis. The university's buildings face each other, their backs to the 21st century. To stroll the campus, start at the **Yale University Visitor Information Center** (149 Elm Street, at College Street; 203-432-2300). The center is in the oldest of three 18th-century wood-frame houses on the Green. Free campus tours leave from here on weekdays at 10:30 A.M. and 2 P.M. and weekends at 1:30 P.M.

Founded in 1701 in Killingworth, with offshoots in Old Saybrook and other neighboring communities, and permanently established in New Haven in 1717, Yale University is a fastidious collection of gothic tracery, grassy parks, and shady courtyards. **Phelps Gate,** facing the green, leads to the Old Campus, built between 1842 and 1928. **Connecticut Hall** is the oldest university building, dating from 1717, but Yale's most ancient-looking buildings were actually erected between 1919 and 1941.

The most architecturally alien presence here is also one of the most glorious, the **Beinecke Rare Book and Manuscript Library,** inside a massive block of Vermont marble and granite, bronze, and glass that is more starship than building. Huge "windows" of translucent marble protect the 180,000 volumes in the central tower, and more than 500,000 books and several million manuscripts reside underground. Padding around the starship *Beinecke,* you circle this book aquarium, admiring ancient bindings and titles while students in the reading room below peruse the daily catch, served up by library staff. In addition to its astonishing general holdings, the library also houses collections of Western Americana, German literature, and English literary and historical manuscripts. The Gutenberg Bible and John James Audubon's *Birds of America* are permanently displayed alongside special exhibitions. Research at the Beinecke may reveal why James Fenimore Cooper was expelled from Yale, why Sinclair Lewis briefly dropped out, and the secrets of other graduates such as Jonathan Edwards, Nathan Hale, and Thornton Wilder. Cole Porter, a cheerleader who graduated in 1913, once confessed, "I delight in being chatty with New Haven's literati." *121 Wall Street; 203-432-2977.*

The nearby **Yale University Art Gallery**—the country's oldest university art museum—exhibits Picasso's *First Steps,* van Gogh's *Night Cafe,* Seurat's tiny *Cow,* and other marvels, not all of them on canvas. The gallery's collection of American furniture and silver is outstanding. *Chapel and High Streets; 203-432-0600.*

Across the street, the **Yale Centre for British Art** (1080 Chapel Street; 203-432-2800) will effortlessly steal your time and thoughts with works by J. M. W. Turner, William Blake, Joshua Reynolds, Anthony van Dyck, Thomas Gainsborough, and others. The museum shop will drive Anglophiles to distraction. The **Yale Repertory Theater** (1120 Chapel Street; 203-432-1234), the nearby **Shubert Performing Arts Center** (247 College Street; 203-562-5666),

(above) Interior courtyard on Yale University campus. (opposite) Yale's Harkness Tower.

built in 1914, and the **Long Wharf Theater** (222 Sargent Drive; 203-787-4282), along the waterfront, make New Haven one of the region's richest theatrical venues—many productions have their pre-Broadway tryouts here.

To get a sense of New Haven's sedate past, follow splendid Hillhouse Avenue past 19th-century mansions, now owned by Yale. Also here is the **Yale Collection of Musical Instruments** (15 Hillhouse Avenue; 203-432-0822). At the **Peabody Museum of Natural History** (170 Whitney Avenue; 203-432-5050), a gigantic brontosaurus skeleton dwarfs the other fine exhibits. The nearby **New Haven Colony Historical Society** (114 Whitney Avenue; 203-562-4183) displays Eli Whitney's cotton gin and mounts exhibits covering 350 years of the city's history.

On the opposite side of the New Haven Green, on Chapel Street, **Wooster Square,** between Academy Street and Wooster Place, is an architectural showplace of 19th-century homes enhanced in spring by flowering cherry trees. **Frank Pepe's** (157 Wooster Street; 203-865-5762), off the square, is where the American version of pizza was invented and where today's version upholds the standard. If the wait is too long at Pepe's, head across the street to the equally atmospheric Sally's.

■ HAMDEN *map page 42–43, C-2*

An exploration of the back roads north of New Haven reveals the unequal struggle between land and concrete. Pockets of farmland, though, have survived the suburban pincer movement from New Haven and Hartford, especially on Route 68 between Wallingford and Durham, where the smell of manure still overpowers that of asphalt.

A surprisingly short distance from downtown New Haven off Route 10 lies the 1,500-acre **Sleeping Giant State Park,** which follows the line of the city's surrounding volcanic hills and allows you to refill your lungs along a 32-mile trail of woodland and rock. For a real workout, hike the entire trail; a casual stroll to the peak yields views of foliage and the surrounding countryside. The park's entrance is opposite Quinnipiac University. *200 Mount Carmel Avenue; 203-789-7498.*

■ BRANFORD AND THE THIMBLE ISLANDS
map page 42–43, C-2

Escape I-95 east of New Haven by taking Route 142 (Exit 53) at Branford and heading east on Route 146. There is traffic on this pleasantly contorted route to Guilford and Madison, and modest houses as well. But the curves and the views impose a soothing dreaminess. Crossing the salt marshes with your window down, you hear the clacking of the reeds and the creak of the bulrushes, and may eavesdrop on duck conversation.

Your ocean view is dominated by the Thimble Islands, which at times seem to be within wading distance. Turn right off Route 146 onto Thimble Islands Road and follow it to **Stony Creek,** a village tucked so neatly into its sheltering cove that it might have been painted onto the outcropping. At summer's height, traffic in the harbor and on the village's narrow streets reaches an impressive peak as SUVs progress, tank-like, to the shore while a nimble flotilla of sailboats, fishing boats, kayaks, and ferries navigates the sound.

To join a fancier throng, hop aboard a tour boat at Stony Creek Dock and cruise around some of the Thimble Islands. Depending on whom you believe and how many rocks you include, the archipelago encompasses up to 365 islands with names like Cut-in-Two, Mother-in-Law, Beers, and Money. Each one has a story, and your captain will happily relate several, including the one about pirate Captain Kidd, who is said to have buried treasure on one of the islands in 1699.

In the late 19th century, wealthy families from New York and Connecticut began to build grand summer houses on the Thimble Islands—during the 1930s there were even a few small resort hotels—and more than 100 of those meticulously restored houses remain to be gawked at from the tour boat. About two dozen of the islands are inhabited, the tinier ones supporting perhaps one cottage apiece. Others, like Money Island, contain a substantial cluster. When it came to mansion building, there was a more subtle vanity at work on the Thimble Islands than there was in Newport. Here the seascape was incorporated into the architecture, not overwhelmed by it, muting both the grandiosity of the mansions and the cloying charm of Victorian cottages that appear to have been here forever.

Strolling back to your car with a sailor's gait, rejoin Route 146, at this point called Leete's Island Road. After the sandy outcropping of Leete's Island, turn right onto Sachem Head Road, another good place to ride a bicycle. **Sachem Head** earned its name when the Mohegan chief, Uncas, exhibited his enemy's head in a tree during the Pequot War. The rugged 600-acre peninsula of salt marsh, beach, forest, rocky bluffs, and vacation houses has become increasingly popular with weekend and summer visitors tired of the Hamptons and attracted by the sophisticated shopping and restaurant activity in neighboring Guilford. Sachem Head reflects the change, but development is curtailed by the presence of wetlands on which building is prohibited. The promontory retains a feeling of remoteness, particularly in early spring, when you can observe nesting cranes instructing their young.

■ **GUILFORD** *map page 42–43, D-2*

After the marshland reveries of Sachem Head, Guilford, to the west on Route 146, feels strikingly solid. Granite from its quarries formed part of the Brooklyn Bridge and the base of the Statue of Liberty, but the town's most impressive rock formation is the oldest stone house in Connecticut. Newly arrived English settlers who had decided to live midway between more established New Haven and Saybrook built the residence for pastor Henry Whitfield.

The **Henry Whitfield House,** on a sloping orchard field just outside town, was part dwelling, part meeting place, and part fortress, erected on land bought in 1639 from the Menuncatuck Indians, a small tribe whose sachem was a woman called Shaumpishuh. Weather was a serious adversary during the autumn of 1639, and legend has it that only the north chimney stack and half of the room now known as the Great Hall had been completed before freezing temperatures halted all masonry work. Spring saw the completion of two floors and the spacious attic. A covenant drawn up on the voyage from England bound the members of the Whitfield contingent to each other, making them pledge "not to desert or leave each other or the plantation, but with the consent of the rest." But Henry Whitfield did leave, in 1650 or 1651. The original structure was altered over the years by later owners and during restorations that began after the dwelling was purchased by the state in the late 1800s. None of the English or American furnishings on display belonged to the Whitfields, but some of the earliest pieces belonged to contemporaries who developed the Guilford settlement.

The Whitfield House, which contains exhibits about the home and the settlement, still exudes the stoical optimism of its builders. The adjacent visitors center has changing exhibits, tourist information, and rest rooms. *248 Old Whitfield Road, at Stonehouse Lane (follow signs from Whitfield Road heading south from the town green); 203-453-2457.*

The stone house blends in with the surrounding land, and it is not alone in that happy circumstance. Spared destruction by the British during the Revolution largely because its militia successfully defended nearby Leete's Island, Guilford retains an intact architectural face. And unlike so many historic houses that sit marooned and humiliated on a commercial strip, Guilford's architectural treasures reside in an intelligently preserved landscape. The heart of Guilford is one of the area's loveliest town greens, bordered by 18th- and 19th-century residences and commercial buildings. The stores here cater mainly to affluent shoppers craving organic-cotton clothing and handmade chocolates. Most of the town's several hundred historic homes are privately owned, but Boston Street (Route 146), off the green, contains two gems, the Thomas Griswold House and the Hyland House, both open seasonally.

On a muggy afternoon, the very sight of the **Thomas Griswold House** is inviting. Trees shade the large, sloping meadow and the white clapboard house lures you inside with dark rooms that still smell of wood smoke. A more surprising delight, once you cross the threshold, is the palpable presence of the Griswolds themselves. The land the building occupies had been in the Griswold family since

Henry Whitfield House, 1639, is the oldest stone house in New England.

1695, when Thomas Griswold II moved from Wethersfield. Around 1774, Thomas Griswold III built the restrained saltbox house for two of his sons, and it remained in the Griswold family until the Guilford Keeping Society bought it in 1958. Following restorations in 1974 and 1995, the house is furnished in the style of the early 19th century. Several items listed in George Griswold's inventory—a parlor mirror, a dressing table—remain in the house. The sense of entering the lives of its former occupants increases as you visit the attic bedroom, with its straw beds.

The changing exhibits in an upstairs room reinforce the intimacy of the tour. A recent one presented the story of Hannah Landon and her daughters, Nancy Griswold, Henrietta Hill, and Mary Ann Tharp, as told through letters that are startlingly immediate in their references to ailments, weather, and loneliness. Behind the house are a large barn, a blacksmith shop, and a Victorian privy. Horticultural purists may notice that the garden is filled only with plants that were available before 1820. *171 Boston Street, at Lovers Lane; 203-453-3176.*

The Thomas Griswold House was built ca. 1774 in the saltbox style.

The **Hyland House** is a saltbox reputedly built between 1690 and 1710, though the height of its rooms has convinced some experts that construction more likely began around 1770. Unperturbed by the debate, the dignified house tolerates visitors crawling around its three walk-in fireplaces and is probably gratified when somebody notices its carved overhang or recognizes the name of its most celebrated occupant, town clockmaker Ebenezer Parmelee. *84 Boston Street; 203-453-9477.*

Guilford's long history includes a childhood visit from Harriet Beecher Stowe, who spent a year on her grandmother's farm, where she met her first African-Americans, the household's indentured servants. Stowe is most famous for her first book, *Uncle Tom's Cabin* (1852), which the Connecticut native wrote while she was living in Brunswick, Maine. Begun as a serial for the Washington antislavery weekly *National Era*, the deeply controversial work focused public interest on the issue of slavery.

Should you begin to feel like a musty old Griswold or Whitfield, or if Guilford's charms become too cloying, you can blow the cobwebs away and restore your sense of geological perspective by driving north on Route 77 to the southernmost tip of the Metacomet Ridge at Bluff Head. This wall of ancient lava deposits runs as far north as the Holyoke Range in Massachusetts, and its dramatic formations provide spectacular, if at times demanding, hikes. Serious footwear and surefootedness required.

Above North Guilford, Route 77 runs through rock hills of lava traprock and schist formed 200 to 400 million years ago. Lake Quonnipaug is on your right, and a parking area for Bluff Head is a half-mile north of the ancient pond (stocked with trout and open for public fishing). A climb to the 500-foot summit—720 feet above sea level—provides an outstanding view of Long Island Sound to the south, Myer Huber Pond to the east, and a collage of fields and hills that look like a child's play farm. Only masochists hike this section of the Mattabesett Trail in hot weather, though, so choose a clear, cool spring or autumn day. Set off early with a packed lunch and plenty of water to enjoy at the summit, and begin your descent in early afternoon: Even hardy climbers dislike scrambling down scree in twilight.

Those who enjoy their hikes spiked with a frisson of danger will be happy to know that the northern copperhead—one of New England's two poisonous snakes, the other being the timber rattlesnake—is most commonly found on the basalt ledges of the Metacomet Range. Snakes are not impressed by screaming.

■ **MADISON** *map page 42–43, D-2*

Returning southward unmolested, you may gratefully follow the snake-free surface of U.S. 1, which curves soothingly across the East River into the equally soothing village of Madison, where the wildest thing you see may be an outdoor sculpture exhibition on the green or a brace of sweating joggers. Originally settled as part of Guilford, Madison has a less rarefied air than its upscale neighbor. There are plenty of antiques shops and galleries on the outskirts, but places like the downtown **Madison Coffee Shop** (765 Boston Post Road; 203-245-4474) still serve blue-plate specials and you'll likely come across friendly locals eager to point you toward Connecticut's best beaches, which form Madison's threshold.

Before kicking off your shoes beachside, though, you should wander around the Madison Green Historic District, a town common regularly enlivened by festivals and concerts. The **Deacon John Grave House,** on the edge of the green, is in a class by itself. Perhaps the best-preserved and documented 17th-century dwelling in Connecticut, the large colonial saltbox began life as a two-room cabin and stands today on its original site. According to early records, John Grave was granted land in East Guilford (now Madison) sometime before 1680. Required to build on the land or pay a sizable fine, Grave quickly erected a simple cabin. In 1685, John Grave II and his new bride moved into the house.

All this and a great deal more is known because the Graves were an archivist's dream: the family members kept ledgers from 1678 until 1933. "I begin to teach school on December 16, 1707," John II wrote, adding that there were nine male students. The Graves family liked facts and recorded them meticulously. By 1717, when John II became a tavern keeper, a large central chimney and a two-story section now called the Tavern Room had been added. We learn from John's ledger that a Nathaniel Holley ran a tab that included ". . . a pot of milk punch, a gill of rum, a pot of cider, a meal of victuals, a tankard of metheglin" (a type of mead).

There is also evidence that these dedicated record keepers were men of action. In the side of the chimney, you can see the narrow steps that led into a secret room used to store firearms and ammunition during the French and Indian War. John III served as a justice of the peace from 1750 until his death in 1763, and the parlor became his courtroom. The atmosphere of both the tavern and the courthouse is still detectable in the low rooms that, on an autumn afternoon, retain the russet light. *581 Boston Post Road; 203-245-4798.*

East of the Grave house, the **Allis-Bushnell House** was built in 1785 in the saltbox style. During the 19th century it was home to Cornelius Bushnell, a founder of the Union Pacific Railway and the chief financier of the Civil War iron-clad ship the USS *Monitor*. Furnished with 18th- and 19th-century pieces and now headquarters of the Madison Historical Society, the house is a good place to learn about the lives of those buried in the nearby smallpox cemetery, or to ask where you might buy a tankard of metheglin. *853 Boston Post Road; 203-245-4567.*

Few subjects divide traveling companions as effectively as that of the beach. For many the very word "beach" means happiness. For others, it means hours of bore-dom punctuated by meaningless sandy chores, such as applying sunscreen, erecting flimsy shanties to protect offspring, or assembling gritty sandwiches. The bad news for the latter crowd is that coastal Connecticut is one long beach stretching from Greenwich in the west to Stonington in the east. The good news is that the beach experience can be astonishingly varied. Madison is the perfect example. A seaside resort since the late 19th century, when shingled cottages began to appear outside town, Madison is a magnet for beach lovers, although from Memorial Day through October, access is limited to residents or guests of the town's hotels. But in the off-season, the sheltered cove at West Beach, outside Madison, is ideal for swimming in waters that retain the summer heat and become satisfyingly theatrical in stormy weather.

Regardless of the season, **Hammonasset Beach State Park,** between Madison and Clinton, welcomes even anti-beach curmudgeons onto its 1,000-acre penin-sula and onto its 2 miles of sand that truly deserves the tired adjective "golden." Fastidious visitors will be delighted by the clean, roomy bathhouses, and aerobic types will breathe easier when they see the imaginatively laid-out biking trails and the inviting wooden boardwalk. Fishermen will rush to cast for bluefish and striped bass from a long jetty that provides plenty of elbow room, and swimmers and sunbathers will do what they always do, but on sand that is smoother than that found elsewhere along the coast.

Those are the immediate surprises (high-season traffic is another, less agreeable revelation). But the park, open from Memorial Day to Labor Day, has other charms. Inland, it is a dreamy composition of marshland and bayberry thickets, irresistible to nesting and migrating birds that mesmerize the humans who rever-ently observe them.

The Hammonasset Natural Area, at the park's eastern tip, encompasses a series of marsh islands—ethereal on a May morning with mist hanging in the salty air—that constitute a major junction for migrating warblers and many other species in spring and autumn. From a series of sturdy observation platforms, visitors can view great blue herons, egrets, and ospreys, while peregrine falcons and sharp-shinned hawks take turns monitoring your movements from above. In May, multicolored ducks sample the marsh's weed of the day, while perfectly poised snowy egrets stand aloof in the reeds. If you are lucky, you'll hear the hysterical giggle of a loon or see osprey chicks.

To get your bearings in this watery landscape and to identify what you are seeing (or what is keeping an eye on you), visit the Meigs Point Nature Center, which houses dioramas, a touch tank, and exhibits on local aquatic and bird life. Nature programs range from bird-watching walks to canoe trips. *Hammonasset Connector off the Post Road (or take I-95 Exit 62); 203-245-8743.*

Continuing eastward from Hammonasset on U.S. 1, you pass through Clinton and Westbrook, which support a ramshackle assortment of fishing shacks, tackle shops, and tiny motels. Filling the town's marinas, though, are fiberglass behemoths that look like futuristic vacuum cleaners ready to sweep up the manmade structures.

■ **FENWICK AND OLD SAYBROOK** *map page 42–43, E-2*

Outside Westbrook, turn right onto Route 154, which loops along the peninsula below Old Saybrook, allowing you to drive—or, better still, to bicycle—between forests of salt-marsh grasses that nod and wave above your head. At Knollwood Beach you can bike along the seawall or cast a line from the jetties. As you speed on the bike path across the long causeway that joins Fenwick and Saybrook Point, your delighted exclamations—"Look, swans! Ah, a heron!"—will prompt those feathered aristocrats to dip their heads underwater. The wildfowl here are a rarified group.

Fenwick is an exclusive old-money summer colony. Instead of trophy houses, there are extravagant summer cottages that look like lace-trimmed dowagers passing judgment on any visitor who dares to penetrate their labyrinth of tiny lanes. When she was a young girl, Katharine Hepburn's family had a cottage in Fenwick that Barbara Leaming, one of the actress's biographers, describes as being

Connecticut soldiers fought at Chancellorsville during the Civil War; each April the battle is reenacted at Hammonasset Beach State Park.

"perched precariously on a sandbar. Howling winds shook the screens and rattled the porches on the lower floors. Waves pelted the stony beach and wooden bulkhead. . . .One occupant compared the cottage to a 'sailing ship' or a 'castle perilous on the ocean.' "

The hurricane of 1938 demolished the Hepburn cottage, but a fire in 1647, not the weather, destroyed the original fortification that occupied **Fort Saybrook Monument Park,** just off Route 154. A second fort built nearby provided defense against the Dutch in the 17th century and the British during the War of 1812.

But all is quiet on this eastern front these days, especially just beyond the fort on Route 154 just before you get to Old Saybrook proper. Look for signs to North Cove Road on your right, and try not to shout when you get there. **North Cove** is a calm little place, ideal for a decorous picnic. Houses from the 18th and early 19th centuries, most of them wooden but a few them made of brick, face a sheltered cove. On a late summer afternoon the only sounds are the mewing of catbirds in the bayberry thickets, the thunking of wooden boats rocking lazily on the water, and the gentle crunch of your cucumber sandwich.

A Dutch contingent from Manhattan Island nailed its coat of arms to a tree in what is now Old Saybrook in 1623 but declined to stay long, perhaps because the indigenous tribes were hostile. When John Winthrop Jr. arrived from Boston in 1635 to create Saybrook Plantation, the Dutch emblem was reportedly ripped from the tree and a grinning face carved in its place. Saybrook Plantation encompassed the seven towns known today as Chester, Deep River, Essex, Lyme, Old Lyme, Westbrook, and Old Saybrook.

During the Pequot War of 1637, Saybrook lost nine men and nearly all its livestock, buildings, and grain. The town lost Yale College less violently. The institution was founded in Killingworth as the Collegiate School in 1701 and moved to Saybrook a few years later. Its trustees voted in 1716 to move the college to New Haven, sparking another Saybrook skirmish. When delegates were sent to transport the books, they found the repository fortified and guarded by armed townsmen. Reinforcements were sent and the books were surrendered, but the move was further impeded when the delegates' horses were let loose and bridges along their return route were sabotaged.

The wind from Long Island Sound that flays this coastline in winter cools demure Old Saybrook on a summer afternoon, and there is nothing in the peaceful

The shoreline and summer beach cottages of Old Saybrook's Fenwick Point Community.

scene that you can imagine having inspired David Bushnell in the late 18th century to start blowing things up underwater. Bushnell experimented in Saybrook's Otter Cove, submerging and igniting gunpowder-filled barrels before testing his submarine, the *American Turtle,* in front of an enthusiastic Benjamin Franklin. Today's aquatic outings from Saybrook Point are less incendiary. **Deep River Navigation Company** (860-526-4954) operates several cruises daily to Essex, Duck Island, and nearby lighthouses. **Mystic Whaler Cruises** (860-536-4218) entices voyagers with lobster-dinner cruises and one- to five-day voyages on the tall ship the *Mystic Whaler.*

The earliest resort development in the area began in 1870 with the construction of cottages and hotels at Lynde Point, where the temperature rarely exceeds the mid-80s and cooling breezes are constant. This 19th-century planned resort set standards that controlled building designs and prohibited amusement concessions.

■ **OLD LYME** *map page 42–43, E-2*

Lyme was set off from Saybrook, which is on the west bank of the river mouth, on February 13, 1665. Its merchants and shipbuilders made Lyme a key player in the West Indies trade, and the wealth created by their enterprise still pervades the town, which has long been an affluent summer retreat. In the fading light of an October evening, the 18th- and 19th-century mansions along Lyme Street seem like ships themselves, anchored by their taut shadows in a harbor of meticulously groomed parkland.

Artist Willard Metcalf came to board at Florence Griswold's house at Old Lyme in 1901 "because he was poor and had heard that she served four vegetables with each meal." Scores of artists were similarly drawn to "Miss Florence's" art colony in the 1817 mansion on Lyme Street to explore a surrounding landscape the colony's founder, Henry Ward Ranger, described as "only waiting to be painted."

The **Florence Griswold Museum** provides the opportunity to see works created by American impressionist painters like Childe Hassam, Will Howe Foote, Matilda Browne, Charles Ebert, and others—and to see how they lived and

worked. The Griswold dining room is lined with more than 30 panels painted by artists who ate the famed four vegetables here. Viewing the landscape scenes and humorous self-portraits is like catching the author Henry James writing his holiday postcards. The Chadwick Studio, overlooking the Lieutenant River a short distance from the house, was the workplace of impressionist William Chadwick from 1920 until his death in 1962. So strong is his presence that you expect him to burst in at any minute and upbraid you for snooping. Indignant catbirds will croon similar accusations when you linger in the museum's gardens. *96 Lyme Street; 860-434-5542.*

Buoys decorate a lobster pound in Noank.

Farther along Lyme Street, the **Bee and Thistle Inn,** built as a private home in 1756, is unrepentantly frilly. As soon as you enter the hallway, with its bumpy floor and well-worn, curving stairway, you begin to relax. A stroll around the 5-acre grounds earns you dozy hours under a leafy beech tree, the perfect place to keep an eye on the equally lazy Lieutenant River as it glides past your vigilant gaze. The sophisticated American cuisine served at the inn's romantic restaurant is uniformly excellent. *100 Lyme Street; 860-434-1667.*

Route 156 north from Old Lyme to Hamburg winds between inviting coves on one side and salt marshes on the other. Swans glide, herons stalk, and reeds catch the afternoon sun. Hamburg Cove is a light-filled composition of glassy water, sloping meadows, and cool forest, and **Selden Neck State Park,** a shady preserve north of Hamburg off tiny Joshuatown Road, inspires even the most reluctant walker with views of the surrounding marshes and creeks.

Route 156 south holds further wonders. Thanks to a providential quirk of nature—in this case, treacherously shifting bars and channels along the Connecticut River—a large seaport was never developed. Consequently, what you see at the **Roger Tory Peterson Wildlife Area** at Great Island, below Old Lyme, is a rarity in the Northeast: the unspoiled mouth of a major waterway. Here, in a setting of unsurpassed beauty, the Connecticut River discharges more water than the Hudson River does at New York City.

A canoe provides an ideal way to get around. You can put in at the public landing on Smith Neck Road and spend the day paddling through the marshes and channels behind **Griswold Point,** spotting egret and osprey nests on one side and a pastoral landscape of small fields and tidy farmhouses on the other. More prosaically, you may walk west to the preserve from the parking area at **White Sands Beach** and observe the same wonders in a less stealthy manner.

Five miles to the east at **Rocky Neck State Park,** the prospect is more rugged and the summer traffic more congested. Two granite projections of land, Giant's Neck and Rocky Neck, shelter a salt pond and marshes that, in turn, support not only such exotic visitors as the tricolor heron but also the delicious blue crab, more commonly found in the Delaware Bay but also spawning in southern New England's shallow estuaries. Contrary to its name, the beach at Rocky Neck is a graceful crescent of soft sand and its gentle waves coax even the most timid swimmer. A large snack bar, a picnic pavilion, and changing rooms are among the amenities. *Off Route 156 (take I-95, Exit 72), East Lyme; 860-739-5471.*

■ WATERFORD   *map page 42–43, E-2*

At **Harkness Memorial State Park,** in the small town of Waterford, the word "amenities" takes on an altogether different meaning. Eolia, the 42-room Italianate mansion built in the late 19th century for oil magnate Edward S. Harkness, is surrounded by 250 acres of groomed parkland that terminates in a flawless beach (swimming prohibited). The moment you leave the paved parking lot and step onto the sloping velvet lawns, you feel your body relaxing, your stride becoming more languorous. You vow that from this day forward you will wear only ankle-length lawn skirts and impractically large straw hats. In this airy, impressionist landscape, even the odd screaming child or barking dog is an artful contrast, not an irritant. Ambling from shade tree to shade tree, you are drawn to the sound of laughter, popping champagne corks, and 1930s dance music. You are not hallucinating. The colonnaded terrace and exquisite garden surrounding the Harkness mansion is a favorite wedding venue. Discreet gawking is permitted. *275 Great Neck Road; 860-443-5725.*

■ NEW LONDON   *map page 42–43, E/F-2*

Still mentally attired in your lawn skirt and straw hat, you will be shocked as you cross the bridge into New London to see not whalers and schooners plying the Thames estuary below but fiberglass yachts and brick-shaped ferries making their way to Fishers Island. The pendulum of decline and redevelopment has eviscerated New London, as it did Norwich, and parking garages and office buildings now dominate much of the waterfront. Not everything of value, though, has been scuttled.

Settled in 1646 by John Winthrop Jr., the son of the first Massachusetts governor, and others, New London commanded the largest and deepest harbor on the coast, profited from the West Indies trade, and became one of New England's largest whaling centers in the early 19th century, when its fleet of 80 vessels was outnumbered only by those of Nantucket and New Bedford, Massachusetts. The *New London Gazette* exhorted as early as 1775, "Now, my horse jockeys beat your horses and cattle into spears, lances, harpoons, and whaling gear, and let us all strike out; many spouts ahead! Whale plenty, you have them for the catching."

On Huntington Street is **Whale Oil Row,** four breathtaking Greek Revival mansions that testify to the golden days when a yearlong voyage could bring

State Street and the Old Ferry Landing, New London, in the late 1900s. (Mystic Seaport)

$150,000 in profit. Capt. Lyman Allyn, however, preferred Williams Street, buying a mansion here in 1851. His home, now called the **Deshon-Allyn House Museum** (613 Williams Street) has as its neighbor the beautiful **Lyman Allyn Art Museum** (625 Williams Street; 860-443-2545), which exhibits contemporary American art, American impressionist paintings, and drawings.

The 1833 **Custom House** on Bank Street is still glorious, as is the 1887 **Union Station** on the waterfront, the latter designed by Henry Hobson Richardson. George Washington and the Marquis de Lafayette visited the **Shaw-Perkins Mansion** (11 Blinman Street; 860-443-1209), built in 1756; it was the state's naval headquarters during the Revolution and is today a museum run by the New London Historical Society. Business here was brisk—and lethal—at its peak. New London harbored more privateers during the Revolutionary War than any other New England port, and was burned and blockaded for its temerity.

The playwright Eugene O'Neill once wrote a daily column for the *New London Telegraph* and spent summers at **Monte Cristo,** his parents' cottage. Now open to visitors, the modest structure overlooks the harbor. The room in which O'Neill set *Long Day's Journey into Night* has been reconstructed from his stage directions. Even today, the somewhat lifeless house seems to exude O'Neill melancholy. *325 Pequot Avenue; 860-443-0051.*

The Joshua Hempsted House is New London's oldest dwelling. (Hempsted Houses)

Joshua Hempsted wrote far jollier prose in his diary than did O'Neill, and visiting the exquisite **Joshua Hempsted House** today you imagine a robust man striding through these plain rooms. This is New London's oldest dwelling—its earliest portions date to 1678—and one of New England's most historic, with heavy framing, casement windows, and simple furnishings that impart an immediate sense of life in the early settlement. The Nathaniel Hempsted House, beside Joshua's, is another rarity, built in the 1750s of granite quarried on the site by Huguenot refugees. *11 Hempstead Street; 860-443-7949 or 860-247-8996.*

If the Hempsted Houses don't dispel the O'Neill gloom, you can always try the **Connecticut College Arboretum,** where the trees, plants, and ducks and even more dignified birds do everything they can to entertain their visitors on 750 verdant acres. *Williams Street across from the college; 860-439-5020.*

New London is the point of embarkation for a number of ferries, including the ones to Block Island, Rhode Island (auto reservations required, one trip daily, operates from June to early September; 401-783-4613); Fishers Island, New York (car ferry, year-round; 631-788-7744); and Montauk, New York (passenger ferry; 888-443-3779).

■ GROTON   *map page 42–43, F-2*

Groton was the site of one of the Revolution's most horrific engagements when more than 80 of the 150 young patriots defending Fort Griswold against Benedict Arnold's assault—and inflicting heavy casualties on the British—were killed when they surrendered. The ramparts at **Fort Griswold State Park** are intact. Students of modern military history will be impressed by the Submarine Force Library and Museum at the Naval Submarine Base, where the world's first nuclear-powered submarine, the USS *Nautilus,* is among the exhibits. *Off Route 12; 860-694-3174.*

■ BLUFF POINT STATE PARK   *map page 42–43, F-2*

On a good map, Bluff Point State Park, east of Groton, is hard to miss; it is the big green blob sticking out into Fisher's Island Sound west of Groton Long Point. The park has in the past, however, been omitted from some state maps, and even today the signs directing you there from U.S. 1 are discreet. All of which is good for Bluff Point and good for you, as it means that one of the most remarkable stretches of the southern New England coast may remain that way.

Shipbuilding, possibly at Eastern Shipbuilding Company, Groton. (Mystic Seaport)

Take U.S. 1 into Groton, turn left after the Town Hall onto Depot Street and follow the unassuming road under a railroad bridge to the Bluff Point picnic ground and parking area. Arriving on a clear June morning, you could be forgiven for thinking that some form of triathlon competition is about to take place. Beside a row of horse trailers, earnest helmeted women and gangly teenage girls groom impeccably mannered horses, who accept the beauty treatment as their due. Bicyclists check the tire pressure of their less elegant mounts while whippet-like runners perform thorough stretching exercises against the trees.

John Winthrop Jr. would have approved of the energy if not of the recreation. This was originally the colonial governor's farm, and the 800-acre preserve—a state park since 1975—encompasses his overgrown fields and the magnificent hardwood trees that bordered those fields for centuries. The largest wild coastline remaining in the state (about half of Connecticut's salt marshes have been lost to development), Bluff Point is a captivating arrangement of forest, rock, and marshland that seems to soak up horse riders, bicyclists, runners, and hikers as soon as they enter its green trails. This allows solitary hikers to feel as if they alone are discovering the bluff overlooking the Sound at the peninsula's tip, the small rocky island of Bushy Point at the tip of the beach, or the shady enclaves of the sassafras forest that fringes the west side of the park.

Following even the most trafficked route—a 4-mile loop that meanders along old cart paths—you quickly reach the euphoric conviction that the most urgent task is to pick wayside bayberries and crush their waxy sweetness onto your fingers while inhaling the succulent scent of beach roses or honeysuckle. Wander off on side trails to the shore or into the forested interior. One may lead you to a piping plover's nest in the dunes, another to an encounter with a bounding white-tailed deer, or with a similarly attired, and equally affronted, cottontail rabbit.

There may also be ghosts—or so you imagine as you pass some stony rubble, the remains of John Winthrop's homestead. To reach the ruined foundation and walls, bear right past Bluff Point Beach onto a side trail that briefly follows the coastline and then veers into the woods, passing the Winthrop site on its descent. Nothing remains of the community of summer cottages that grew up along some of Bluff Point's cart paths. They were wiped out in one blow by the ferocious hurricane of 1938. The countryside surrounding Groton has also witnessed plenty of human violence. Some of the region's bloodiest tribal wars were fought here on the hunting grounds of the Pequots, who fiercely resisted both the rival Narragansetts and later—with poorer results—the invading Europeans.

Take your mind off these bloody events by visiting **Abbott's Lobster in the Rough,** in Noank, the small port east of Bluff Point. Sitting at a picnic table on the dock or on the screened-in porch, tackling one of the finest lobster dinners in the region—or on the Atlantic seaboard, some insist—you quickly feel benevolent, even toward the gulls that swoop in to sneak a beakful. *117 Pearl Street, Noank; 860-536-7719.*

■ MYSTIC   *map page 42–43, F-2*

Allow at least a full day to tour one of the nation's finest living-history maritime museums, **Mystic Seaport.** A visit here is bewitching at any time of year, but try to come in early spring, late autumn, or in winter, when the crowds have thinned and the only sounds along the waterfront and the 19th-century streets are the screeching of gulls and the creaking of the port's leviathans, rocking gently at anchor.

Mystic Seaport is best known for its 19th-century village and waterfront, and for its three largest ships: the 1841 *Charles W. Morgan,* America's last surviving wooden whaling ship; the 1882 training vessel *Joseph Conrad;* and the 123-foot fishing schooner *L. A. Dunton,* built in 1921. The museum includes a preservation shipyard, a research library, exhibition galleries, a planetarium, and a children's museum. The range of daily activities, many of them seasonal, is equally impressive, including steamboat cruises on the 1908 *Sabino,* whaling reenactments, carriage rides, garden tours, nautical demonstrations, concerts on the green, and conversations with meticulously researched 19th-century characters. You can even sample the definitive New England chowder at the museum's Columbus Day weekend Chowderfest.

Standing outside the Spouter Tavern, looking back at Mystic harbor as a chilling November mist shrouds the masts of the *Charles W. Morgan,* you feel as if a hand is about to land on your shoulder, condemning you to a five-year whaling voyage. The museum is a working institution, and in 1998, its shipyard staff completed a replica of the 80-foot-long *Amistad,* these days on view (when it is in port) at New Haven's Long Wharf. *75 Greenmanville Avenue, (take I-95, Exit 90 and follow signs); 860-572-5315 or 888-973-2767.*

Another major delight in Mystic is the **New England Carousel Museum,** which displays antique carousel art and miniature carousels and has a carving shop. *193 Greenmanville Avenue; 860-536-7862.*

(opposite) A schooner docked at the Steamboat Wharf in Mystic. (above) African black-footed penguins at the Mystic Aquarium.

The **Mystic Aquarium and Institute for Exploration** is an unlikely apparition, particularly when approached on the small woodland roads caught in the slip-stream of I-95. A spiky futuristic disk served by a vast (and, in summer, packed) parking lot, this research, educational, and exhibition center has much more to offer than dolphin acrobatics. The discovery of ancient Roman shipwrecks in the Mediterranean and seal rehabilitation are just some of the institute's activities. But there are also shameless somersaulting dolphins, applause-hungry beluga whales, strait-laced penguins, baby alligators, and finny creatures swimming around you in a wide range of imaginatively designed exhibits. *55 Coogan Boulevard (take I-95, Exit 90); 860-572-5955.*

The adjacent **Denison Pequotsepos Nature Center** (109 Pequotsepos Road, off Jerry Browne Road; 860-536-1216), a 125-acre sanctuary encompassing 7 miles of hiking trails, houses feathered exhibitionists in its outdoor flight enclo-sures, where swooping birds of prey attempt to upstage their watery relatives.

■ STONINGTON *map page 42–43, F-2*

Follow U.S. 1 and then U.S. 1A to Stonington. Well-worn descriptions in countless travel articles make this old fishing and whaling port sound unbearably charming, an upmarket version of an imaginary theme park: "Olde New Englande Village," all gingerbread and picket fences. Do not be put off. Stonington is an old whaling and fishing port that still has workboats in its harbor and magnificent Greek Revival mansions lining the narrow streets that lead to the water. Stonington is one of New England's prettiest historic villages, its rough edges smoothed by the steady infusion of tourist dollars. Many houses built by sea captains have been snapped up by affluent urban refugees, and some outlying homesteads are now the weekend pastime of recreational farmers. But Stonington takes all of this in stride and remains a real place.

Having scandalous down-to-earth Rhode Island as its neighbor may partly explain the town's contrary side. Dr. Timothy Dwight, writing in his *Travels in New England and New York* (1821–22) observed that "Stonington and all its vicinity suffers in religion from the nearness of Rhode Island," which he considered "missionary ground." The Narragansett tribe, which called it Pawcatuck or Mistack, originally occupied the outcropping on which the town stands. In 1649, a group of colonists arrived from Plymouth, Massachusetts. In 1658, they named the settlement Souther Towne. Connecticut renamed Stonington in 1666 after winning the tug-of-war with Massachusetts over the barren land.

Stonington's merchant vessels opened up foreign markets for the colony's fledgling industries; one of America's first whaling franchises was granted to a Mr. Whiting in 1647 for the waters between Stonington and Montauk Point. A target of British bombardment in both the Revolutionary War and the War of 1812, the port supported a shipbuilding industry that flourished through the post–Civil War years. In the late 19th century, the village became the terminus of the newly completed shore railroad, and it was here that train cargo was loaded onto the steamships, which were becoming the flagships of American trade. The village is still a seafaring place. A commercial fishing fleet continues to operate out of the harbor and the Blessing of the Fleet each summer remains one of the port's largest and most colorful celebrations.

An American flag with 16 stars hangs from the Ocean Bank Building.

Through the 1940s, Stonington retained its small manufacturing base. Many of the mill and factory buildings—not all of them renovated—now visible produced everything from velvet to silk-throwing machinery to rubber molds. You will still find exotic fabrics and maybe even some industrial artifacts on Water Street, the town's main thoroughfare, but they will be displayed in craft galleries or antique stores. Like every tourist destination, Stonington caters to recreational shoppers, and a stroll along Water Street will satisfy practically every taste, if not every pocketbook. On a summer weekend you may find yourself stalled in minor traffic jams, although in compact Stonington the very idea seems incongruous. Avoid the traffic by parking at Stonington harbor or on a quiet side street and exploring on foot or two wheels. Either way, you will find the gradients kind and the rewards great.

Stonington's long-lived prosperity is most obvious on commercial Water Street and on Main Street, where tree-shaded 18th- and 19th-century mansions sit harmoniously amid exquisite gardens. Their serenity is soothing. Walking or pedaling slowly along Main Street or on the quieter parts of Water Street, you realize that you have jettisoned not only your car but also your concerns.

Old Lighthouse Museum (Stonington Historical Society).

The **Old Lighthouse Museum,** inside a sturdy stone structure, displays whaling, nautical, and military equipment, along with portraits, scrimshaw carvings, and artifacts from the China trade. Everyday life in a coastal region is illustrated in six rooms of historical materials dating as far back as 1649. Climb the tower, which dates from 1823, for views of three states—New York, Connecticut, and Rhode Island. *7 Water Street; 860-535-1440.*

Leaving the museum on an autumn evening, you should linger on the quay until sunset, perhaps contemplating the words of Chief Canonchet, who was executed here in April 1676, declaring, "I like it well that I should die before my heart is softened and I say things unworthy of myself." If that seems too maudlin, try chanting the defiant cry that became Stonington's anthem when its two cannons defeated 140 British naval guns in 1814: "It cost the King ten thousand pounds to have a dash at Stonington."

Follow any narrow side street here and you will find examples of earlier, humbler dwellings, whose slightly cockeyed walls and tilting roof pitches may make you feel as though you have just returned from a five-year whaling voyage. You may even need to lie down. If so, follow Water Street to its southern tip, where you can recover on tiny DuBois Beach. Facing Stonington Harbor and hidden between two short jetties, the pebbly cove offers sand, seclusion, and beautiful views. Propped on one elbow, take in the 270-degree panorama from Fishers Island, New York, to Watch Hill, Rhode Island.

Stonington does not have this soporific effect on everybody. Nathaniel Palmer, for example, couldn't wait to get moving. The 21-year-old captain sailed from Stonington in 1820, commanding the sloop *Hero,* the smallest ship of a fleet of eight that set out for the Antarctic Ocean to find new seal rookeries. Later that year he identified an uncharted piece of land that today we call Antarctica. This and other exploits are recounted in the exhibits at the **Captain Nathaniel B. Palmer House,** the 16-room mansion he commissioned in 1852. You don't have to be a sailor to be astonished, or even moved, by the collection of maritime memorabilia here. *40 Palmer Street, at North Water Street; 860-535-8445.*

The leafy roads surrounding Stonington may not be uncharted, but they can feel that way if you pedal or cruise along them at the right time. Choose a spring or autumn day (although summer heat will not tax you on these gentle rises), preferably during the week, when traffic is light. Follow North Main Street as it winds along under generous shade trees and past pristine horse farms and tidy fields bordered by stone walls. Tiny wrens buzz at you from ferny crevices in the rock, and the smell of freshly mown grass instantly rewinds your mind to childhood.

Should you need to reclaim your adult self, a right turn at the end of North Main Street puts you on the Connecticut Wine Trail. A converted 1880 dairy barn now houses the **Jonathan Edwards Winery,** where you can taste wines and tour. *74 Chester Main Road, North Stonington; 860-535-0202.*

If any place can be called defiantly sleepy, **North Stonington** is it. The village center, with its small municipal buildings, school, churches, library, and modest houses, is compact, and the surrounding countryside is an appealing arrangement of dairy farms, horse farms, and small woodlots.

South of the village, the less bucolic side of town on Route 2 presents the usual shopping and fried-food temptations. But it also leads you to **Randall's Ordinary Landmark Inn and Restaurant,** an establishment that makes you realize what seems so phony about so many other "historic inns." To be fair, though, few such establishments date back to 1685. John Randall bought this piece of land in 1680, and the Randall family occupied the farm for more than two centuries. Ardent abolitionists, the Randalls were among the first in Connecticut to free their slaves, and their house was an important refuge for fugitives on the Underground Railroad.

Its adventurous namesake commissioned the 16-room Captain Nathaniel B. Palmer House.

On 250 wooded acres, Randall's quietly makes it clear that it is the real thing. The 17th-century house presents a plain face to the world. You'll see no architectural sugar frosting, no fussy plantings, and no wicker porch chairs. If Randall's Ordinary were a dog, it would be a grizzled old black Labrador. There is nothing grizzled, however, about the guest rooms, with their canopy beds and antique furniture, and nothing ordinary about the Nantucket scallops and similar delicacies cooked on an open hearth. *Route 2; 877-599-4540.*

On a perfect summer day, when the air is dry and the breeze cool, take an early evening drive or bicycle ride on winding Route 49 north of North Stonington, which skirts the Pachaug State Forest and terminates in a junction with Route 14. In 1938, the Federal Writers' Project *Guide to Connecticut* noted a common scene along Route 49: "A barefoot boy sits in the shade of a giant maple with a bunch of pond lilies, hopefully awaiting a customer, or two little girls hold up a pail of huckleberries and smile at the motorist who applies brakes and backs up to price their wares." Driving along this quiet, undulating road, through farmland and forest that remains unmarred by strip malls or trophy houses, you would not be surprised to encounter the barefoot boy or the little girls around the next bend.

Climbing a gentle rise that promises a view, you pass between an old sawmill on one side and a wheat field on the other, bounded by a stone wall. A sign ahead reads "Piglets For Sale" and you slow down, idly speculating how you might alter your life to accommodate one.

■ TRAVEL BASICS

Getting Around: Interstate 95 slices through the coastal area, and though it is often the quickest route between two points, you should repair to back roads whenever possible. U.S. 1 and the scenic Merritt Parkway (and, east of Milford, the Wilbur Cross Parkway) travel more or less parallel to I-95.

Climate: Coastal Connecticut typically has hot summers, with temperatures in the 80s and 90s Fahrenheit. Winters can be stormy, with daytime temperatures ranging from the 20s to the 40s. Offshore winds can make moderate spring and autumn days feel chilly. Bring several layers of clothing.

CENTRAL AND EASTERN CONNECTICUT

Viewing the most rural part of the Connecticut River Valley today—with its lush meadows and gentle curves—you see what attracted Native Americans and the first European colonists. To the Nipmucs of northeastern Connecticut, to the Saukiogs of present-day Hartford, and to the neighboring Tunxis, Poquonocks, and Podunks, the valley was an ideal farming, fishing, and hunting site. But fertile land is also enviable land. The Pequots had invaded the territory of the Connecticut Algonquins before 1600, and the Mohawks attacked the area repeatedly. The territory remains coveted, though the encroachments upon the land these days take the form of subdivisions that gobble up farmland. But little Connecticut—only Rhode Island and Delaware are smaller—still has space and surprises left. Its leafy interior is an old hand at soothing visitors with its charm. There is real grit in cities like Hartford and Waterbury, but the overall impression is one of softness. Emerging from a morning hike along the Nipmuck Trail or an evening stroll by the Farmington River, you realize how smitten you are when you forget not only where you parked your car, but that you even had one.

■ HARTFORD *map page 104*

When you leave Bradley International Airport on a midsummer day, everything seems suspiciously easy. There are no traffic snarls, no tunnels, and no tollbooths. Best of all, you seem to be in the country. On either side of the airport road, shade tobacco grows under acres of white gauze, giving the fields the look of a maiden aunt wearing a hair net. Hartford is just 15 minutes away.

As you approach the city, however, traffic often grows thick and sluggish. A gigantic landfill, locally known as Mount Refuse, fills one horizon. The highway circling the city becomes a challenging work-in-progress that seems inspired by an Escher puzzle. The blue onion dome of the old Colt armory, once the worldwide symbol of Hartford's genius and energy, still stands out. But the building it crowns seems neglected and the famous Colt weathervane is now in the Museum of

A statue of Nathan Hale stands near the historic Center Church.

Connecticut History on Capitol Avenue. (A legendary symbol of endurance, the gilded colt holding a broken spear in its mouth represented the warhorse fighting the losing battle after its rider has fallen.)

During Hartford's heyday as a manufacturing center, few could have foretold the present state of affairs. In 1860, Hartford's population was about 29,000, with European immigrants who had arrived since 1845 making up almost a third of the total. One of the city's biggest employers by this time was Samuel Colt's Patent Arms Manufacturing Company, the maker of the Colt revolver. Between 1850 and 1900, the city's manufacturing work force grew by almost 250 percent, and as late as 1937 almost 70 percent of Hartford's population worked in its 300 manufacturing companies. Every imaginable item—from axes to aircraft engines—has been manufactured here; since the Patent Office opened in 1790, more patents have been filed on behalf of Connecticut residents and companies than their counterparts in any other state.

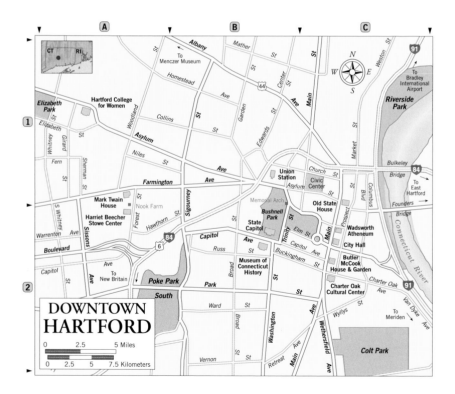

DOWNTOWN HARTFORD

DAMN HARD-WORKING YANKEE

I am an American. I was born and reared in Hartford, in the state of Connecticut—anyway, just over the river, in the country. So I am a Yankee of the Yankees—and practical; yes, and nearly barren of sentiment, I suppose—or poetry, in other words. My father was a blacksmith, my uncle was a horse-doctor, and I was both, along at first. Then I went over to the great arms factory and learned my real trade; learned all there was to it; learned to make everything: guns, revolvers, cannon, boilers, engines, all sorts of labor-saving machinery. Why, I could make anything a body wanted—anything in the world, it didn't make any difference what; and if there wasn't any quick new-fangled way to make a thing, I could invent one—and do it as easy as rolling off a log. I became head superintendent; had a couple of thousand men under me.

—Mark Twain, *A Connecticut Yankee in King Arthur's Court,* 1889

Colt-era Hartford long ago lost its battle against the forces of redevelopment, although the Colt building itself is slated for restoration. Expressionless office buildings dominate the city's skyline like extraterrestrial slabs. Several redevelopment plans have failed to revitalize the city, though its leaders hope that a new one, the first stages of which are slated for completion by 2005, will lead to a renaissance. Despite the aesthetic damage Hartford experienced during the 20th century, the city retains a satisfying symmetry. "They have the broadest, straightest streets in Hartford that ever led a sinner to destruction," Mark Twain once wrote. Even on a stifling July day, when those streets are clogged with cars, the sense of space and airiness persists. Hartford may sit on a low bluff, but its wide thoroughfares and Connecticut River breeze make it almost seem lofty. And with its arts-oriented and historical attractions, a stop in the state capital makes a worthy beginning to a Connecticut River Valley visit.

■ DOWNTOWN

Old State House *map page 104, C-1*
Glassy high-rises dwarf the Old State House, completed in 1796. The building, designed by Charles Bulfinch, replaced the 1720 State House, which accidentally caught fire in 1783 during the celebrations following the American colonists' victory in the Revolutionary War. Costumed staff members here attempt to re-create

The Great Senate Chamber of the Old State House, where the first Amistad *trial was held.*

the past, and though some of them are mediocre actors, one gets into the spirit after bumping into George Washington as he plans Revolutionary strategy with the Comte de Rochambeau, Roger Sherman Baldwin as he defends the *Amistad* prisoners, or Joseph Steward as he launches his distinctly strange museum in the Old State House. "The patronage of the curious is still solicited to increase the collection," urged Steward, a deacon and painter when, in 1797, he sought a two-headed calf. That double-topped calf and other stuffed aberrations glower at you from the walls of Steward's one-room museum, defying you to keep a straight face.

The first trial of the *Amistad* slaves began in the magnificent Senate Chamber in 1839, and the twice-weekly, half-hour reenactment, based on the original transcripts, is both enlightening and stirring. Earlier in 1839, 53 Mende-speaking Africans who had been kidnapped in western Africa and illegally enslaved in Havana seized control of the slave-ship *Amistad,* but were tricked into sailing into Long Island Sound, where they were arrested and charged with murder and piracy.

A dramatic legal battle, first in the Old State House and later in the U.S. Supreme Court, freed the Africans, by then being housed in nearby Farmington. Hartford's *Amistad* awareness predates Steven Spielberg's 1997 film, by the way, and the city's Connecticut Freedom Trail has long included several *Amistad*-related sites.

A practical as well an inspirational starting point for a tour of the city, the Old State House has extensive tourist information, including details about guided and self-guided tours, and many of the city's notable sites are within walking distance. *800 Main Street; 860-522-6766.*

Wadsworth Atheneum Museum of Art *map page 104, C-2*

Once you enter the Wadsworth Atheneum Museum of Art, America's oldest continuously operated public art museum, time evaporates. Founded in 1842 by the businessman and philanthropist Daniel Wadsworth and opened in 1844, the museum has many "first in the United States" credits. This was the first American museum to acquire artworks by Caravaggio, Frederic Church, Salvador Dalí, and Alexander Calder, among others. It organized the first comprehensive Picasso retrospective, began screening films in 1929, and staged the first public performances by George Balanchine's American Ballet Theatre in 1934. This is also the home of the earliest dated American portrait painting: *Elizabeth Eggington,* (artist unknown), completed in 1664.

Perhaps even more impressive is the relationship between Daniel Wadsworth and the artists he collected in the 19th century. The label beside a Frederic Church painting, for instance, notes that Wadsworth had seen promise in the artist's early work and arranged for him to apprentice to another Wadsworth friend—the great landscape painter Thomas Cole, who is well represented in the museum's Hudson River Galleries, said to be the largest collection of its kind in the country.

When Samuel Colt died in 1862, his widow Elizabeth inherited more than $3.5 million and control of the Patent Arms Manufacturing Company. As one of several memorials to her husband, Elizabeth formed a private art gallery at Armsmear, the Colts' Hartford mansion. A believer in the redemptive power of art, she favored works that emphasized serenity and pastoral beauty. Controversisal she wasn't, but with her good taste and the advice of Frederic Church and others she amassed an impressive collection. In 1905, she bequeathed more than a thousand objects to the Wadsworth Atheneum, including paintings and her husband's firearms collection. The painting collection provides a glimpse of America's post–Civil War taste.

Hooker and Company Journeying through the Wilderness in 1636 from Plymouth to Hartford *(1846), by Frederic Church. (Wadsworth Atheneum)*

The Wadsworth's collection spans 5,000 years and includes Greek bronzes, American furniture, and contemporary mixed-media installations. To modernize its exhibition spaces, the museum is slated to break ground in 2004 for a makeover by the design architect Ben van Berkel, of the Amsterdam-based UN Studio. The renovation is scheduled for completion by 2006; until then, part or all of the museum may be closed. *Main Street and Atheneum Square North; 860-278-2670.*

Butler McCook House & Garden *map page 104, C-2*
The modest Butler McCook House, built in 1782, is the last of the dwellings that lined Main Street. The house stayed in the McCook family until 1971, and its small memento-crowded rooms make you feel as though Mrs. McCook might bustle in any moment, offering tea. The ornamental garden out back reflects the Civil War era. Much of the neighborhood surrounding the house and garden was demolished during one 20th-century redevelopment project or another, but the house survived unscathed until 2002, when an errant vehicle rammed into the front. *394–396 Main Street; 860-522-1806.*

THE GUNMAKER WHO MADE MEN EQUAL

"It is better to be the head of a louse than the tail of a lion," Samuel Colt always replied when asked his family's motto. Born in Hartford in 1814, the inventor and industrialist who revolutionized American manufacturing was a willful 16-year-old recently expelled from the Amherst Academy in Massachusetts when his father sent him to sea to learn discipline. En route to Calcutta, he whittled a wooden model of the revolver that would become the world's first repeating firearm.

"The gun that won the West" started out as an engraved prototype in 1835 and was refined into the famous 1860 Army Revolver, a sleek weapon with just seven moving parts. Demand from the U.S Army and from the westward-bound pioneers made Colt a fortune practically overnight. His best-selling gun was one of his cheapest: a .31-caliber pocket pistol costing $10. "God made all men," a popular Civil War slogan had it, "And Samuel Colt made them equal."

In 1855, Colt built the world's largest armory on a reclaimed flood plain that is still dominated by the onetime factory's blue onion dome. Producing 1,000 arms daily, Colt's enterprise transformed manufacturing by mass-producing gun parts on steam-powered, belt-driven machines, using interchangeable parts, and instituting a rigid division of labor. Before Colt, one gunsmith, working by hand, performed as many as 200 tasks. After Colt, each worker concentrated on a single part. The industrialist also revolutionized the workplace itself, building high-quality housing for his workers, as well as Charter Oak Hall for their instruction and entertainment.

Colt built the ostentatious Italianate mansion Armsmear for his bride, Elizabeth Hart Jarvis. A private rest home today, Armsmear was once surrounded by elaborate gardens and commanded Hartford's finest view of the Connecticut River and of Colt's factory. Armsmear, at 80 Wethersfield Avenue, sits on the edge of Colt Park—originally the campground of the Saukiog tribe, later a Dutch trading post, and now enlivened by the sounds of multinational soccer players competing on multiple fields.

Samuel Colt died in 1862. Mrs. Colt's wedding cake had been decorated with pistols, and as a widow she remained faithful to the motif. Consequently, Hartford's Church of the Good Shepherd, dedicated to her husband's memory in 1869, is surely the only church decorated with revolvers, gun sights, bullet molds, and other firearm motifs.

Bushnell Park *map page 104, B/C-2*

From certain angles, downtown Hartford can seem all stone, concrete, and glass, and the mating call of throbbing muscle cars can grate on the ears. The nearest antidote is the grassy retreat of Bushnell Park. A few joggers pad laboriously by, and a leafy rustle replaces the traffic's hum. A **carousel** built in 1914 by Solomon Stein and Harry Goldstein—and said to be only one of three remaining by the renowned Coney Island–based craftsmen—twirls mid-park. Closer to the state capitol, which sits in the park to the west, is the Gothic-style **Soldiers and Sailors Memorial Arch,** dedicated in 1886. A terra-cotta frieze above the archway portrays scenes from the Civil War, and statues underneath it depict individuals representative of the 4,000 Hartford residents who participated in the war. On the arch's west side is a statue of a slave, his chains broken, holding a tablet with the upper- and lower-case letters ABC on it. (Teaching slaves and former slaves to read was a major preoccupation of New England abolitionists.) Due west of the statue, on the sloping north lawn of the State Capitol, is a fountain honoring donated by John Corning in 1899 to honor his father, who operated a grist mill here. A stag (or "hart," for Hartford) tops the 30-foot-tall monument. On the lowest tier are bronze statues of Saukiog Indians, Hartford's first inhabitants. *Trinity Street, two blocks west of the Wadsworth Atheneum.*

State Capitol *map page 104, B-2*

Connecticut's exuberant Gothic Revival–style capitol, completed in 1878, is one of the country's most surprising public buildings, grand and yet perhaps a tad too playful for a house of representatives. "Nobody would ever imagine such a building to be intended for a State House," railed the *Hartford Times* in an 1872 review of the design. "These plans are architectural delirium tremens." By the next decade, though, the critical winds had changed direction. In an 1885 poll, the peers of the structure's architect, Richard Upjohn, rated the capitol "one of the ten best buildings in the United States."

The capitol building's highly theatrical halls, with their marble walls, granite columns, inlaid-marble floors, and brass chandeliers, contain fascinating historical exhibits—the Marquis de Lafayette's camp bed, a cannonball-encrusted tree trunk from a Civil War battlefield, battle flags of Connecticut regiments from the Civil

Hartford police patrol Bushnell Park. The State Capitol stands in the background.

War to the Korean War, and a plaster model of the winged *Genius of Connecticut* statue. The original 3.5-ton bronze *Genius,* which topped the Capitol dome and wobbled erratically in high wind, was removed in 1938 and melted down for armaments during World War II. The restored plaster model, painted bronze, is on view in the north lobby. The capitol's exterior is decorated with outstanding sculptures of state notables. *210 Capitol Avenue, at Trinity Street; 860-240-0222.*

The holdings of the **Museum of Connecticut History,** across Trinity Street from the capitol, include about 1,000 firearms and Colt-related documents, along with items relating to the state's military, industrial, and political past. The state royal charter of 1662 is here, as are Thomas Hooker's Fundamental Orders and the 1818 and 1964 state constitutions. *Connecticut State Library, 231 Capitol Avenue; 860-757-6531.*

Nook Farm   *map page 104, A-1/2*
In 1853, the lawyer and abolitionist John Hooker and the playwright Francis Gillette established Nook Farm, a community of like-minded intellectuals who built about two dozen homes on 150 acres beside the Park River. Harriet Beecher Stowe and Samuel Clemens (just becoming famous as Mark Twain) were among those who called Nook Farm home. "Every bush has its hair cut and face washed daily," Stowe wrote. "The evergreens are clipped into most precise decorum, the grass duly manured, rolled and shaved. . . .Hartford is a very beautiful city." Driving the short distance from the city center to Stowe's house on Forest Street today, you see little of the gentility the writer described. But the Stowe House and its neighbor, the Mark Twain House, still transmit the charm and taste of a prosperous, highly cultivated 19th-century city. To reach Nook Farm from downtown Hartford, take Asylum Street to Broad Street and make a left and then a quick right onto Farmington Avenue, heading west.

Stowe, most famous for *Uncle Tom's Cabin,* was the author of 29 other books, including one she wrote with her sister about housekeeping. She spent her final years at the Stowe House, now the centerpiece of the **Harriet Beecher Stowe Center,** arriving in 1873 when she was 62 years old. She loved gardening and the grounds still show traces of her sensibility. The atmosphere was not completely restful for Stowe, however. During her time here, one of her sons was missing in California, her husband's health failed him, and she was disabled by a stroke late in life. Her neighbor Mark Twain recalled that earlier in her tenure, "she would slip up behind a person who was deep in dreams and musings and fetch a war

The Case against Corsets

It is a difficult duty of parents and teachers to contend with the power of fashion, which at this time of a young girl's life is frequently the ruling thought, and when to be out of the fashion, to be odd and not to dress as all her companions do, is a mortification and grief that no argument or instructions can relieve. The mother is often so overborne that, in spite of her better wishes, the daughter adopts modes of dress alike ruinous to health and beauty.

. . . It is a singular fact that the war of fashion has attacked most fatally what seems to be the strongest foundation and defense of the body, the bones. . . . The consequence of tight dress around the waist is a constant pressure of the spine toward the unsupported part where the stomach lies. . . . Many a school-girl, whose waist was originally of a proper and healthful size, has gradually pressed the soft bones of youth until the lower ribs that should rise and fall with every breath, become entirely unused. . . .

It is hoped that the increase of intelligence and moral power among mothers, and the combination among them to regulate fashions, may banish the pernicious practices that have prevailed. If a school-girl dress without corsets and without tight belts could be established as a fashion, this would be one step in the right direction.

—Catherine E. Beecher and Harriet Beecher Stowe,
The American Woman's Home, 1869

whoop that would jump that person out of his clothes." Stowe's home—airier than others of the Victorian period, owing to her philosophy about the benefits of natural light—and gardens transmit not gloom, but the palpable sense of an agile life. Stowe wintered in Florida and traveled elsewhere, but this was her primary residence until her death in 1896. *77 Forest Street, near Farmington Avenue; 860-525-9317.*

"To us our house was not insentient matter," Samuel Clemens wrote in 1896; "it had a heart and a soul and eyes to see us with . . . we were in its confidence and lived in its grace and in the peace of its benediction." So indelible is Clemens's mark that the **Mark Twain House,** where the author lived and worked from 1874 to 1891, still seems sentient. Touring the Gothic Revival extravaganza, another concoction of Richard Upjohn, who designed the State Capitol, you feel as if each lavishly decorated room is amused by your enthusiastic reaction. Built in 1874 at a

The photo was taken early in Mark Twain's tenure at Nook Farm. (Mark Twain House)

cost of $40,000, the vermilion and black confection has interiors by Louis Comfort Tiffany and seven exterior balconies. Its oddities include a window over a fireplace that enabled Clemens to watch snowflakes and flames at the same time. The author wrote some of his best-known works here, including *Tom Sawyer, Life on the Mississippi, The Adventures of Huckleberry Finn,* and *A Connecticut Yankee in King Arthur's Court.* He also found time to invest heavily in the doomed Paige typesetting machine, which led to his losing his home. The Twain house can only be seen on guided tours. *351 Farmington Avenue; 860-493-6411.*

Elizabeth Park *map page 104, A-1*

"Money is another kind of poetry," Wallace Stevens once wrote, perhaps after he had walked the 3 or so miles from his office at the Hartford Accident and Indemnity Company through glorious Elizabeth Park to his house (still private) at 118 Westerly Terrace. The poet's daily walk through the park passed by its rose garden, whose blooms peak in late June, when more than 14,000 rose bushes compete to intoxicate visitors. *Prospect and Asylum Avenues.*

If Elizabeth Park causes symptoms of chronic euphoria, you can always visit the nearby **Menczer Museum of Medicine and Dentistry**, where displays of instruments and medications from the 18th to the 20th century prove an excellent corrective. In 1844, Hartford witnessed the first use of nitrous oxide gas as an anesthetic, by Dr. Horace Wells. *230 Scarborough Street; 860-236-5613.*

■ TOWNS NEAR HARTFORD

■ WETHERSFIELD *map page 117, B-2*

In this artfully preserved 18th-century town, people appear immune to modern activity. Strolling along Main Street on a balmy spring evening, they greet you as you sit on a bench, listening to the clock in the 1764 meetinghouse strike the half-hour. You might even see a rider on horseback. Like so many old Connecticut towns, Wethersfield is blessed with huge maples that provide its broad streets with shade, birdsong, and soundproofing. But life was not always this peaceful. In April 1637, the "Wethersfield Massacre" by the Pequots sparked the Pequot War; the Ancient Burying Ground behind the stately Congregational Church on Main Street has some early settler graves. Ideally situated on the Connecticut River, Wethersfield prospered from the West Indies trade until the mid-19th century, gaining particular fame for its red onions, which tolerated long Caribbean voyages.

The same skills that produced ships here starting in 1649 created some of the region's finest 18th-century houses, and Wethersfield's historic area—Connecticut's largest such district—contains more than 140 of them.

The Wethersfield Historical Society runs the **Wethersfield Museum,** whose exhibitions survey life in the town from 1634 to the present. One of the permanent exhibits describes many nearby historical sites, making this a good first stop on a visit here. *200 Main Street; 860-529-7656.*

The **Webb-Deane-Stevens Museum** comprises three houses on their original sites: a Georgian mansion built for the patriot and merchant Joseph Webb in 1752; the adjacent 1766 home of lawyer and diplomat Silas Deane, who married Joseph's widow, Mehitable Webb; and the humbler 1789 house built for leather-worker and saddler Isaac Stevens. The star of the trio is the Webb House, where George Washington stayed in 1781 when he came to Connecticut to discuss strategy with the Comte de Rochambeau for what eventually took place as the Battle of Yorktown. Ten years after Deane moved into his house, he was also involved in the Revolutionary War, traveling to France to lobby for arms and supplies. Between the Webb House and its nearby barn is the exquisite garden, where many 18th-century flower varieties bloom. The simpler Stevens House has one room set up as though a group of middle-class 18th-century women were about to meet. *211 Main Street; 860-529-0612.*

The **Hurlbut-Dunham House,** built in 1793, is a brick Federal house updated in the Italianate style during the Victorian period. One clue that this isn't an entirely Federal affair is the cupola, part of the 1860s makeover. A Captain Hurlbut owned the house in the early 19th century, and the Dunhams—including Henry Dunham, who was a Connecticut insurance commissioner in the early 20th century—lived here until 1970. The house is decorated to reflect the 1930s, but earlier eras bleed through. *212 Main Street; 860-529-7656.*

The **Capt. James Francis House** was the home of a man who built more than 20 Wethersfield houses. He finally got around to erecting one for himself in 1793. It remained a

Treenware and other 18th-century utensils. (Buttolph-Williams House)

Francis home for seven generations and today provides a rare peek at one family's changing tastes over 170 years. *120 Hartford Avenue; 860-529-7656.*

Built decades earlier than the other homes open to the public, the **Buttolph-Williams House,** with its hewn overhang and casement windows that evoke medieval English building styles, looks like a 17th-century construction but probably dates to 1711. Whatever its age, its plain grace is indisputable. The best-restored museum house of its period in the Connecticut River Valley, the home reflects 18th-century upper-middle-class tastes. The kitchen, its table set with treenware (wooden plates and utensils), contains a large fireplace and culinary-related implements of the era, among them a butter churn, a cylindrical grain bin, and a clockjack—an early version of a rotisserie. *249 Broad Street; 860-529-0460.*

The **Cove Warehouse,** which looks like a giant Cape Cod–style house, was completed in 1690. Overlooking Wethersfield Cove, it is one of the nation's few surviving 17th-century warehouses. You may well emerge from its nautical exhibits expecting to see a forest of wooden masts. Sadly, most vessels in the cove today are of the fiberglass variety. *Cove Park, north end of Main Street.*

CENTRAL & EASTERN CONNECTICUT

Elevation
in feet
1,500
1,000
500
0

10 Miles
5
0
15 Kilometers
10
5

RHODE ISLAND

MASSACHUSETTS

To I-90 &
Boston
Thompson
West
Thompson
Reservoir
Quaddick
Reservoir
North
Foster
To
Providence

North
Woodstock
Woodstock
Putnam
Pomfret
Dayville
Danielson
Brooklyn
Moosup
East
Killingly
South
Killingly
Thompson

Union
West
Woodstock
Woodstock
Valley
Phoenixville
Abington
Hampton
Canterbury
Plainfield
Jewett
City

Stafford
Springs
Westford
West Ashford
Storms
University of
Connecticut
Willimantic
Scotland
Baltic
NORWICH

Crystal Lake
Tolland
North
Coventry
Coventry
Andover
Fairview
Gilead
Lebanon
Colchester
Uncasville
Montville

Somers
Melrose
VERNON
MANCHESTER
EAST
HARTFORD
Glastonbury
East
Glastonbury
South
Glastonbury
Marlborough
Hebron
Amston
Westchester
Moodus
East
Haddam
Gardner
Lake
North Plain
Hamburg
Old Lyme

Scitico
Suffield
Windsor
Locks
Bradley
International
Airport
East
Granby
Granby
Simsbury
Avon
WINDSOR
South
Windsor
Rocky
Hill
Wethersfield
Portland
MIDDLETOWN
Haddam
Higganum
Shailerville
Chester
Deep River
Essex
Old Saybrook

West
Granby
North Canton
Collinsville
Burlington
Station
Farmington
New
Britain
Berlin
Middlefield
Durham
North
Guilford
North
Madison
Clinton

East
Hartford
West
Hartford
HARTFORD
WEST
HARTFORD
BRISTOL
SOUTHINGTON
MERIDEN
Cheshire
Prospect
Durham Center
Northford
Guilford
Branford
Madison

Winsted
Torrington
Terryville
WATERBURY
Waterbury
HAMDEN
Montowese
Montowese
NEW
HAVEN
Shelton
Seymour

New
London
Waterford
Niantic
Groton
Mystic
Pawcatuck
Westerly

Ledyard
Mashantucket
Pequot Museum
and Research Center
Foxwoods
Casino

Mohegan
Sun

Pachaug
Pond
Hale
Voluntown

■ GLASTONBURY *map page 117, B/C-2*

Glastonbury was part of Wethersfield until 1693 and became famous for fruit and hygiene—Hale peaches and commercial soap were first produced here—but also for the five forward-thinking Smith sisters. The women—Hancy, Cyrinthia, Laurilla, Julia, and Abby—fought for the abolition of slavery, suffrage for women, and other causes. As elderly ladies, Julia and Abby created a stir in 1873 by demanding the vote and refusing to pay their taxes because doing so amounted to taxation without representation.

You can learn about the activities of the Smith sisters and other historical events at the **Museum on the Green** (1944 Main Street; 860-633-6890), most easily reached by taking the Main Street exit off U.S. 2 East. The Historical Society of Glastonbury, which runs the museum, also arranges tours of the **Welles-Shipman-Ward House** (972 Main Street), a 1755 Colonial with three barns, a garden, and a collection of hearses, carriages, and other horse-drawn vehicles.

To explore the area's natural history, head out along the 4-mile **Shenipsit Trail** (Hebron Avenue and Hill Street), where glacial boulders, many of them studded with tiny garnets, litter the ridges, giving the impression that you have interrupted a giant in the middle of his tidying.

■ ROCKY HILL *map page 117, B-2/3*

More prehistoric celebrities—not to mention 200-million-year-old fossil tracks and plants native to the Jurassic era—lurk across the Connecticut River at **Dinosaur State Park,** in Rocky Hill. Hundreds of tracks were uncovered here in 1966, at what is said to be the largest dinosaur track site in North America. A mammoth geodesic dome protects the ancient footprints and related exhibits. The full-size model of the carnivorous *Dilophosaurus* may dissuade you from exploring the park's 70 bird-filled acres of gardens and trails, but if you daren't venture into the wilderness you can always make your own cast of a dinosaur footprint in the perfectly safe track-casting area. The only supplies you need are 10 pounds of plaster of Paris and a quarter-cup of vegetable oil. *West Street (follow signs from I-91, Exit 23); 860-529-8423.*

You can reach Dinosaur State Park from Glastonbury by taking the **Glastonbury–Rocky Hill Ferry** (Route 17 off Route 2, Glastonbury; 860-443-3856). Billed as the country's oldest continuously operating ferry, it first sailed in 1655; today's vessel accommodates 20 passengers, three automobiles, and numerous bicycles, and sails from May through October, weather permitting.

■ **NEW BRITAIN**   *map page 117, B-2/3*

New Britain graduated from making sleigh bells to earn the nickname "Hardware City," but the somewhat lifeless town is better known today for the **New Britain Museum of American Art.** A stucco mansion is home to an exceptional American collection that includes works by John Singer Sargent, Winslow Homer, Childe Hassam, Thomas Hart Benton, and members of the Hudson River School. Frederic Church's painting *West Rock, New Haven* and Hassam's *Lejour du Grand Prix* are always on display. Also here are Georgia O'Keeffe's *East River from the 30th Story of the Shelton Hotel,* Benton's mural *The Arts of Life in America,* and works by American illustrators from the 19th century to the present. Small rooms ward off gallery fatigue, and most are furnished with a large book-strewn table where you may sit in a comfortable Windsor chair reading about art or staring out the tree-filled windows. *56 Lexington Street (take Route 72, Columbus Boulevard Exit); 860-229-0257.*

■ **BRISTOL**   *map page 117, A-2/3*

Bristol presents mechanical delights: 3,000 timepieces, at the **American Clock and Watch Museum** (100 Maple Street, off U.S. 6; 860-583-6070). Try to drop in at 11 A.M. or noon, when about 120 clocks chime more or less together. A few are set a bit slow, others a little fast, so that the chimes of individual pieces can be detected above the cacophony. Also in town is what is said to be the nation's oldest amusement park, **Lake Compounce** (Enterprise Drive and Middle Street, 860-583-3300), where the 1911 carousel still turns and the wooden Balderdash and Wildcat roller-coasters still prompt screams from riders. Bristol is also where, in the 1880s, Everett Horton invented the collapsible fishing rod, which allowed him to slip from house to river without being seen carrying a pole—indulging in leisure activities on the Sabbath was still considered bad form in the late 19th century.

■ **FARMINGTON**   *map page 117, A-2*

Reaching Farmington, you enter a landscape that is green with trees, fields, and money. In its early days, Farmington was known as "Tunxis Plantation," after the Tunxis Indians, who inhabited the region then. The town was founded in 1640 as "an ideal Christian commonwealth."

Fortunes were made here from manufacturing, commerce, and trade, and the town was further enriched by the completion of the Farmington Canal in 1828. But the stories behind the 18th- and 19th-century mansions lining shady Main

Street demonstrate that principle and profit were not mutually exclusive. Samuel Smith built the 1769 **Smith-Cowles House** (27 Main Street), a white Georgian colonial that in the 1800s was owned by Horace Cowles, a noted abolitionist. One of three little girls among the *Amistad* passengers is believed to have been a guest at the house, which later became a famous stop on the Underground Railroad, the secret route by which fugitive slaves in the South escaped to freedom in the North.

Other *Amistad*-related sites in town include **Union Hall,** where abolitionists rallied support for the captives; **Samuel Deming's Store** (still a store), where the Africans were educated; the **Austin F. Williams House,** the home of the man who built a dormitory for them on his grounds; and **Foone's Grave** in Riverside Cemetery, where a Mende leader who drowned in the Pipkin Basin is buried. This and other town history is covered on the walking tours arranged by the **Farmington Historical Society** (860-678-1645).

The first stop on the walking tour is the sublime **1771 Meetinghouse** (75 Main Street; 860-677-2601), now the First Congregational Church. The Mende Africans worshiped here during their eight-month stay in Connecticut. The tour also takes in America's first all-girls school, **Miss Porter's School** (60 Main Street),

The Riverside Cemetery grave of Foone, an Amistad *African who died while the group was living in Farmington.*

The 1771 Meetinghouse, now the First Congregational Church.

founded in 1843. The exclusive school has educated many famous Americans, among them Theodate Pope Riddle, one of America's first female architects, and Jacqueline Bouvier Kennedy.

Not far from Miss Porter's is the **Stanley-Whitman House,** a minor gem whose oldest parts date to 1720. The rooms here are furnished to shed light on the lifestyles of the mid-18th century. To represent the earlier time, the set-up is utilitarian, reflecting the tasks—farming and weaving—around which life revolved for the house's first inhabitants, Tom and Mary Smith. In the 1730s, Solomon Whitman and his wife, Susannah Cole Whitman, moved in. Among other occupations, Solomon was an arbitrator, a justice of the peace, and a shoemaker, and the furniture and other artifacts have been selected to illustrate their more refined existence. *37 High Street; 860-677-9222.*

Leaving the center of Farmington on Mountain Road's gentle incline, you encounter one of Connecticut's absolute treasures. The **Hill-Stead Museum,** a 33,000-square-foot Colonial Revival house set amid 152 acres of fields, gardens, and woodland, contains an extraordinary collection of French impressionist masterpieces by Degas, Monet, Manet, Cassatt, and Whistler, all exhibited in their original domestic setting. Before you even reach the paintings, though, you may be distracted by the estate's circa–1920 sunken garden—designed by Beatrix Farrand, the niece of the writer Edith Wharton—and the sloping, tree-fringed meadows. Theodate Pope Riddle designed Hill-Stead as a retirement home for her parents, and she clearly had as fine an eye for proportion as her father, the Ohio iron industrialist Alfred Atmore Pope, had for art. Theodate survived the sinking of the RMS *Lusitania* off the Irish coast in 1915, and went on to design, among other projects, the Avon Old Farms School in neighboring Avon, completed in 1927. *35 Mountain Road (follow signs from Route 10); 860-677-4787.*

Take practically any side street in town, and you will quickly reach the **Farmington River.** In 1994, Congress added 14 miles of the waterway's west branch to the National Wild and Scenic Rivers System, but the Farmington River was remarkable long before legislators made it official. Otters and bald eagles raise their young along its banks; the river also accommodates sedate canoeists.

An early Monet canvas hangs in the Morning Room at Hill-Stead. (Hill-Stead Museum)

■ **SIMSBURY** *map page 117, B-1*

Simsbury's first settlers were attracted in 1640 by the area's pine trees, which were critical to the shipbuilding industry, and the town later prospered with the discovery of copper in neighboring East Granby. Today the giant pines are gone, the old railway station has become the **One Way Fare** (4 Railroad Street; 860-658-4477) restaurant, and Simsbury wears the pastel gloss of an affluent suburb. It is relaxing, however, to sit at a shady table on the old station platform, eating an exceptionally good hamburger while you summon the energy to walk the few hundred yards to **Massacoh Plantation** (800 Hopmeadow Street), the small historic district run by the Simsbury Historical Society. Here the furled bark of enormous sycamores crunches explosively underfoot as you proceed from the 1771 Phelps Tavern to the icehouse, a meeting house from 1683, and several other buildings.

■ **TALCOTT MOUNTAIN STATE PARK** *map page 117, B-2*

A more eccentric sight, **Heublein Tower,** awaits you if you hike the hilly, 1.25-mile **Talcott Mountain Trail.** The seven-story concrete-and-steel castle was built for the food and liquor merchant Gilbert Heublein in 1914. On a clear day you can see five states from the tower, which is open to the public part of year. The hillsides of Talcott Mountain State Park are pockmarked with modern condominium-castles, but the park supplies pleasant views as you walk or ski its forested trails. *Off Route 10/U.S. 202 south of Simsbury; 860-242-1158.*

■ **OLD NEWGATE PRISON** *map page 117, B-1*

When the copper mine at East Granby ceased production in 1773, another use was immediately found for the bleak underground warren: it became Newgate Prison. Wrote one inmate, "Finding it not possible to evade this hard cruel fate, they bade adieu to the world and descended the ladder. . . . Here they found the inhabitants of this woeful mansion who were exceedingly anxious to know what was going on above."

Visiting the small Newgate complex on Newgate Road on a breezy, clear July morning, you feel the chill long before you explore the dripping labyrinth. Standing on the site of the whipping post and the treadmill, you try to look on the bright side. The maximum allowance was 10 lashes, and prisoners spent 30 minutes on the treadmill, working 10 and resting five. Cider was provided daily, and rum for good behavior. Then you see a ladder disappearing into the ground and imagine surfacing each morning at 4 A.M. from the hellish depths. The small museum tells the stories of several prisoners—the admittance ledger is a catalog of rape, incest, and petty crime. When Tories incarcerated during the Revolutionary War staged a mass escape in 1781, 16 of the 28 escapees were recaptured within a week. A resident vulture hovers over the picnic area, which overlooks a rolling, wooded valley. *115 Newgate Road (follow signs from Route 20); 860-653-3563.*

■ **SUFFIELD** *map page 117, B-1*

The Newgate Prison museum has a crude sketch on stone by one of Newgate's inmates depicting a man smoking a cigar, and driving along the quieter roads of the Connecticut River Valley above Hartford you see why. Tobacco has a long history here, beginning with the Native Americans who taught the settlers how to grow the crop that made this valley's worldwide reputation for premium cigar-wrapper leaf.

Though the recent cigar fashion revitalized the industry, it's unlikely this valley will ever again see 1,600 square miles of tobacco planted—as there were after World War II. But it is astonishing to see tract housing and mini-malls interrupted by broad green swaths that launch perfumed waves at you as you drive by. The fertile red soil on either side of the road north from Granby to Suffield may now grow mostly lawn, but many fields around Suffield itself are still productive. On a spring afternoon, the town center even smells of manure. Stare long enough at the **Gay Manse** (on Main Street), built in 1743 by Rev. Ebenezer Gay of the First Congregational Church of Suffield, and you begin to wonder if the rolling fields behind it did not partly inspire the exquisite curves of its restrained Connecticut Valley doorway.

Old Newgate Prison.

New England tobacco is used primarily for premium cigar-wrapper leaf.

Among the 11 rooms of the **King House Museum** (232 South Main Street; 860-668-5256) is a fine tobacco and cigar collection. But South Main Street itself is Suffield's chief delight—a broad, shady thoroughfare where even the outbuildings are splendid. Behind its gigantic sycamore and ornate fence, the regal **Hatheway House** (55 South Main Street; 860-668-0055), completed in 1760, has presided over the street since it was a dusty Common. Its original furnishings include rare 1790s hand-blocked French wallpaper, and its restful garden is a treat to behold in spring.

■ **WINDSOR LOCKS** *map page 117, B-1*
When a canal was built in 1829 to bypass the rapids of the Connecticut River at Windsor Locks, that town quickly became known as the bawdiest in New England, thanks to the scandalous behavior of its river men. Today, Windsor Locks is a respectable Hartford suburb and its waterway supplies more innocent pleasures. Walking or bicycling its paved towpath, you pass the exhilarating Enfield Rapids, one of the best shad fishing spots in New England, and encounter wildflower and butterfly delights at every turn.

Intermittent rumblings remind you that the towpath is on Bradley International Airport's flight path. "Even in my childhood . . .I dreamed about the possibility of going straight up," remarked the late Igor Sikorsky, the inventor of the helicopter and a longtime Connecticut resident. Those harboring similar fantasies will want to visit the **New England Air Museum** and see how Sikorsky and other innovators turned theirs into reality. A new hangar opens in 2003 to showcase *Jack's Hack,* a restored B-29A Superfortress bomber from World War II. *Bradley International Airport, Schoephoster Road off I-91, Exit 40; 860-623- 3305.*

■ **WINDSOR** *map page 117, B-2*
Windsor has a long tradition of being first. Its settlers were the first Americans (in 1633) to transport a prefabricated frame house (from Plymouth, Massachusetts to Windsor) and the first New Englanders (in 1647) to hang a suspected witch, Alice Young. The town's historic **Palisado Avenue** (Route 159) and **Palisado Green** are named after the settlement's original stockade. The **Oliver Ellsworth Homestead** (778 Palisado Avenue; 860-688-8717) was the residence of Connecticut's first U.S. senator, one of the framers of the United States Constitution.

On tours given by the Windsor Historical Society, visitors take in the 1758 **John and Sarah Strong House** (96 Palisado Avenue; 860-688-3813), which contains a wealth of furnishings from the 18th and 19th centuries. On the **Palisado Green** is the Founders Monument, listing the names of Windsor's founding families of 1633, and a statue of Maj. John Mason, a 17th-century military leader in the Pequot War. Across Palisado Avenue are the 1794 meetinghouse and **Palisado Cemetery,** with its Puritan gravestones.

Tobacco has grown around Windsor for centuries, the native tribes having introduced the crop in the 1630s. Cultivation started early, but tobacco's heyday was the first half of the 20th century, when Havana seed tobacco grown under shade tents occupied more than 30,000 acres. Today, only about 2,000 acres remain under cultivation in the Connecticut River Valley. During tobacco-drying time, from late summer through autumn, you can still see long barns filled with what appear to be thousands of sleeping bats hanging upside down. The **Luddy/Taylor Connecticut Valley Tobacco Museum** (145 Lang Road; 860-285-1888), which has a tobacco-curing barn, explains the history of the local crop.

Native tribes introduced tobacco to Connecticut in the 1630s, and the plant is still grown here.

■ **NORTHEAST CORNER** *map, page 117, C/E-1/3*

Connecticut's Quiet Corner in the northeast is not as quiet as it once was. There are fewer "tractor crossing" signs these days and more "horse crossing" ones, fewer silos and more antique barns. But in much of the Woodstock Valley, pleated farmland still falls away from the road as you drive along winding old Route 169 from Woodstock to Canterbury.

■ **WOODSTOCK** *map, page 117, E-1*

You may, of course, never leave the starting gate if you succumb to the beguiling garden at Woodstock's **Roseland Cottage,** which has survived intact since 1850. Wispy cosmos, playful petunias, exuberant snapdragons, and other flowery exhibitionists wave at each other across immaculate boxwood hedges, luring you through the green maze to a summerhouse that begs to host a romantic assignation. Also known as the Bowen House, the 1846 Gothic cottage, with its blushing walls, stained glass, pointed arches, and peerless Victorian interior, remained in the Bowen family until 1970. The barn contains one of the country's first bowling alleys, and the October Festival held on the property is one of the region's most spirited arts and crafts events. *556 Route 169; 860-928-4074.*

Roseland Cottage, with its blushing walls, stained glass, and pointed arches, has survived intact since 1850.

■ **PUTNAM WOLF DEN** *map, page 117, E-1*
Putnam Wolf Den memorializes the shooting during the winter of 1742–43 of what became known as the last wolf in Connecticut. The event came to symbolize the end of Connecticut's wilderness era. The triggerman, Israel Putnam, later became one of the Revolutionary War's heroes as Major General Putnam ("Old Wolf Putnam" to his men). Follow the trail in **Mashamoquet Brook State Park** as it slopes toward Putnam Wolf Den, midway down an impressive cliff, and then relax in the Indian Chair, a natural stone couch perched on a 20-foot-high ridge. A suitably heroic statue of Israel Putnam on horseback dominates the pretty agricultural town of Brooklyn, to the south. *U.S. 44 south of Pomfret; 860-928-6121.*

■ **CANTERBURY** *map, page 117, E-2*
Canterbury, south of Pomfret on Route 160, is yet another now-sleepy Connecticut town that made history. A little less than a century after Israel Putnam shot the state's last wolf, Prudence Crandall brought another era to a close in 1832—or so she thought—by admitting a young black woman to her school for girls. Exhibits in the three small rooms of the **Prudence Crandall Museum,** inside the circa-1805 mansion that served as the Canterbury Female Boarding School, tell the larger-than-life story of Crandall, whose experiment in desegregation resulted in her closing her academy after irate townsfolk began withdrawing their daughters. She reopened it as a school for "young ladies and little misses of color," but ceased operations altogether 18 months later because the locals were still up in arms and the state legislature had passed a bill in 1834 prohibiting such institutions. *Routes 14 and 169; 860-546-9916.*

■ **WILLIMANTIC** *map, page 117, D-2*
Swooping Route 14 travels west from Canterbury to Willimantic, darting under trees and between lush meadows, throwing up scents of hay and honeysuckle along the way. The feel is altogether grittier in Willimantic, where the bartenders at the **Willimantic Brewing Company** (967 Main Street; 860-423-6777), in a lofty old postal building, pour some outstanding beers.

Nearby to the southeast is the 12,500-acre **Natchaug State Forest,** known for its rhododendrons and the Silvermine Horse Camp, an area set up for equestrian camping. *Pilfershire Road, Eastford; 860-974-1562.*

■ **COVENTRY**   *map page 117, D-2*

When gardening became a competitive sport, nurseries became merciless testing grounds, with frowning customers inspecting serried ranks of eager-to-please plants. But **Caprilands Herb Farm** is the opposite—an idiosyncratic 50-acre garden of herbs and woodland that soothes and inspires as it leads you from scented corner to scented corner, following its own eccentric logic. Much of what you see and smell is for sale in the farm's shops. *534 Silver Street, off U.S. 44, North Coventry; 860-742-7244.*

Stone-walled meadows and the 500-acre Hale State Forest surround the **Nathan Hale Homestead,** filled with original furnishings and family memorabilia. Connecticut's hero was executed as a spy by the British before the 1776 structure was completed. *2299 South Street, off U.S. 44 East and U.S. 6 West; 860-742-6917.*

The British executed Nathan Hale before his house was completed. (Nathan Hale Homestead)

■ **STORRS** *map page 117, D-2*

The biggest surprise on the graceful **University of Connecticut** campus at Storrs (Route 195, 1 mile south of U.S. 44) is not the 15-foot white shark in the fine Museum of Natural History, but the cattle grazing nearby as part of the agricultural program. Hikers with a taste for wilder life should hike 3 miles or so along the **Nipmuck Trail,** which can be entered at Gurleyville Road and may present, if you're lucky, acrobatically gifted troupes of flying squirrels.

■ **HARTFORD TO OLD SAYBROOK**   *map page 117, B/C-2/4*

Traveling southeast from Hartford, following the Connecticut River to its destination on Long Island Sound, you enter an amphibious world where even the Goodspeed Opera House in East Haddam, a national treasure that opened in 1876, has one foot in the water. Soon you are in the same condition. Lured by watery temptations that shimmer around each bend, you find yourself coaxing your car or bicycle onto a ferry regardless of the destination. Finally you abdicate responsibility, abandon your burdensome wheels, and submit to a steamboat ride or an island cruise.

■ **MIDDLETOWN** *map page 117, B-3*

Middletown, a former shipbuilding and trading port, earned its name by being the halfway point along the Connecticut River between inland Hartford and coastal Saybrook. This was Connecticut's wealthiest town in the mid-18th century, though today it presents a blank face to the visitor, particularly in its arid, tree-starved downtown, where the few remaining 19th-century commercial buildings seem to have washed up on an alien, concrete shore.

If the structures could manage the short journey uphill to **Wesleyan University,** they would feel completely at home. Founded by Methodists in 1831 but nonsectarian from the outset, Wesleyan is small enough to be explored in a leisurely walk and grand enough to necessitate frequent stops to admire the varied architecture. Its grassy, tree-shaded thoroughfares also present fine lolling opportunities. The **Davison Art Center** (Alsop House, 301 High Street; 860-685-2500) displays prints and photographs in a home built in 1838; the adjoining **Zikha Gallery** (283 Washington Terrace; 860-685-2684) exhibits contemporary art; and the **General Mansfield House** (151 Main Street), an 1810 mansion, contains period furnishings and Civil War memorabilia.

Its trees and architecture are among the grace notes of the Wesleyan University campus.

■ HADDAM   *map page 117, C-3*

Rather than vaulting back onto Route 9 to travel south from Middletown, meander along the old highway—an extension of Main Street—that turns into Route 154 (signed much of the way as Saybrook Road) and shadows the river to Long Island Sound.

In the town of Haddam, which was incorporated in 1668, is **Thankful Arnold House.** Built in 1794 and restored to its 1810 appearance, the house has period furniture, a small garden, and restrained decoration that present a striking contrast to the modern trophy houses now lining many of the region's back roads. The museum houses the Arnold family's Civil War correspondence. *14 Hayden Hill Road, off Route 154; 800-522-7463.*

The Connecticut River is at its most sedate on the outskirts of Haddam, sliding between the broad expanse of Haddam Meadows on one side and the defunct Connecticut Yankee nuclear power plant on the other. If the bulbous power facility unsettles you, picnic by the lily pond or head downstream on one of the narrated **Camelot Cruises.** *Route 154, west bank of river; 860-345-8591.*

■ **EAST HADDAM** *map page 117, C-4*

Crossing the Swing Bridge (Route 82) from Haddam to East Haddam, you are greeted by one of Connecticut's most exuberant edifices. The **Goodspeed Opera House,** a six-story Victorian music hall, looks like an overdressed bathing beauty about to take the plunge. The tallest wooden building on the river when shipping and banking entrepreneur William H. Goodspeed built it in 1876, the structure served various purposes before being restored in the 1960s. One of the nation's most whimsical-looking musical theater venues, it has a cozy Victorian Bar and Ladies' Drinking Parlor. The Goodspeed's resident company produces three musicals from April through December in East Haddam and develops new musicals at Goodspeed-at-Chester, an old factory building. You can tour the Goodspeed Opera House from June through October. *Route 82 (follow signs from Route 154 or Route 9, Exit 7); 860-873-8668.*

To enjoy East Haddam's countryside, visit **Devil's Hopyard State Park,** where water and rock produce the exquisite Chapman's Falls. *Hopyard Road off Route 82.*

The Goodspeed Opera House, ready for a plunge.

■ **GILLETTE CASTLE STATE PARK** *map page 117, C-4*

The wonders at Gillette Castle, southeast of East Haddam, are manmade, the product of the imagination of the actor and playwright William Gillette, who grew up next door to the Mark Twain House at Nook Farm in Hartford, an experience that may have contributed to the youngster's eccentricity. The teenage Gillette built his first steam engine at home and fully indulged his mechanical passion when theatrical success—in particular his portrayal of Sherlock Holmes—allowed him to build Seventh Sister, now known as Gillette Castle, in the 1910s.

Viewed from the river below or approached by road, the fieldstone Rhenish castle seems to lurk in its wooded grounds, daring visitors to probe its secrets—an effect that the playful Gillette doubtless intended. The interior, designed by Gillette himself, is heavy on stone and wood, with raffia wall coverings and art-nouveau lighting sconces and other fixtures. Having specified in his will that the property not fall into "the possession of some blithering saphead who has no conception of where he is or with what surrounded," Gillette would no doubt be delighted today by the astonishment greeting his innovations. An elaborate mirror system allows someone in the bedroom to monitor the entrance below, furniture runs on railway-like metal tracks, and intricate locks and ingenious lighting challenge even the most sleuth-like visitor. Tantalizing river views can be had from the castle or the trail, which is dotted with stonework and bridges. *River Road off Route 82; 860-526-2336.*

Set yourself and your car adrift on the tiny **Hadlyme-Chester Ferry,** which materializes like an eager dog whenever it is summoned and is content to fetch and retrieve passengers between April and November. The four-minute ride provides the best angles for photographing Gillette Castle. *State Pier; 860-443-3856.*

Fantasy is a permanent fixture at Gillette Castle.

■ CHESTER   *map page 117, C-4*

Once known for manufacturing and shipbuilding, pretty little Chester is today dominated by theater and art. The town's **Connecticut River Artisans Cooperative** is an eclectic gallery in an old house that formerly served as a church. The Great Room here has an arched ceiling with an oval skylight to illuminate the art, sculpture, prints, toys, textiles, and jewelry. *5 West Main Street, Route 148; 860-526-5575.*

The **Goodspeed-at-Chester** (North Main Street; 860-873-8668), which presents musicals, occupies a former knitting-needle factory. The **National Theater of the Deaf** (55 Van Dyke Avenue; 860-724-5179), which has won a Tony Award for its efforts, presents plays in sign and spoken language throughout the year.

■ COCKAPONSET STATE FOREST   *map page 117, C-4*

If the ferry trip whetted your appetite for less confined spaces, the 15,652-acre Cockaponset State Forest, stretching from Chester north to Haddam, is the perfect destination. You can wander the Cockaponset Trail for hours, through snowdrifts of mountain laurel in the spring or ankle-deep in golden leaves during the autumn. The electric blue flash catching your eye by a riverbank may be a kingfisher. *Route 148, 3 miles west of Chester.*

■ DEEP RIVER   *map, page 117, C-4*

Nourishment of an equally transcendent sort is available in the small town of Deep River, to the south on Route 154. The **Pasta Unlimited** (159 Main Street; 860-526-4056) shop here provides not only superb pasta dishes and sandwiches to take out (the chicken salad would convert any meatball extremist), but also picnics that may be ordered, from spring through autumn on the morning of your excursion. Seating is limited to a few chairs on the busy street, but you will be spending most of your time on your knees anyway, adoring the almond bars and raspberry tarts.

Casting about for a reason to stay in Deep River for another snack, you will be relieved to discover the **Stone House** (245 Main Street; 860-526-1449), a museum of local history that reveals, among other things, the area's time as the nation's center of ivory cutting. Combs, toothpicks, piano keys, and other ivory items are on display.

■ **ESSEX**   *map page 117, C-4*

If you find regression distasteful then you should bypass Essex, where the steam locomotives of the Valley Railroad turn responsible adults into enthralled children. Standing beside Engine No. 40 as the 1920 giant does some preparatory breathing exercises, you wonder if it is too late to become an engine driver.

The **Essex Steam Train and Riverboat Ride** takes you on a two-and-a-half-hour journey, first on rail, then on water as the train hands you over to a steamboat at Deep River—you'll see Gillette Castle and the Goodspeed Opera House from the water. The Dinner Train serves meals during a luxurious two-hour ride. *Railroad Avenue, a quarter-mile west of Highway 9, Exit 3; 860-767-0103.*

Essex was a major shipbuilding town from the mid-18th to the mid-19th century and has the oldest continuously operating waterfront in the country. In 1987, archaeologists from Wesleyan University uncovered evidence of Robert Lay's wharf, built in 1650 on the site of the present-day Steamboat Dock. The dockside **Connecticut River Museum** focuses on maritime and river history and includes a replica of the 1775 *American Turtle,* America's first submarine, which David Bushnell built in Old Saybrook. *67 Main Street; 860-767-8269.*

The Essex Steam Train.

Main Street, Essex.

To observe more about local reality, visit the Essex Historical Society at **Hill's Academy Museum** (22 Prospect Street; 860-767-0681) or the **Pratt House** (19 West Avenue), part of which may date to 1648. Or just sit on the spacious porch of the 1776 **Griswold Inn** (36 Main Street; 860-767-1776) and watch Essex go leisurely about its business. If you continue south to the coast, you'll arrive in Old Saybrook, described in the COASTAL CONNECTICUT chapter.

■ NORWICH AREA   *map page 117, D/E-3/4*

An alternate journey from Hartford to the coast begins on soothing Route 2, which takes you to Norwich, at the head of the Thames River (pronounced "Thaymes" here, not "Tems"). Working farms flank much of Route 2, as they did 30 years ago. But Norwich, gloriously situated on a rocky bluff overlooking the river, has declined since its glory days in the 1850s, when the town had the world's largest paper mill and the country's largest cotton mills.

■ **NORWICH** *map page 117, D/E-3*

Downtown Norwich is a patchwork of elegant facades and boarded-up store-fronts. There are, however, remarkable survivors. The Leffingwell Inn, built in the late 1600s and a meeting place for patriots including George Washington, peeps out shyly from under the highway at the junction of Route 2 and Route 169. Now known as the **Christopher Leffingwell House Museum**—its namesake was a financier and an ardent supporter of the American Revolution—it still has clay pipes by the fireplace and a fine collection of period furniture. *348 Washington Street; 860-889-9440.*

Eighteenth-century houses ring the neighboring **Norwichtown Green.** The site of the first English settlement in Norwich, the Green was part of the "nine miles square" given by Uncas, chief of the Mohegans, to Thomas Leffingwell, a Saybrook soldier and the great-grandfather of Christopher Leffingwell, as payment for English assistance in routing the attacking Narragansetts in 1645. Uncas is buried in the Indian Burial Ground at Sachem Street and commemorated with an 1833 obelisk. Reminders of Norwich's past affluence are everywhere as well. Broadway is the most evocative: an airy thoroughfare lined with 19th-century houses in styles from Greek Revival to English Gothic.

The gardens that once surrounded these houses earned Norwich the title "Rose of New England," and the **Memorial Rose Garden** in Mohegan Park, on Judd Road, maintains the fragrant tradition from June through September. A more tangible legacy is displayed at the 19th-century **Slater Memorial Museum** (108 Crescent Street, 860-887-2506), whose extensive collection ranges from Greek, Roman, and Renaissance casts through American, European, and African art, Native American artifacts, furniture, and firearms.

Following Route 12 south along the river, turn east onto leafy Route 214 to visit **Ledyard,** which has a water-powered, up-and-down sawmill in a pleasant park to the east of the town. The site is open on weekends in April, May, October, and November, water levels permitting. Once famous for a late-18th-century female preacher named Jemima who sprang out of her own coffin to impress her zealous "Jemimakins," Ledyard now attracts different believers, praying for different miracles, at **Foxwoods Casino** (Route 12), where the gaming area alone covers 314,000 square feet.

Fireworks (opposite) over the Thames and boats (following pages) along it.

BASTION AGAINST VULGARITY

Helen had a way with houses. She could buy one in a rundown condition, move in, vigorously improve its value and sell it at a profit. . . . But their present house, the seventh, was a different story. . . . they doubted if they would ever move away. . . .

It was one of the few authentic pre-Revolutionary dwellings left in the district, flanked by one of the few remaining wine-glass elms, and she liked to think of it as the final bastion against vulgarity. . . . she might have to stand smiling in the kitchens of horrid little ranch houses and split levels, dealing with impossibly rude people whose children ran tricycles against her shins and spilled Kool-Aid on her dress; she might have to breathe the exhaust fumes and absorb the desolation of Route Twelve, with its supermarkets and pizza joints and frozen custard stands, but these things only brightened the joy of her returning. She loved the last few hundred yards of shady road that meant she was almost there, and the brittle hiss of well-raked gravel under her tires, and the switching off of the ignition in her neat garage, and the brave, tired walk past fragrant flowerbeds to her fine old Colonial door. And the first clean scent of cedar and floorwax inside, the first glimpse of the Currier and Ives print that hung above the old umbrella stand, never failed to fill her with the sentimental tenderness of the word "home."

—Richard Yates, *Revolutionary Road,* 1961

Suddenly filling the horizon like a candy-colored spaceship, Foxwoods is an enterprise of the Mashantucket Pequot Tribal Nation and Connecticut's biggest individual source of revenue. Should the casino's immense attractions overwhelm you, catch a shuttle bus to the nearby **Mashantucket Pequot Museum and Research Center.** The high-tech exhibits here will transport you from the glacial period to the present, illustrating Native American life not only in traditional villages, but also in the trailers that were the pre-casino homes of many Pequots. *110 Pequot Trail; 800-411-9671.*

Across the river at Uncasville, the **Mohegan Sun** (Mohegan Sun Boulevard) and the **Tantaquidgeon Indian Museum** (Route 32) are more modest gaming and historical institutions.

Foxwoods Casino fills the horizon like a candy-colored spaceship.

■ TRAVEL BASICS

Getting Around: Bradley International Airport lies 12 miles north of downtown Hartford on I-91. Amtrak's rail service from Boston and New York serves Hartford, New Britain, Windsor, and Windsor Locks; Metro-North serves New Haven from Grand Central Terminal in New York City; and Connecticut Commuter Rail runs between New London and New Haven. By car, it is difficult to avoid I-91 and I-84 around Hartford, where rush-hour delays are lengthy. Routes 169 and 14 in the Woodstock Valley provide a restful contrast. Choose minor roads that shadow the Connecticut River and skirt I-95 along the coast, following U.S. 1 and its offshoots. A river ferry serves Glastonbury and Rocky Hill, and the Hadlyme-Chester river ferry operates from April through October.

Climate: Hartford and Central Connecticut seem to boil in summer (temperatures average in the high 80s) while the Woodstock Valley is slightly cooler. Winter can be cold, and sudden blizzards and ice storms occasionally close stretches of the interstates. Spring and autumn are typically moderate, with pleasantly warm days and chilly nights.

NORTHWESTERN CONNECTICUT

Connecticut is a noticeably tilted place. From the heights of Bear Mountain, in the state's northwestern corner, the land tumbles down to form the rugged slopes and alpine meadows of the Litchfield Hills before finally reclining along the shore of Long Island Sound. The contrasts in northwestern Connecticut are dizzying as well. You can spend the morning exploring hill country that has been scarified by glaciers, and then pass the evening at decidedly civilized chamber music festivals.

New York—just an hour away—creates its own gravitational field. Some parts of northwestern Connecticut are a commuter's paradise, and its hills have long been summer retreats. Appearances here are deceptive. That grain silo is actually an art gallery, the Victorian farmhouse beside it is a conference center, and the general store is exclusively gourmet. But any region with a thousand lakes is sure to keep a few charms in reserve. To discover some of them, wander through the Litchfield Hills during spring or autumn, taking back roads whenever possible, and explore the coast when the elements, not the crowds, are in charge.

This corrugated landscape encourages even the most disciplined visitor to lose a few days in its upland meadows and comfortable inns. Anxiety and urgency drain away as the road lulls you with gentle, rhythmic curves. In this chapter, we make a circuit from Winsted, reached from Hartford on U.S. 44, down to Litchfield and New Milford, returning north on U.S. 7 and Route 41 to U.S. 44 and the towns of Canaan and Norfolk.

■ HISTORY

Traversing the northwest corner's quiet back roads today, it is hard to imagine that this was once one of New England's most industrialized regions. But following the early 18th-century discovery of iron-ore deposits near Kent, Lakeville, and other towns, area hills were quickly stripped bare and valleys were turned into roaring, puffing blast furnaces. Metal objects of an astonishing variety—everything from firearms to cooking pots—were manufactured here, with factories popping up in even the smallest towns.

Out for a stroll (and a roll) on West Street in downtown Litchfield.

Evidence of the colonial past is thin and scattered, thanks in part to devastating British raids during the Revolution, a conflict to which this small western corner, long since reforested, made a significant contribution. Most eligible men enlisted in the Connecticut Army, and the area's list of Revolutionary War heroes is impressive. The patriot Ethan Allen was born in Litchfield County and manned his forge in Lakeville, and George Washington chose Benjamin Tallmadge of Litchfield as one of his closest advisers.

■ TOURING THE LITCHFIELD HILLS   *map page 147, B/C-2/4*

■ WINSTED   *map page 147, C-2*

The hill region bred strange beliefs. Winsted, for example, was a hotbed of superstition and outlandish sightings in the early 18th century. "Wild men" reportedly roamed the hillsides, along with five-legged cows and talking owls. It all started when the Beach family found cloven hoof tracks in the snow and "a slight mark as if a forked tail had been drawn across the powdery surface"—enough to have a parishioner whipped for practicing witchcraft.

Today's visitors must content themselves with admiring the 19th-century mansions on Main Street, among them the Greek Revival **Solomon Rockwell House,** completed in 1813 for the owner of an area iron forge and other businesses. With its sturdy Ionic columns, the house continues to strike a commanding pose. On exhibit inside are original Rockwell family furnishings and a Civil War military collection. *225 Prospect Street, off U.S. 44; 860-379-8433.*

The wilderness also harbored outlaws and outcasts. In **Barkhamsted,** east of Winsted, Molly Barber, a white woman from Wethersfield, and her Narragansett husband, James Chaugham, established an outcast village in 1740 where Native Americans, African-Americans, and wayward whites found refuge. An archaeological site in **People's State Forest** (West River Road off Route 118) recalls the community, which survived until 1860.

■ TORRINGTON   *map page 147, C-2*

Heading south from Winsted on Route 8, you come to the once heavily industrialized town of Torrington. Known as Mast Swamp for its exceptional pine trees used in shipbuilding, Torrington was one of the region's early brass towns, producing the country's first machine-made brass kettles and cartridge brass for export to Spain and Russia, as well as other goods.

John Brown, the famous abolitionist, was born in Torrington in 1800. The pikes used by Brown and his men during their 1859 raid on the U.S. arsenal at Harper's Ferry, Virginia, were made by the Collins Company in Canton. A marker on John Brown Road, which is accessible from University Road off Route 4, commemorates his birthplace.

At the northern end of Main Street is the Torrington Historical Society, which occupies the 18-room **Hotchkiss-Fyler House,** built in 1900. Orsamus Roman Fyler, a Civil War veteran and the town's postmaster for years, lived here with his wife, Mary, and his married daughter Gertrude Hotchkiss. The mansion contains family furnishings and paintings by Connecticut artists and has elaborate woodwork of maple, mahogany, birch, and ash. A circa-1885 residence next door contains an exhibit about Torrington history that focuses on industry and immigration, and the carriage house has a re-created machine shop with equipment manufactured at Torrington's Hendley Machine Company, in business from the 1870s to the 1950s. *192 Main Street; 860-482-8260.*

■ THOMASTON *map page 147, C-3*

More legends lurk to the south at **Leatherman Cave,** named for the Old Leatherman, a Connecticut wanderer who first came to notice in 1862. A Frenchman named Jules Bourglay, who had failed in the leather business and had been jilted by a lady friend, the Old Leatherman traversed the state in all seasons wearing nothing but leather clothing and sleeping out-of-doors, often in caves. A mile southwest of Thomaston, you can hike along the **Mattatuck Trail** to the cave, the most famous of Bourglay's retreats. The trail passes through the cave at the foot of Crane Lookout, which affords spectacular views. *Off Reynold's Bridge Road.*

To let someone else do the driving, visit the **Railroad Museum of New England.** The Naugatuck Railroad Company will take you on an 20-mile ride along the river, through state forest and across the face of the dramatic Thomaston Dam—an excursion that is particularly memorable in October, when outrageous autumn leaves do their best to distract the stolid locomotives. Under the supervision of a certified instructor, you can learn how to drive the train. *Off East Main Street (Route 8, Exit 38); 860-283-7245.*

■ **LITCHFIELD AREA** *map page 147, B/C-3*

From Thomaston, take Route 109 to Route 63 to Litchfield, whose broad tree-lined streets and large shady green dominate a generous hilltop. Long popular as a summer retreat for affluent New Yorkers, Litchfield in the 1600s was Indian territory. In 1667, two Farmington residents bought part of the town's acreage from the Tunxis Indians, and in 1715 or 1716 people from Hartford and Windsor bought nearby land in what is now called Bantam from the Potatucks.

Litchfield was settled in 1721, but not peacefully. The town was repeatedly attacked. In 1722, one Joseph Harris was captured and scalped on what is now known as Harris Plain. The atmosphere was no less bellicose during the Revolution, when many Litchfield residents, including Oliver Wolcott, held key military and governmental positions. A Continental Army store on the main route to Boston, Litchfield prospered after the Revolution and became an intellectual center of Federalist New England.

(above) Tapping Reeve opened the first U.S. law school. (Litchfield Historical Society) (following pages) Autumn colors add to the visual charm of the Litchfield Hills.

When railroads bypassed the town in the 19th century, Litchfield became a sedate backwater. In 1938, the *WPA Guide to Connecticut* noted: "When the mail comes in, townsfolk gather at the post office. . . . Just across the Green . . . is the county jail, seldom occupied except by some backwoodsman who has been intemperate. . . . The warden usually basks in the sunlight near the harness store . . . his golden badge polished bright."

The scene today along the **Litchfield Green** is a little different. All-terrain vehicles circle at lunchtime and chalkboards outside the many restaurants announce a daunting assortment of pastas, salads, and vegetarian alternatives. To savor the setting on a summer afternoon, take the easy way out. Buy a sandwich at **Litchfield Gourmet** (33 West Street, 860-567-4882), which occupies an 1880 building that was the Granniss and Elmore General Store, and lunch under a tree, watching elderly gentlemen in shirtsleeves playing boccie ball nearby, and a motorcyclist, probably a vacationing CEO, blatting back and forth on his Harley.

The **Litchfield History Museum,** housed in a handsome beaux-arts building, is a good starting point for more strenuous exploration. The collection includes paintings of Litchfield notables by Ralph Earl, a leading portraitist of the early 19th century, along with textiles, photographs, clothing, and furniture. *7 South Street; 860-567-4501.*

Museum admission includes entrance to the nearby **Tapping Reeve House and Law School,** America's first law school, which was founded in 1774 and played a pivotal role in shaping the new nation. Until Judge Tapping Reeve opened his school, lawyers learned their profession by apprenticing to other lawyers. Reeve organized a curriculum and gave lectures on various topics. Standing in the small one-room structure, it's hard to imagine that as many as 25 men at a time huddled together here to learn from Reeve. And an impressive group they were: the school's graduates include two U.S. vice presidents, 102 representatives, 28 senators, and three justices of the United States Supreme Court. Tapping Reeve is also known for championing more enlightened legal status for married women, working toward legislation that would eventually allow wives to transfer property without their husband's permission. *82 South Street.*

Litchfield's other prominent residents included Pastor Lyman Beecher, the father of Harriet Beecher Stowe and the Rev. Henry Ward Beecher, and Benjamin Tallmadge, chief of the Intelligence Service during the Revolution and a friend of Nathan Hale. The **Tallmadge House** on North Street, like most of the town's

White Flower Farm.

Federal and Colonial Revival houses, is a private residence. If you're in town on Open House Day, the second Saturday in July, you can see the interiors of the some of the town's mansions, but a walk around the Green and down South Street at any time of the year will give you a sense of the town's uninterrupted prosperity.

Five minutes from downtown Litchfield in Morris, the **White Flower Farm** is the leading nursery in a region where competition is tough. Heading south of the town center, passing equestrian centers that look more like luxury condominiums, you turn into a modest parking lot and immediately change from a rational person into a creature ruled by the senses. Colors and scents erupt from every corner of the 10-acre display garden and from the 30 acres of growing fields, drawing you past glorious perennial beds, through arbors, and under copper beeches until you stumble upon the nationally famous display of English tuberous begonias. These outrageous plants, which look like roses on steroids, are in bloom all summer and into the early fall. Amid the show-offs are subtle varieties as well. *167 Litchfield Road (Route 63); 860-567-8789.*

Topsmead State Forest is harder to find but even more intoxicating than White Flower. Apple trees line the rustic path leading to an English cottage perched in a highland meadow—the former summer home of Edith M. Chase, the heiress to a brass-industry fortune. After the grandiosity of Litchfield, the 1920 Tudor Revival cottage's dainty walled gardens and exquisite architectural details, the work of the prominent Boston architect Richard Henry Dana Jr., restore the human perspective. The most perfect picnic spot imaginable, the park also tempts you with woodland walks. The house is open to visitors on two weekends a month. *Buel Road (head south on Route 118, turn right on Clark Road, and go to the right at the end); 860-567-5694.*

Tastefully Tudor: Edith Morton Chase's house in Topsmead State Forest.

The 4,000-acre **White Memorial Foundation** provides challenging trails and has a campground, a marina, and a nature museum. Every preference—whether for meadow, river, forest, or marsh views—is accommodated with an accompanying seasonal soundtrack: cricket, grasshopper, and cicada harmonies in summer; the rustle of leaves during autumn; and an icy crunch in winter. *U.S. 202, 2.5 miles west of Litchfield; 860-567-0857.*

■ SMALL-TOWN DETOURS

■ WASHINGTON AND WASHINGTON DEPOT *map page 147, B-3/4*

U.S. 202 dips and climbs its way southwest from Litchfield to New Milford, but you may want to make a detour south on Route 47, to quiet Washington and Washington Depot. Among the attractions is the **Gunn Memorial Library and Museum,** which mounts local-history exhibitions in a 1781 house. *5 Wykeham Road, at Route 47, Washington; 860-868-7756.*

Behind the **Institute for American Indian Studies** is its main attraction, a re-created 17th-century Algonquin village, with two huts and a longhouse made of bark, with branches as framing. The nearby Medicine Wheel garden, with indigenous healing and flowering plants, is laid out in symbolic quadrants of red, white, yellow, and blue flowers, in tune with the four directions. In the modest museum are arrowheads, spear points, pottery shards, and other artifacts found in the Northeast. *38 Curtis Road, off Route 199, Washington Depot; 860-868-0518.*

■ **BETHLEHEM**   *map page 147, B-3/4*

Pleasant back roads head east from Route 47 at Washington to Bethlehem. Take Wykeham Road from the Gunn House; it eventually becomes Carmel Hill Road. At Guilds Hollow Road make a left. The site of the first theological seminary in the country, Connecticut's "Christmas Town"—people come in droves in December to have their Christmas cards postmarked "Bethlehem"—is famous for the preaching of the pastor of the First Church of Bethlehem, Rev. Joseph Bellamy. The reverend was at the forefront of the "Great Awakening" religious revival in the 18th century and was locally dubbed "the Pope of Litchfield."

The 18th-century **Bellamy-Ferriday House** sits on property whose history spans from 1744 to the present. The house was constructed in phases for Reverend Bellamy and his son, David, and numerous outbuildings were added to the farm by the four generations of Bellamys that lived here. The Ferriday family bought the site in 1912. In addition to Reverend Bellamy's writings, the extensive manuscript collection includes documents related to the Ferriday family's involvement with the U.S. Sanitary Commission during the Civil War and Miss Caroline Ferriday's support for the French Resistance during World War II. The formal garden in back is a work of art. *9 Main Street North; 203-266-7596.*

■ **WOODBURY AND ROXBURY**   *map page 147, B-4*

South of Bethlehem (take Route 132 from Bethlehem to U.S. 6) is Woodbury, whose restaurants and lengthy Antiques Row attract an upscale crowd.

For much of the year a startlingly large centuries-old elm shades **Glebe House,** built around 1750 and beginning in 1771 the residence of America's first Episcopal priest, the Rev. John Marshall. A handsome variation on saltbox-style architecture, the farmhouse has a gambrel roof pitched so precipitously in back it seems to tumble into the small outbuilding behind it. Gertrude Jekyll, a major influence on 20th-century landscape architecture, designed the small garden here, though only in recent years has work begun on completing the entire project. *Hollow Road (follow signs from U.S. 6); 203-263-2855.*

Roxbury, west of Woodbury on Route 317 (or south of Washington on Route 199), is the high, isolated, and very exclusive enclave to which writer James Baldwin retreated in 1961 while working on his novel, *Another Country.* The task probably prevented him from appreciating the pretty sweep of Route 67 between Roxbury and New Milford.

■ **NEW MILFORD**   *map page 147, A-4*

Settled in 1707 by John Noble of Westfield, Massachusetts, who moved here with his eight-year-old daughter, New Milford attracted Roger Sherman, the only individual to sign all of the United States's founding documents: the Declaration of Independence, the Articles of Confederation, the Articles of Association, and the Constitution. Sherman arrived here from Newton, Massachusetts, in 1743 and opened a cobbler's shop. He served as New Milford's congressman and was also elected to the U.S. Senate.

The properties of the **New Milford Historical Society Museum** include a reconstruction of the 1796 Elijah Boardman Store, moved up the hill from the town common to its present location. According to local accounts, the store was *the* place for settlers heading out west to pick up supplies. These days the building exhibits landscapes of the surrounding countryside by Woldemar Neufeld, a Russian immigrant who in 1949 established a studio and art school in New Milford. The furniture, clocks, buttons, pottery, pewter, tools, and other artifacts on exhibit in the main museum building were all created in New Milford—the legacy of an era when a town's self-sufficiency was a matter of course. *6 Aspetuck Avenue; 860-354-3069.*

■ **HOUSATONIC RIVER AREA**   *map page 147, A/B-1/4*

U.S. 7, one of the region's most scenic roads, runs north from New Milford to Connecticut's border with Massachusetts, following the course of the Housatonic River for much of its run and competing for beauty with the equally engaging Route 41 and U.S. 44 to the west. "There is no tonic like the Housatonic," U.S. Supreme Court Justice Oliver Wendell Holmes once observed. He was right: dawdling is the point here. The road's curves and the sleepy villages along the way demand it. You may, of course, drive single-mindedly through unassuming **Gaylordsville.** But then you would miss Brown's Forge, an authentic 1871 blacksmith shop on Brown's Forge Road.

COVERED BRIDGES

At one time covered bridges were as much a part of any journey as are today's traffic signals. Most country roads followed the banks of a river and at every bend there was one or more of these barnlike structures thrown across the water like drawbridges over a moat to some little kingdom. . . .

Although Connecticut has only three covered bridges left, the Housatonic River alone had eighteen fine examples, each marking a community of mills that has since grown into a riverside town. Connecticut was proud of its bridges, particularly because the two most famous names in bridge engineering, Theodore Burr and Ithiel Town were born there. But ambitious men of those days spread their work in far places: although Burr and Town designed hundreds of covered bridges in almost every state, Connecticut never had more than fifty.

The reasons for covering bridges varied with the builder, but they had primarily to do with strengthening the structure and making the wood season properly and last longer. . . . A reason for covering a bridge, which has seldom been mentioned, is for appearances. When toll-collecting was an entirely private enterprise, there was something distinct about using a covered structure which seemed to make a bridge passage worth that much more. The added expense would seem unnecessary today, but bridges were often built for resale and they were therefore made to look as attractive as possible.

—Eric Sloane, *Our Vanishing Landscape*, 1955

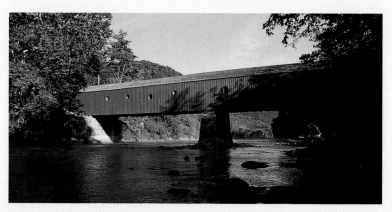

Cornwall Bridge spans the Housatonic River.

This rugged terrain is ideal ambush country, and weaving your way north to Kent on a spring afternoon you become a willing victim. The glinting Housatonic River makes repeated forays at the road, and banks of purple loosestrife suddenly catch your eye; finally, **Bulls Covered Bridge** forces you to stop and admire both river and foliage framed in its tiny, dark windows.

One of the apparently natural beauties in this area, the 6,000-acre **Candlewood Lake** is actually manmade. To create hydroelectric power in the late 1920s, the Connecticut Light and Power Company dammed the Rocky River near where it joined the Housatonic, flooding entire towns and farms in the process. The lake is a popular summer recreation spot, especially with scuba divers, who enjoy tracing old roads and peering into abandoned houses. *U.S. 7/202, south of New Milford.*

■ **KENT** *map page 147, A-3*

Fine-art and crafts galleries and, in good weather, outdoor cafes provide the man-made distractions in Kent, settled in 1738. For most of the 19th century, this was one of Connecticut's leading iron-producing towns.

The ruins of the Kent Iron Furnace, completed in 1826 and in operation for about 70 years, can be seen just below the **Sloane-Stanley Museum,** which exhibits early-American tools—axes, nail-making devices, silage choppers, wooden shovels and hay forks, hide scissors, and other implements—many of which you've probably never heard of. The museum is named for the 20th-century writer and illustrator Eric Sloane, who lived most of his adult life in Connecticut and donated his tool collection (he also helped arrange the exhibits), and for the Connecticut-based Stanley Works company, which donated the site on which the facility sits. Sloane's studio has been re-created here, and his paintings are on display. *U.S. 7, a mile north of Route 341; 860-927-3849.*

■ **FLANDERS** *map page 147, A-3*

Just north of Kent, at **Flanders Cemetery,** you can see what attracted landscape painters of the 19th century such as George Inness. Here you can also contemplate the gravestone of Capt. Jirah Swift, killed during the Revolutionary War; it reads, "I in the Prime of Life must quit the Stage or Nor see the End of all the Britains Rage." *U.S. 7 and St. John's Acre Road.*

Part of the **Appalachian Trail** crosses the Schaghticoke Indian Reservation west of Kent off Route 341, providing a steep hike that affords fine views of the

Familiar tools and ones you've probably never heard of. (Sloane-Stanley Museum)

Housatonic Valley, especially from Indian Rocks. More than 100 Schaghticoke warriors, descendants of the Pequots, joined the Continental Army. Acting chiefly as a signal corps, they relayed messages from Stockbridge, Massachusetts, to Long Island Sound, using drumbeats and fires on Candlewood Mountain, Straits Mountain, and Pickett Rock. Far less rugged than the steep trail ridges is the terrain at **Kent Falls State Park** (U.S. 7), a few miles north of Kent. A ¼-mile stepped pathway leads to the top of the cascades.

■ **CORNWALL AREA**   *map page 147, A/B-2*

"Only the very poor or the very brave settled here," the *WPA Guide to Connecticut* observed of rocky, icy Cornwall in 1938. An updated assessment would, however, include the very gifted and the very rich. A favorite summer retreat of New York intellectuals and even the occasional movie director, this isolated town deep in the

Taconic highlands attracted writers like the fabled *New Yorker* contributor and humorist James Thurber. The writer and his wife, Helen, settled in Cornwall in 1945, and he lived here until his death in 1961, completing *The Thurber Carnival* and other books in the house, which still stands near the Cathedral Pines section of the **Mohawk Mountain State Park** (off Route 4, east of U.S. 7).

The summit tower atop 1,683-foot Mohawk Mountain commands a 360-degree view, but various hiking trails, some originating from the dramatic Cathedral Pines stand, provide equally fine perspectives as they cross swamps, woodland, escarpments, and abandoned villages. The sleepy villages of **Cornwall Bridge** and **West Cornwall,** both on U.S. 7, and Cornwall, to the east on Route 4, form a triangle of treats that includes a one-lane covered bridge in West Cornwall and the Housatonic Meadows State Park. During fishing season you may see people up to their waists and higher in the Housatonic, fly-fishing for trout. Tiny West Cornwall has a few streets of shops and galleries.

■ SHARON   *map page 147, A-2*

The town of Sharon, founded in 1739, provides further diversions. (From West Cornwall, the most scenic route is West Cornwall Road, which you can pick up near the covered bridge.) Workers in this manufacturing center produced shoes, tools, mousetraps, and many other items. Benjamin Hotchkiss invented exploding shells here, a fact that is hard to imagine when you walk down Sharon's inordinately tranquil Main Street.

Main Street's showpiece is the magnificent **Gay-Hoyt House Museum.** Built in 1775, the magnificent brick structure is named after its first occupant, Ebenezer Gay, a politician, Revolutionary War soldier, and merchant, and the last owner, Anne Sherman Hoyt. American furniture, decorative arts, and iron and iron-industry related artifacts are on display here, along with five portraits by the folk artist Ammi Phillips, an itinerant painter from Colebrook, Connecticut, who received many commissions from middle- and upper-middle-class families during the 19th century.

At the 1,200-acre **Sharon Audubon Center,** the loudest sound is usually that of bees on assignment in the wildflower and herb gardens. A wildlife sanctuary, the center has a butterfly garden, a birds-of-prey aviary, and 11 miles of hiking trails through various habitats. *325 Cornwall Bridge Road (Route 4); 860-364-0520.*

Kent Falls State Park.

■ **LAKEVILLE**   *map page 147, A-1*

Ethan Allen became a co-owner of the Lakeville iron forge during the 1760s, before he moved to Vermont. So critical was the output of cannons and shot to the Revolution that Lakeville's ironworkers were fortified with unlimited supplies of meat and rum to keep the factories in full production.

In the early 1950s, the Belgian-born writer Georges Simenon, the creator of Inspector Maigret, lived at Shadow Rock Farm, in Lakeville, part of Salisbury township, producing *Maigret and the Headless Corpse* and many other novels. "In the United States I learned shame," Simenon wrote, referring to the "alcoholic consciousness" that overcame him when he traded wine for martinis. Shadow Rock remains in private hands.

Iron and rock are constant presences as you reach Salisbury. Depending on your fitness level, you may choose either a hike following the Appalachian Trail to the peak of **Bear Mountain** (start from the Undermountain Trail parking area off Route 41), or a more leisurely exploration of the early-19th-century **Mount Riga Ironworks Site,** home of the oldest remaining blast furnace, off U.S. 44. High and mighty in its own right, the furnace occupies a 1,000-foot ledge, and in its day manufactured anchors for the USS *Constitution* and other warships. It may be viewed from the road only. Bear Mountain, on the other hand, welcomes explorers, particularly in the kinder seasons when wild blueberries and mountain laurel decorate the slopes.

That the **Holley-Williams House** is less perfectly coiffed than many other northwestern Connecticut house museums only adds to its peculiar allure. Built in 1768 but expanded in 1808, it feels simultaneously lived-in and utterly 19th-century. Some say this is because the place is haunted, but the less ethereal evidence includes old toys original to the house and a window pane onto which one resident used her diamond engagement ring to scratch a memo of contentment ("Home Sweet Home, June 1847"). After the decline of the iron forge, the Holley family revitalized the Lakeville area's economy with a pocketknife factory, and a room on the ground floor includes a display of knives that was part of the company's presentation at the 1876 Centennial Exposition (the nation's first world's fair) in Philadelphia. Also on the grounds are a carriage house, an icehouse—the ice came from the nearby lake—and the Salisbury Cannon Museum, a Revolutionary War museum for children. *15 Millerton Road, off U.S. 44, Lakeville; 860-435-2878.*

Collin's Diner has been a fixture in North Canaan for more than half a century.

■ CANAAN   *map page 147, B-1*

Advertised as "a land flowing with milk and honey" when it was auctioned off at New London in 1738, the town of Canaan, northeast of Salisbury, was a mountainous outcropping redeemed only by some fertile valleys along the Housatonic River. Any trace of early hardship has been erased by prosperity, though, as has the Sunday drinking and brawling that earned neighboring Sodom its name in the 18th century. More respectable pleasures are provided these days at **Music Mountain** (Music Mountain Road, off Route 63 or Route 7; 860-824-7126), the nation's oldest continuous summer chamber-music event.

■ NORFOLK   *map page 147, B-1*

Once a wild, rugged outpost, compact Norfolk, sheltered by surrounding hills, is perhaps best known today for the summer and autumn **Norfolk Chamber Music Festival–Yale Summer School of Music,** held in the Music Shed at the Ellen Battell Stoeckel Estate. Mrs. Stoeckel and her husband, Carl—the son of Gustav Stoeckel, the first professor of music at Yale University—founded the Litchfield

County Choral Union in 1899 and built a music festival around its concerts. The event attracted composers like Coleridge Taylor, Sibelius, and Henry Hadley. Internationally renowned ensembles and artists continue to play for audiences who are usually sated with the estate's beauty and with the traditional picnics on the lawn. *June–August, 860-542-3000; September–May, 203-432-1966.*

The divertingly fishy **Joseph Battell Memorial Fountain,** on the Norfolk Green's south end, commemorates the philanthropist whose bequest to Yale paved the way for Gustav Stoeckel's appointment. The New York City–based architect Stanford White designed the fountain, portions of which were created by the sculptor Augustus Saint-Gaudens.

■ **WATERBURY** *map page 147, C-4*

Route 63 winds southeast from Norfolk to New Haven, passing by Goshen, Litchfield, and Watertown, where you can detour on Route 69 to visit Waterbury, a town that presents a sharp contrast to the Litchfield Hills. Comfortably lodged in the valleys of the Naugatuck and Mad Rivers, it tempts you with its soaring display of red brick mill buildings and church spires. Known originally to the Native Americans as Mattatuck, meaning "badly wooded region," the area was surveyed— somewhat pessimistically—in 1674 by English settlers who expressed doubts that it could support more than 30 families. Today, it appears to support twice that number of shopping malls, and brick now shares the skyline with concrete. The country's leading brass-producing city from the 19th century through the early 20th century, Waterbury provided America with about five million of Robert Ingersoll's famous Yankee-brand, one-dollar pocket watches annually until 1922; it also supplied copper and brass for the Boulder Dam in Colorado and coinage for South America, and revolutionized metallurgical technology in its own factories. Remnants of that industrial legacy are still visible. Grand Street, with its venerable municipal buildings, is still rather grand, and the Green is still green despite the traffic.

The Brass Roots and other exhibits at the **Mattatuck Museum** provide a comprehensive and imaginative view of the city's history, and the museum has airy galleries containing three centuries of American art, including works by Frederic Church, Josef Albers, Arshile Gorky, and Alexander Calder. Many of Calder's sculptures and mobiles were cast by local foundries. The Button Museum displays 10,000 buttons, most of them brass, donated by Waterbury manufacturing companies. *144 West Main Street; 203-753-0381.*

The **Waterbury Visitors Center** (on Church Street) is across the Green from the Mattatuck Museum. Turning from the Green onto Central Avenue, you reach Hillside, where wealthy 19th-century industrialists built homes, and just above it, Overlook, a 148-acre suburban community laid out in the 1890s and completed by 1930. Fulton Park, designed by Frederick Law Olmsted, is still the chief recreation area here, and streets like Buckingham, Pine, Willow, and Upper Fiske have a lived-in rather than a preserved appearance. No two houses are alike, and the array represents practically every American architectural style.

Descending into Waterbury's challenging one-way traffic puzzle, you understand why James Thurber's hero, Walter Mitty, lapsed into one heroic fantasy after another as he negotiated the city to run his nagging wife's errands in the short story "The Secret Life of Walter Mitty."

■ TRAVEL BASICS

Getting Around: Driving at a relaxing pace, you can see much of the Litchfield Hills in a couple of days. Whether your starting point is New York, Boston, or somewhere in between, the main routes are easily plotted. Route 8 heads straight up through the region, Route 63 runs on a southeast to northwest angle, and U.S. 7 skirts the western edge of the state heading north–south. Route 4 and U.S. 202 are the main east–west routes.

Climate: Temperatures in the Litchfield Hills are not unlike those in the Berkshires to the north. Summer temperatures often rise to the 90s Fahrenheit during July and August, with high humidity, while winter temperatures can drop well below zero at night and into single digits in the daytime. Autumn is colorful, with moderate temperatures.

NORTHERN RHODE ISLAND

When you think of America's smallest state, it is hard not to think of water. How could it be otherwise? One look at a map of Rhode Island tells you that water, salty or fresh, is everywhere. It is surprising, then, to learn that more than 60 percent of Rhode Island is wooded—not with the giant spruce of Maine or the white oak of Massachusetts, but with vegetation nonetheless. There is, in other words, an interior Rhode Island. You can explore it in a day or two if you meander north from Providence to Pawtucket and Woonsocket, and west to Slatersville and Chepachet, tracing the industrial revolution that turned agrarian communities into mill towns and villages, and exploring rugged parkland and historic river valleys. This modest region will hold your attention, not because it is spectacular—a word both irrelevant and tasteless here—but because this section of the state preserves a unique social history in a remarkably unspoiled landscape.

The contrast with neighboring Connecticut could not be more striking or more immediate. Enter Rhode Island at its northwestern corner, for instance, and everything will seem to have shrunk. The fields and houses are smaller, the roads narrower and quieter. You'll see fewer of the roadside produce stands and immaculate horse farms so visible in Connecticut; instead you'll find tiny roadside eateries and small cockeyed dwellings that look as if they are emerging from or subsiding into their surroundings.

Your first impression may be that residents of this quiet corner sell firewood cheap, fix their automobiles constantly, and prefer the specials at the local diner. Thanks to the influence of Italian immigrants and to a vibrant regional culinary tradition, those diner specials are likely to be very good. On the haute cuisine front, the students at Johnson and Wales University's College of Culinary Arts have moved far beyond traditional New England cookery, but even in Providence, the school's home and the state capital, traditional foods like cornmeal johnnycakes are also served. But before you begin eating your way across Rhode Island, stop first in Providence, where fresh water meets salt. The English clergyman Roger Williams founded the city in 1636 on the twin causes of religious liberty and individual freedom.

Landing of Roger Williams *(ca. 1886), by Alonzo Chappel. (Museum of Art, Rhode Island School of Design)*

■ PROVIDENCE *map page 168, and page 183, C-2*

Viewed from the heights of I-95, Providence looks beehive busy, especially at rush hour, when the city's vehicular circulation system stalls and you can be slowed down in its main arteries. At street level, however, Providence is small and compact, and its chief attractions—among them Benefit Street, Federal Hill, and the waterfront area—are within walking distance of one another. Following the example of *Independent Man,* the bronze symbol of Rhode Island's freedom, which stands 14 feet tall atop the State Capitol, liberate yourself from your car and proceed on foot as much as possible. The **Welcome Center** (1 Sabin Street; 401-751-1177), on the first floor of the Convention Center, is a good place to pick up maps and receive touring advice.

If you have a car, though, consider staying auto-bound long enough to get your bearings. Slip off I-95 onto Exit 22A, Memorial Boulevard, and cross the river on

Thomas Street, which becomes Angell Street. Bypass for the moment the historic Benefit Street district and turn left on Congdon Street. You'll shortly come upon Prospect Terrace, the **burial place of Roger Williams,** where a larger-than-life statue of him gazes westward at the superb view of the city below.

To find out more about Rhode Island's founder, head back downhill to the **Roger Williams National Memorial Park** (282 North Main Street; 401-521-7266), 4.5 acres on the original site of Providence. The visitors center here stocks relevant publications and presents a video about the clergyman. Ejected from the Massachusetts Bay Colony in 1635, the robust freethinker settled near a spring on

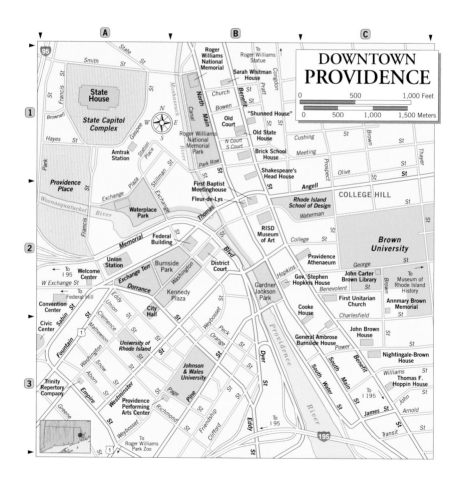

the site of the present memorial. "Having a sense of God's merciful providence unto me called this place Providence," Williams later wrote, "I desired it might be for a shelter for persons distressed for conscience." One early convert to Williams's views was the Rev. Chad Browne, who arrived in Providence in 1638 and whose descendants would become the city's most prominent citizens. Roger Williams's house is believed to have stood opposite the park on North Main Street. A plaque commemorates that site.

■ COLLEGE HILL HISTORIC LANDMARK DISTRICT
map page 168, B/C-1/3

Providence is built on three steep inclines, and the earliest English settlement arose above Benefit Street on the slopes of College Hill. This area is one of America's loveliest historic neighborhoods, rivaling Boston's Beacon Hill and Salem's Chestnut Street. Beyond appreciating the astonishing variety and beauty of the architecture—from early-18th-century houses, mansions, and churches to Brown University's 19th-century campus—you can also take pleasure in strolling at such an airy height in a place that seems to truly enjoy its visitors. Walking south along **Benefit Street** from its intersection with Jenckes Street, for example, you notice that even the dignified State Capitol across the river cannot resist playing peek-a-boo, filling each gap between the houses with its enormous white dome.

Tree-lined and entirely golden on an autumn morning, Benefit Street forbids you to hurry. Edgar Allan Poe learned how to linger in the garden at the Quaker poet **Sarah Helen Whitman's home.** Poe's stories supposedly caused in Whitman "a sensation of such intense horror that I dared neither look at anything he had written nor even utter his name"—

Benefit Street near Brown University.

though she did send him a poem and later became a staunch defender of his work. Vowing "never again to taste wine" and having attempted suicide in despair of winning her, Poe, who wrote two poems titled "To Helen," won a betrothal to Whitman in 1848 after an intense courtship. But she broke off the engagement, and within one year of his disappointment, Poe was dead. It is easy to imagine the rejected suitor, hurrying blindly down Church Street to the river, the poetic scar tissue already forming over his romantic wound. *88 Benefit Street, at Church Street.*

Something about this turf attracts fantasy and horror writers, for a short distance away is the **"Shunned House"** (135 Benefit Street). H. P. Lovecraft made the residence famous in his 1924 novel of the same name, in which a house is haunted by a malevolent presence. The writer was born at 454 Angell Street in 1890. Following the 1926 failure of his marriage, Lovecraft lived with his aunt on Barnes Street, where he wrote "The Dunwich Horror" (1928) and other tales. His final dwelling was 66 College Street, a house later moved to **65 Prospect Street,** at the corner of Meeting Street. Poetry, nonfiction, fiction, and aptly named "ghost-writing" for others occupied his brief life. Lovecraft was buried at Swan Point Cemetery, on Blackstone Boulevard, beneath a gravestone proclaiming "I Am Providence." Across the street a bit south of here, Alpheus Morse built the Italianate-style **Old Court** (144 Benefit Street), originally a rectory and now a well-run B&B.

The **Old State House,** built in 1762, was the seat of state government until 1904 and now houses the Rhode Island Historical Preservation and Heritage Commission. On May 4, 1776, Rhode Island renounced its allegiance to the English crown here, and George Washington, Thomas Jefferson, and the Marquis de Lafayette were all entertained at dinners and balls in the building. The building was greatly remodeled during the 19th century. *150 Benefit Street; 401-222-2678.*

The small **Brick School House,** downhill from Benefit Street, can been seen but not visited. It played a role in the Revolutionary War, serving as a munitions dump and as a Brown University classroom when French troops occupied the campus. *24 Meeting Street; 401-831-7440.*

Across the street, the equally modest **Shakespeare's Head House** was erected in 1772 and used as the print shop for the *Providence Gazette,* the city's first newspaper. Its publisher, John Carter, apprenticed with Benjamin Franklin. The

Sturdy yet ornate architecture graces Providence's Jackson Park area.

Providence Preservation Society (401-831-7440) has its offices at Shakespeare's Head House, whose name derives from a sign of the playwright's head that hung outside the printing shop. The society sells booklets with walking tours of Benefit Street and other parts of the city. *21 Meeting Street.*

Roger Williams founded the country's first Baptist congregation in 1638, although he later became disillusioned with organized faiths and died an unrepentant "seeker." The glorious, wood-frame **First Baptist Meetinghouse** was built in 1775 as the third building to be used by Providence's Baptist community and is open to the public. *75 North Main Street, extending east to Benefit Street; 401-454-3418.*

Waterman and Thomas Streets were the early center of Providence's costume-jewelry industry, and the streets later became the city's 19th-century arts district, a development that is most whimsically commemorated in the medieval-style **Fleur-de-Lys** building, the studio that artist Sydney Richmond Burleigh had built in 1885. *7 Thomas Street.*

An even grander arts presence has been the **Rhode Island School of Design,** or RISD (pronounced "rizdee"), founded in 1877 by a women's art collective. In 1878, the school offered its first class in downtown Providence. The Waterman Building, first campus building at the present site, went up in 1893, and the school has sub-sequently expanded its presence without dwarfing its neighbors on Benefit Street and the surrounding hillsides. Notable contemporary graduates include Cara Walker, known for her silhouettes and shadow plays of slave-era behavior; glass artist Dale Chihuly; fashion designer Nicole Miller; David Macaulay, the author of *The Way Things Work;* and filmmakers Gus Van Zant and Martha Coolidge. *62 Prospect Street; 401-454-6100.*

American decorative arts at the Pendleton House. (Museum of Art, Rhode Island School of Design)

The College Hill district is reflected across Waterplace Park.

The **RISD Museum of Art** houses a collection that ranges from the ancient, medieval, and Renaissance eras to the present, and includes one of the world's largest wooden Japanese Buddhas and galleries of impressionist paintings. The Pendleton House displays American decorative arts, including outstanding period furniture. The museum presents a deceptively modest face to the street. But don't be misled by the shallow entrance pavilion. The architects of this five-story establishment made clever use of its hillside site. *224 Benefit Street; 401-454-6500.*

The moment you enter the **Providence Athenaeum,** a cozy temple dedicated to books, you can see what attracted the courting couple Edgar Allan Poe and Sarah Helen Whitman. On raw winter afternoons, the warmly lit corners and reading galleries invite a prolonged stay and whispered confidences. Founded in 1753, this is one of the nation's oldest libraries, designed by one of the first American-trained architects, William Strickland, in the Greek Revival style. The Athenaeum was established as a public library dedicated to all readers, and it has catered to its users' changing tastes throughout the centuries. Its holdings include a complete original set of John James Audubon's *Birds of America,* a first edition of Charles Darwin's *Origin of the Species,* and intriguing accounts of 19th-century travel and exploration. *251 Benefit Street; 401-421-6970.*

The granite **First Unitarian Church,** built in 1816, combines Renaissance and Federal elements. After the intimacy of the Athenaeum, the marvelous structure seems almost melodramatic. *1 Benevolent Street; 401-421-7970.*

John Quincy Adams judged the three-story **John Brown House** "the most magnificent and elegant private mansion that I have ever seen on this continent," a conclusion that would doubtless have pleased its first owner. A large, energetic, ruthless man and ardent patriot, Brown died in 1803 leaving an estate valued at $600,000—most of it from the West Indies and China trade and from his life as a privateer, preying on enemy (then British) ships. Referring to himself as "the cleverest boy in town," Brown monitored his ships entering the harbor below and surrounded himself with the finest available furniture from America and Europe, much of which is still displayed. A man of action as well as guile, he led one of the earliest strikes of the American Revolution, the 1772 raid on the English revenue ship *Gaspee,* which took place 7 miles south of Providence. He burned the vessel but emerged with souvenirs, among them six silver wine goblets now on display in the house. Brown's deed has not been forgotten: Providence still celebrates Gaspee Days with parades, a colonial muster, and a gala ball during May and June.

Guided tours of the red brick 1788 house are informative, lively, and honest. Brown's lengthy involvement in the slave trade, for example, is candidly discussed, as is the lawsuit that abolitionists—including John's brother, Moses Brown—initiated against John in 1797 when he continued to import slaves after Congress had closed such trade to United States citizens. But it is hard to imagine the era's misery when you contemplate the beauty of a unique 18th-century, nine-shell, blocked-front bookcase and desk of Santo Domingo mahogany, not to mention the meticulously restored French wallpaper, and the perfect sweep of the elaborate staircase. Traces of the house's subsequent owners remain, most noticeably in the exotic bathroom additions by the utility tycoon Marsden J. Perry, who reportedly entertained Sophie Tucker and other spirited ladies here. Tall American elms flank the Brown house, a rarity because so many of the trees have succumbed to Dutch elm disease. *52 Power Street, at Benefit Street; 401-331-8575.*

The spire of the First Baptist Meetinghouse.

The striking **General Ambrose Burnside House,** the residence of the Civil War commander, United States senator, and Rhode Island governor, curves sinuously around its hilly corner. Burnside's other accomplishments include being the namesake of sideburns and the first president of the National Rifle Association. *314 Benefit Street.*

The three-story **Nightingale-Brown House,** completed in 1792, was the residence of John Brown's brother Nicolas, one of the founders of Brown University. Parts of the house, which is now the headquarters of the John Nicholas Brown Center for the Study of American Civilization, an affiliate program of Brown University, contain furnishings exactly as the last Brown to occupy the house left them in 1985. Tours are given of four original rooms: the dining room, parlor, drawing room, and library. Among the many family heirlooms are a 9-foot-tall mahogany, block, and shell desk, one of 11 made by the renowned cabinetmaker John Goddard of Newport. *357 Benefit Street; 401-272-0357.*

Other houses of note include the **Thomas F. Hoppin House** (383 Benefit Street), an Italianate palazzo built for the painter and sculptor, who died in 1873; and the **Gov. Stephen Hopkins House** (15 Hopkins Street, at Benefit Street; 401-421-0694), built in 1707, with an addition in 1743. The latter's namesake, a signer of the Declaration of Independence, was Rhode Island's governor in 1776. The house is now a museum run by the Society of Colonial Dames.

Brown University   *map page 168, C-2*

Much of College Hill's vitality is attributable to Brown University. Founded in nearby Warren in 1764 by John Brown's brother Nicolas and moved to Providence in 1770, Brown now dominates the hill. A loftier place than low-lying Yale or Harvard, Brown has a pleasantly windblown atmosphere. On a blustery autumn afternoon, when leaves rush the Van Wickle Gates, the harmonious buildings lining College Green seem to be the only things tethering the campus to the ground. Along with RISD, the university is chiefly responsible for the sight of tattooed, body-pierced youths emerging from some of the nation's most decorous buildings.

But behavior that deviates from the norm is foreign neither to Rhode Island nor to Brown University. From its beginnings as sanctuary from governmental interference in the freedom of worship, Rhode Island attracted practitioners of many organized religions and allowed many new ones to flourish. In his book *A History of Brown University,* Walter Bronson, a professor of English at Brown from 1892 to 1927, wrote that the "afflicted and the eccentric from various quarters,

Banners announcing upcoming events at Brown University.

Antinomians, Quakers, 'Seekers,' and Anabaptists of all stripes, had lived here together in tumultuous amity, attacking one another's heresies but steadily respecting everybody's right to preach heresy without any restraint from the civil power."

The 1904 **John Carter Brown Library** (George and Brown Streets; 401-863-2725) is considered the university's jewel, but University Hall is its oldest building on the Green, dating from 1770 and used to billet American and French troops and their mules and horses during the Revolution. European and American art and a collection of British swords are among the displays at the **Annmary Brown Memorial** (21 Brown Street; 401-863-1994).

The humorist S. J. Perelman grew up in Providence, graduated from Brown University in 1925, and later married Laura West, the sister of his college chum Nathanael West—who in the next decade wrote the novella *Miss Lonelyhearts* and the novel *The Day of the Locust.* Perelman went on to write for the Marx Brothers in Hollywood and for the *New Yorker* magazine. "From the moment I picked up your book until I put it down, I was convulsed with laughter," Groucho Marx wrote in a blurb for Perelman's *Dawn Ginsbergh's Revenge.* "Some day I intend reading it."

Federal Hill is Providence's Italian-American neighborhood.

■ **FEDERAL HILL AND ATWELLS AVENUE**

If the mention of food—even ancient food—has a predictable effect, slip over to Federal Hill, Providence's Italian-American neighborhood. Running the gauntlet of impatient traffic is worth the risk when you reach Atwells Avenue and pass underneath the street's arch, which has an enormous pinecone in the center. Italians began arriving in Providence in the 19th century, but the largest immigration occurred between 1900 and 1915, when new arrivals chiefly from Naples, Palermo, Campobasso, and Frosinone formed the tight communities that continue to flourish in a city proud of its Italian influence.

On Atwells Avenue, you may eat, shop for plaster saints and smoky Chianti, speak Italian, and contemplate some of the snappiest hairstyles in town. The doorman at the traditional Italian **Blue Grotto** (210 Atwells Avenue; 401-272-9030) restaurant is sure to have a prize-winning look, but the coiffed grandmother presiding over a family lunch party at **Angelo's Civita Farnese** (141 Atwells Avenue; 401-621-8171), which opened for business in 1924, is also in the running. Angelo's is a noisy, no-frills place that has valet parking because it makes sense, not because it makes an impression.

Perched on a hill, the state capitol holds its own against Providence's skyscrapers.

L'Epicureo (238 Atwells Avenue; 401-454-8430), farther up the avenue, started out as a butcher shop and is now one of Providence's most sophisticated bistros, serving prime steaks, veal chops, and seafood. Wherever you stop on "the Avenue," you will be hard-pressed to find bad food. Restaurants are not the only culinary stops, however. There are bakeries, food markets, and wine stores to be inspected, among them **Venda Ravioli** (265 Atwells Avenue; 401-421-9105), an irresistible Italian deli, and **Gasbarro's** (361 Atwells Avenue; 401-421-4170), a liquor store that claims to have the largest selection of Italian wines in the country.

■ STATE CAPITOL *map page 168, A-1*

"There was nothing you could do about anything, but then nothing was so bad that you felt a burning urge to do anything about it," the writer A. J. Liebling wrote of Providence when he began working there as a journalist in 1925. Liebling was referring to the city's often scandalous government, whose participants typically behaved as if they were auditioning for the role of a colorful thug in a bad Hollywood movie. Bad government and economic and other calamities had so overtaken Providence by the 1970s that Philip Gourevitch described the city in the

New Yorker as looking in that era "like a railroad yard. In fact, it was a railroad yard. A broad delta of converging tracks sliced right through the city center and under the back door of the state capitol—a luminous palace of white marble crowned by an immense dome that looked like nothing so much as an extravagant tombstone against the surrounding desolation."

Much of the credit for Providence's renaissance has gone to former mayor Vincent "Buddy" Cianci, who helped assemble the public-private coalition that erected new hotels, an upscale shopping mall, and the elegant Waterplace Park to replace the rail yards. Despite his many good deeds and immense popularity, Cianci was convicted in 2001 for corruption.

An oft-seen bumper sticker during Cianci's trial read, "This state has the best politicians money can buy," but at least on the outside the luminous State Capitol shows no signs of ethical wear and tear. Designed by the New York City–based architectural firm McKim, Mead & White and completed in 1904, the giant structure is topped by the second-largest unsupported dome in the world (after Saint Peter's Basilica in Rome) and holds its own against the new high-rise buildings studding Providence's skyline.

■ **WATERPLACE PARK** *map page 168, A-2*

Waterplace Park, a highlight of the massive reconstruction of downtown Providence during the 1990s, altered the course of two rivers—the Woonasquatucket ("river where the tide ends") and Moshassuck ("river where the moose watered")—that converge to form the Providence River. Today, the Woonasquatucket edges the 4-acre **Waterplace Park,** an artful composition of cobbled walkways, grassy promenades, Venetian-style bridges, and even gliding gondolas. Compliments of a fire sculpture by the artist Barnaby Evans, the river area blazes on some summer Saturday evenings, lighted by 100 bonfires that appear to float on its surface. Although this may sound like something more appropriate for Las Vegas, the effect is wondrous, not kitschy. Contemporary sculpture dots the riverwalk landscape, and many festivals take place here. On a hot summer night, as music echoes from bridge to bridge, you can float along in a gondola or sit at a riverside cafe and inhale cedar smoke.

Filled with the music and art of Waterplace Park, you can round out your cultural experience by visiting one of the theaters in downtown Providence. The **Providence Performing Arts Center** (220 Weybosset Street; 401-421-2787), in a

Saturday evening bonfires blaze along Providence's river walk.

glorious former Loews movie palace, provides live performances of touring plays and music concerts year-round. Another refurbished movie theater has been transformed by the **Trinity Repertory Company** (201 Washington Street, 401-351-4242), which presents new works and old standards.

■ **ROGER WILLIAMS PARK ZOO**   *map page 168, A-3*
On the other side of the river, reassuringly natural spectacles take place at the Roger Williams Park Zoo, where polar bears, giraffes, elephants and more than 100 other creatures perform their eating and sleeping routines. Don't miss the Australasia animal display of tree kangaroos and other exotic species. The park covers 430 acres and includes an event facility, called the Roger Williams Park Casino, built in 1896 for special events and weddings, as well as an antique carousel, the Museum of Natural History, and a Queen Anne–style boathouse. The Benedict Temple to Music hosts outdoor concerts in summer. *1000 Elmwood Avenue; 401-785-3510.*

■ BLACKSTONE RIVER VALLEY HERITAGE CORRIDOR

map page 183, A/C-1/2

The Blackstone River has been a part of American history since 1635, when William Blackstone settled in Rhode Island in what is now Cumberland. For much of its 46-mile course the Blackstone behaves like any other lazy, occasionally restless waterway. But when its falls turned the first wheels of the industrial revolution at Pawtucket, the river transformed American life. By the late 1700s, many communities were located on the river near small water-powered mills, and by 1820 the valley was home to a booming textile industry.

Covering nearly 400,000 acres between Worcester, Massachusetts, and Providence, the Blackstone River Valley Heritage Corridor encompasses not only marshes, meadows, and forests but also 24 cities, towns, and villages. Nearly one million people live here. The valley's roads, trails, dams, mill buildings, and ethnic neighborhoods hold important clues to the region's past, and the agricultural and natural landscapes provide precious habitats for indigenous and migrating species and recreational opportunities for humans. One note about traveling the area: as in parts of Connecticut, the townships here are composed of various villages, which can be confusing. Lonsdale, Ashton, and Arnold Mills, for instance, are all part of the town of Cumberland, and Slatersville is part of North Smithfield township.

■ PAWTUCKET *map page 183, C-2*

As you head north from Providence on Route 114, evidence of Rhode Island's industrial history along the Blackstone River begins to materialize. To the Narragansetts, Pawtucket meant "the place by the waterfall," a favorite fishing and camping ground. The first white settler is thought to have been Joseph Jenckes Jr., a blacksmith who set up a forge by the river in 1671. Jenckes produced agricultural equipment and household utensils for the farmers in nearby Providence, and other blacksmiths soon joined him. In March 1676, at the height of King Philip's War, practically all dwellings and forges were destroyed during the Wampanoag chief's attack. The settlers hid in the surrounding woods, however, and returned after the war ended to rebuild their homes. During the Revolution, the settlement supplied the Colonial army not only with men and money, but also with ammunition and firearms made by descendants of those first Pawtucket blacksmiths. (The tradition continued: army records note that in 1810 Stephen Jenckes made 10,000 muskets for the government.)

To Samuel Slater, who arrived in 1789, Pawtucket's "falling water" spelled money. A former manager at England's innovative Arkwright Mills, Slater constructed America's first successful water-powered cotton-spinning mill at the Pawtucket Falls in 1790, expanded it in 1793, and initiated one of the biggest transformations in American society. Farmers who once sold products they had grown began instead to sell their time and labor. Whole families worked in the mills, their housing, clothing, food, education, religious worship, and recreation provided for and controlled by the mill owners. Some workers spent much (and sometimes all) of their lives at the mills. The overseer of the Pawtucket Thread Company in 1826, for example, was a 19-year-old man who already had 11 years' experience.

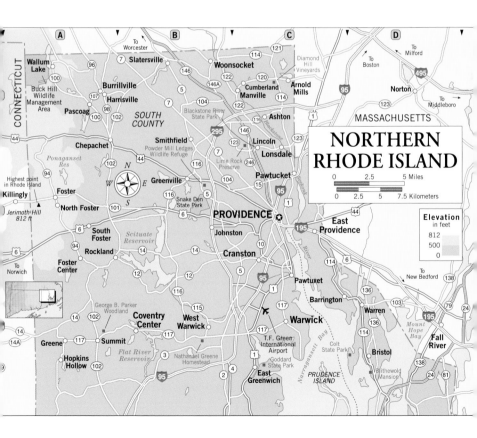

NORTHERN RHODE ISLAND

Water diverted from the Blackstone River powered the Slater Mill.

Pawtucket may be fractured and faded, but the Blackstone River still roars impressively at the **Slater Mill Historic Site,** a celebration of the birthplace of American industry that consists of the 1793 Slater Mill (which replaced the original water-powered mill built here in 1790), the 1810 Wilkinson Mill, and the 1758 Sylvanus Brown House, moved to the site in the 1960s. The three buildings, which can only be viewed on the daily tours, contain exhibits that illustrate various stages in the industrial development that made the Rhode Island cotton-cloth industry possible. The Sylvanus Brown House, where Samuel Slater stayed when he first arrived in the area, recalls the hand-powered spinning-and-weaving era soon to be erased by the mills. Brown, who was essential to Slater's success, was a master craftsman who made machine patterns and wooden machine parts for Slater's textile mill. At the Slater Mill itself, replicas and actual machinery from the 18th to the 20th century refine cotton, create thread and bobbins, and perform other tasks. Workers at the machine shop in the Wilkinson Mill made most of the parts for the Slater Mill. The tour guides here adeptly demonstrate the machinery and explain mill history and labor relations. Children played a major part in New

England's industrial revolution. In the early 1800s, the Slater Mill's employees included 53 children and 17 adults, all of whom worked 12 hours a day during the week and six hours on Saturdays. *67 Roosevelt Avenue; 401-725-8638.*

The hilly city that grew up around the textile industry exhibits signs of industrial decline, and evidence of Pawtucket's 19th-century heyday are visible chiefly in architectural details—the curved facade of the 1892 **Toole Building** (230 Main Street), for example, or the terra-cotta inscription on the corner block of **North Union Street,** which reads "How Do The Beasts Groan!" The biblical reference is an appropriate one for the site of the former Summer Street Stables, which could accommodate 176 horses when completed in 1891.

The **Pawtucket Preservation Society** (67 Park Place; 401-725-9581) distributes tour maps of the Quality Hill and Church Hill historic districts. The **Blackstone Valley Visitor's Center** (175 Main Street and Roosevelt Avenue; 401-724-2200) has exhibits, publications, tour maps, video tapes, and a theater, and arranges Blackstone River excursions aboard the flat-bottomed boat the *Explorer.*

Slater Memorial Park, Pawtucket's largest recreation area, provides a bit of history along with some fun. The city's oldest residence, the 1685 Daggett House (401-722-6931 or 401-724-5748 for tour information), is open on some weekends for tours. Maintained by the Pawtucket chapter of the Daughters of the American Revolution, it displays antique furniture, needlework, and china; some of the pewter dates back to the Revolutionary War era. Nearby, an 1895 carousel by Charles I. F. Looff will twirl you into the slightly more recent past for a nominal fee, and across the street from the Daggett House at the J. C. Potter Casino, you can view the exhibits curated by the Rhode Island Watercolor Society. *Entrances at Armistice Boulevard (Route 15) and Newport Avenue (U.S 1/A).*

Not all of Pawtucket's glory lies in the far-distant past. You can eat cheaply and well at the first diner to be listed on the National Register of Historic Places, and then saunter over to watch some of the best baseball in New England. The **Modern Diner** (364 East Avenue; 401-726-8390), in a working-class neighborhood on the city's outskirts, is a 1941 dining car that has expanded its traditional menu of breakfasts, burgers, roast chicken, and meatloaf to include weekend breakfast specials such as lobster Benedict, eggs Beaujolais, and Belgian waffles.

Spiffy **McCoy Stadium** is the home of the Pawtucket Red Sox, the AAA minor-league farm team of the Boston Red Sox. Wade Boggs, Mo Vaughn, and Roger Clemens all played for the Pawsox, as the team is affectionately known, before moving on to the majors. You don't have to know or care much about baseball to

Old mill building in Pawtucket.

enjoy a game. Just sitting in the intimate stadium—it feels like a small-town version of Boston's Fenway Park—is worth the ridiculously low price of admission. Between April and September the team plays about 70 home games, and tickets are usually available up to the last minute. *1 Ben Mondor Way; 401-724-7300.*

■ SMITHFIELD *map page 183, B-1*
The exertions of industrial Pawtucket may leave you yearning for the bucolic contentment northern Rhode Island confers. If so, head west on Route 15 and U.S. 44 to the **Powder Mill Ledges Wildlife Refuge,** a modest but lovely nature preserve. Three mild walking trails here lead through abandoned farmland and mature hardwood forests to a charming pond, where you may see a family of muskrats frisking about on the shore, or surprise a blue heron waiting to stab its prey. Walking the refuge's entire loop of trails takes less than two hours and concludes at the headquarters of the Audubon Society of Rhode Island, which has a nature center and an extensive library with information about bird life. Here you can also learn about tours of the society's other Rhode Island preserves. *Sanderson Road/Route 5 (turn left at second driveway south of U.S. 44); 401-949-5454.*

A superb examination of human habitat occurs at the **Smith-Appleby House,** 4 miles north of Powder Mill Ledges near the Georgiaville Pond. Constructed in 1696, the 12-room farmhouse was later spliced with a larger dwelling moved here from Johnston in the early 18th century. The original deed to the land was given by Roger Williams to John Smith, one of the original party of six who, with Williams, formed the first settlement in Rhode Island. The Smiths and the Applebys lived in the house from 1696 to 1958.

The completely furnished house provides a glimpse into everyday life in rural Rhode Island. The old couch and piano in the sitting room look as if they were recently used, and when you climb to the smoke room on the second floor, you may fancy that you can taste the home-cured meat. After touring the house, wander around the 7-acre site afterward to see the caretaker's cottage and the minute shed that once served as the Smithfield train depot. The house is open periodically throughout the year, and group tours can be arranged. *220 Stillwater Road, off Capron Road (take Route 5 north to Route 104); 401-231-7363.*

■ LINCOLN AREA *map page 183, C-1/2*

Lime Rock Preserve, a botanical powerhouse, an often soggy haven 4 miles east of the Smith-Appleby House, is especially beautiful in late spring and early summer. On huge outcrops of dolomite marble, the preserve supports lilies, ladyslippers, trilliums, baneberry, and other shy beauties. It's a little hard to find, and you might have to ask 10 locals where it is before you find one who knows, but it's worth seeking out. Head east on Stillwater Road, which becomes Ridge Road, and continue east on Limerock Road, which becomes Wilbur Road. (If you reach Route 246, you've gone too far.)

Back to reality on Wilbur Road, about a half-mile east of the preserve at Route 246 (also signed as the Old Louisquisset Pike) is the North Gate Toll House, for nearly two centuries an important landmark on this former toll road. As you continue east on Wilbur Road, you cannot miss the shining limestone quarries and extensive buildings of the Conklin Limestone Quarry, established in 1640 and said to be the oldest continuously operated industrial concern in America.

A bit farther along on the left, the solid red brick building that commands immediate attention is the **Mount Moriah Lodge No. 8** (1093 Great Road, at Anna Sayles Road). You're now on the **Great Road,** originally a Native American trail and one of the country's earliest roads. The thoroughfare dates to the 1650s, retaining its antiquarian character to this day. An hour is sufficient for a leisurely exploration of the area. The houses of note that are not private residences are open only on special occasions or by appointment, but you can peer into the ground floors of a couple of the public ones.

Diagonally across from the lodge (just before the horse farm) is the former **Mowry Tavern,** now a private residence, which opened in 1686 and served Great Road travelers for more than a century and a half. Continue east on the Great Road from the lodge, turning left when you see straight ahead the **Butterfly Mill** (700 Great Road), also a private residence. Built between 1811 and 1813, it was named for the shape of two stones on its wall that resembled a butterfly. The mill, built by Stephen H. Smith, was one of the state's first stone textile mills.

Smith also built one of the Great Road's most majestic residences, **Hearthside,** which has an intriguing history. According to local romantic lore, Smith commissioned this massive stone house, which was built between 1810 and 1811, after he won $50,000 in the Louisiana lottery. At the time, he was besotted with a woman who craved the grandest house in Rhode Island. Hearthside failed to persuade her, however, and Smith died a bachelor. With its bowed roof and four-columned portico, the house impresses today, even if it didn't back then. Owned by the town of Lincoln, Hearthside is sometimes open for tours. *677 Great Road; 401-333-1100.*

To get your bearings straight and to commune with the locals who run their dogs here, stop a bit east at the **Chase Farm** (669 Great Road). One of Lincoln's last working farms, it ceased its dairy operations in the mid-1960s but is being preserved as a farm by the town. A map posted outside the **Hannaway Blacksmith Shop** (671 Great Road) shows the entire Great Road in detail and has more information about the area. Farther east, **Moffett Mill,** on the north side of Great Road across from No. 590, was built circa 1812, making it one of the rare surviving wooden mills from the Blackstone River Valley's initial period of industrialization. The stone dam, visible behind the building, was erected in the early 1850s.

Less ostentatious than Hearthside but no doubt a stunner in its day is **Eleazer Arnold House,** Lincoln's oldest dwelling, built circa 1687. A wooden "stone-ender" building, it is remarkable not only for its tiny windows and stone-end wall and fireplace but for the curiously moving traces of its builders. In the attic, you can see not only the hewing marks on the original timbers used to frame the house but also graffiti left by subsequent work crews, including a painter who worked here in 1911. *487 Great Road; 781-891-4882 for tour appointments.*

The sublimely plain **Friends Meeting House** was built by the Quakers in 1704 and enlarged in 1740. Still active, it is New England's oldest meetinghouse in continuous use. The lovelorn Stephen H. Smith is buried in the adjacent cemetery. *374 Great Road (turn right onto Route 126 South); 401-245-5860.*

Backtrack a few blocks north and take Route 123 east, and you'll soon arrive at the southern entrance to **Blackstone River State Park,** which shadows the Blackstone River. The park contains one of the longest remaining sections of the Blackstone Canal, which once powered turbines but now glides unobtrusively through the woods with what you imagine to be an air of well-earned relief. Dug by Irish immigrants during the 1820s, the canal was once vital to the region's industrial growth, as evidenced by the textile mill and brick row houses in the towns of Lonsdale and Ashton.

Today, however, walkers, cyclists, and canoeists are attracted to the tranquil 3-mile stretch, which is shaded by some of the state's largest sycamores. Head north on the riverside footpaths, lured by the sound of rushing water and by tantalizing flashes of the Blackstone River oozing its way smoothly down to Pawtucket. For athletic travelers, the Blackstone River Bike Path is accessible from the park at Lower River Road off Route 116 and runs for 7 miles alongside the river, where the foliage display in autumn is particularly colorful. *Off Routes 116, 122, and 123 east of Lincoln; 401-723-7892.*

■ **CUMBERLAND** *map page 183, C-1*

Roger Williams is recognized as Rhode Island's founder, but the hefty burial stone that dominates tiny **Blackstone Memorial Park** honors Rhode Island's first white settler. An Anglican clergyman who came to the state in 1635, William Blackstone is credited with planting the first orchards in Rhode Island and Massachusetts. He had left what is now Boston's Beacon Hill—his cattle grazed on what is now the Boston Common—having run afoul of the Puritans. His parting shot made clear what caused his departure:

> I left England to get from under the power of the lord bishop, but in America I am under the power of the lord brethren. I looked to have dwelt with my orchards and my books, and my young fawn and bull, in undisturbed solitude. Was there not room for all of ye? Could ye not leave the hermit in his corner?

Blackstone, who lived from 1595 to 1675, apparently wasn't as reclusive as he intimated, but he did have books: when his will was probated his estate included 189 books, making his library the largest in North America at the time. He also had a bull; late in life he was said to have traveled the countryside on a white one, dispensing apples—perhaps of the Yellow Sweeting strain, which he developed—to astonished children. Though Blackstone's burial stone is here, his remains aren't. They and the stone were moved a few times over the years. The last time, in the 1940s, they were lost. *Broad Street (Route 114) and Blackstone Street, Lonsdale.*

Man of culture that he was, Blackstone would no doubt be pleased to know that his memorial is adjacent to the **Blackstone River Theatre,** a performing-arts center in a sturdy-looking 1928 brick structure. The fare is nothing if not eclectic, and sometimes involves the audience: French-Canadian quadrilles, traditional Irish dancing, bands playing vintage country music, a cellist performing Bach suites. *549 Broad Street, Lonsdale; 401-725-9272.*

The theater and memorial sit on what Blackstone called Studio Hill. His house was here, facing the river. The view now is two large and mostly abandoned buildings that were part of **Lonsdale's textile mill,** which closed in 1936. To the north is the mill housing, which is being rehabilitated. From Studio Hill one gets a sense not only of the enormous size of the mills but also their overpowering presence in the employees' lives—home, for which one paid rent to the company, was mere steps away from work.

The mill workers' leisure options most assuredly did not include afternoon wine tastings. Fortunately, the present-day choices have improved; you can drive east a few miles on Route 114 to sip the wines at **Diamond Hill Vineyards.** Watch for the sign on the east side of the highway and follow the narrow gravel road to a late-18th-century farmhouse. The Bernston family has been growing pinot noir grapes here since 1976 and produce an imaginative variety of wines, some flavored with other fruit grown on the farm, such as cranberry-apple, blueberry, peach, and plum. *3145 Diamond Hill Road (Route 114); 401-333-2751.*

From the vineyards, continue north on Route 114 to the Nate Whipple Highway, Route 120, which heads east into sleepy **Arnold Mills.** But the village wasn't always so sleepy. The 1937 *WPA Guide to Rhode Island* records that it hosted "the annual summer clambake of the Cumberland Detective Society, now a social club, founded over a century ago as a protection against livestock thieves."

Mill buildings and the falls in Woonsocket.

Arnold Mills, settled in 1734 when a sawmill was built here, was named for Amos Arnold, who erected a gristmill in 1747. The few churches and the remaining 18th- and 19th-century dwellings form a picturesque scene. The foundation of Arnold's gristmill can be seen behind ramshackle **Pentimento** (322 Sneech Pond Road; 401-334-1838), a tantalizingly chaotic antiques and collectibles shop where the prices are extremely reasonable. Equally inviting is the elm-shaded deck, which hangs over a small waterfall created by the stone dam built in the gristmill days— to the right of the dam you can see the chute into which water was diverted to power the mill. The setting is irresistible on a summer afternoon, and you're welcome to sit a spell, even if you don't partake of the pastries, gourmet coffee, and ice cream for sale. Arnold's house, built in 1750, is a few yards away. Several roads labeled Sneech Pond intersect with the Nate Whipple Highway, which is named for an Arnold relative. Look for the Pentimento sign; the correct Sneech Pond Road is east of Route 114 on the north side of the road.

■ **WOONSOCKET** *map page 183, B-1*
Backtrack west on Nate Whipple Highway to Route 122 and head north on Route 126 to Woonsocket. By 1820, when the industrial revolution reached this tough, hilly town, the mills had come to rely on Irish, English, and Scottish immigrants. But from 1860 onward, many new workers were French Canadians who had left their Québéc farms for New England's mills, so French names dominate Woonsocket's downtown businesses and French faces seem familiar. The town is long past its prime, and residents often look baffled when they see visitors following the self-guided walking tour, published in brochures available at the visitors center in Market Square.

The historic square also contains one of New England's finest museums: the **Museum of Work and Culture,** which is interactive in the best (not gimmicky) sense of the word. It primarily tells the story of the French Canadians, but it also charts the rise of the Independent Textile Union, which once dominated the town, and it explains the events that prompted the violent National Textile Strike of 1934. Entering the museum, you cross the threshold of a Québécois farmhouse, briefly acquainting yourself with the preindustrial era, before passing by the replica of the Catholic Church of the Precious Blood. The next stop is the old textile mill's factory floor, where a spinning mule (used to create bobbins) and a weaving machine from the early 1900s are on display. On the museum's second floor are re-

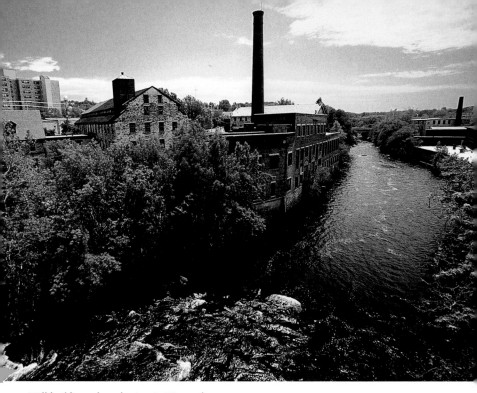

Mill buildings along the river in Woonsocket.

creations of a typical apartment in the three-decker tenements that remain ubiquitous in Rhode Island; a Catholic parochial schoolroom; a corporate boardroom; and the meeting hall of the Independent Textile Union.

Labor organizations expanded in the late 19th century and early 20th centuries, and many workers were radicalized by the severe depression of 1921, which, along with Southern competition, resulted in pay cuts of as much as 40 percent. On January 23, 1922, 11 mule spinners in Pawtucket walked out, prompting a nine-month-long national textile strike. In Rhode Island alone, 34 mills employing 18,000 workers were involved. Both this work stoppage and the one in 1934 were ended by compromise, but by the 1930s many companies had either closed or were taking advantage of cheaper labor in the South. These developments and the increase in textile imports spelled the end of the revolution that Samuel Slater had wrought. *42 South Main Street; 401-769-9675.*

A high-fat reminder of the area's agricultural roots resides south of Woonsocket in North Smithfield. **Wright's Dairy Farm** is a working Holstein dairy that has been in the Wright family for a little more than a century and has probably been fatten-

Rhode Island mill girls stand next to a weaving machine, ca. 1909. (Library of Congress)

ing up its visitors even longer. The milk in the dairy shop is never more than 48 hours old, the cream on your pastry is decadently thick, and the blueberry muffins have been voted the best in Rhode Island. All these delights may make it difficult for you to concentrate on the learning experience the Wrights so graciously supply. Come around at the afternoon milking session, from 3 to 5, and you can watch the process and read placards with the absolute bovine truth: that fully grown Holsteins eat 100 pounds of food a day, drink from 40 to 50 gallons of water a day, have four stomachs to digest all that, and produce from 3 to 14 gallons of milk a day. Now you know. *200 Woonsocket Hill Road (west off Route 146A); 401-767-3014.*

■ **SLATERSVILLE** *map page 183, B-1*
As you head back north on Route 146A and west on Route 102 toward Slatersville, you can imagine the hardscrabble life that drove settlers here to extremes of belief and superstition. This is poor rocky ground that doubtless produced its first few harvests grudgingly. In many cases in northern and western Rhode Island, when disillusioned farmers moved on, all development stopped. Consequently, today's pretty rural scene—the crumbling stone wall, the small, hilly field—owes its existence as much to poverty as it does to preservation.

Weaving machine exhibit. (Museum of Work and Culture)

By 1807, Samuel Slater was ready to expand on his success in Pawtucket and elsewhere, and Slatersville, founded that year, represents the culmination of his theories about mills, mill towns, and mass production. Slater and his brother John opened a large cotton mill along the Branch River here and provided housing, schools, and churches for their workers. The **John Slater House** (16 School Street), where John and his wife, Ruth, lived while he oversaw the millworks for the next 35 years, still stands, though it was moved to its current location in 1843 from a few blocks away. There have been two obvious additions, but in keeping with Samuel Slater's philosophy, the circa 1810 structure differs only a little from the houses of his workers—the house next door, No. 20, a workers' house, has fanciful winged urns carved on the doorway. (Slater's house may have been the cat's meow in the early 1800s, and it still looks substantial on the outside, but new owners bought it in 2002 as a fixer-upper.)

The **Slatersville Library** (20 Main Street; 401-767-2780) has walking-tour brochures—if the library has run out, you can make a copy of the one the library keeps on file—but you won't be able to miss the **Slatersville Mill,** near where Church, Green, and Main Streets intersect. One wooden building remains from the original mill, but the main building, its bricks painted white, dates to the mid-

THE SLATER METHOD

Samuel Slater, born in 1768 in Derbyshire, England, has been called both the "Father of the American Cotton Industry" and the "Founder of the American Industrial Revolution." At age 14, he began a seven-year apprenticeship with Richard Arkwright, who after years of experimentation succeeded in developing machinery that could card, draw out, and spin cotton in one, continuous flow. Taking his knowledge of the new mill technology with him to America, young Sam Slater stepped off the boat at New York and immediately went to work for a textile company. Before long, he heard of William Almy and Moses Brown, in Pawtucket, Rhode Island, who were experimenting with Arkwright's designs, so he headed north to join them.

After much discussion and compromise, the machinery at the Almy and Brown mill was replaced in 1790 with workings that Slater built and operated. By the end of 1792, Almy and Brown had become so successful that Slater was made a partner in the firm. Construction started on a new mill, built expressly for the purpose of completely mechanized textile manufacture. This is the mill that we know today as Old Slater Mill. Its architectural style, management structure, and workforce were replicated throughout southern New England.

After Samuel married, he moved north, following the Blackstone River. Though not big enough to support the large mills that became common in Massachusetts, the Blackstone had a steep drop and numerous falls that proved ideal conditions for the development of small textile mills. When Samuel and his brother John opened a mill west of the river in Slatersville in 1807, Sam refined his organizational method even further. He enlisted entire families, many of them poor and just off the farm, and provided them with company-owned housing near the mills, company stores, and company schools and churches. In Slatersville and other mill towns, the overseer was usually the owner, who lived on a level not much higher than his laborers, making for a tight-knit community.

Slater was able to employ children in his mills because the early Arkwright machines were so simply constructed that the unskilled could easily operate them. Children earned about a dollar a week and worked from 12 to 14 hours a day in unhealthful conditions, often ending up with respiratory problems. By the mid-1820s, more than half the labor force in textile production consisted of children between four and 14 years old.

1820s. With its five-story stair tower and red doors, the structure feels vaguely fanciful, though certainly not playful. Across from the library are some more workers' houses, including 27 and 29 Main Street.

As in other mill towns, the Slaters provided diversions for the few waking hours their workers weren't on the job. The company had a monopoly on the town's entertainment market, so it is unlikely the offerings were touted by means as extravagant as the big neon sign on Route 146 that announces the presence of the **Rustic Tri-View Drive-In,** near North Smithfield. The admission to Rhode Island's last drive-in cinema is by the carload, so loners can round up a surrogate family, pack some blankets, and bring a portable radio to tune in the movie. Even Hollywood's worst seems bearable when you are stretched out on the grass. *Louisquisset Pike; 401-769-7601.*

■ **BURRILLVILLE** *map page 183, B-1*
In most cases, it's sound advice to steer clear of eating establishments that advertise "family-style" dining. In northern Rhode Island, however, the family-style chicken dinner is an authentic tradition—one that originated out of a Woonsocket social club's need to efficiently feed as many hungry working people as possible.

In six dining rooms that can accommodate 1,200 people, **Wright's Farm Restaurant,** 2 miles west of Slatersville, has been serving family-style chicken dinners—bread, salad, roast chicken, pasta, potatoes—for more than 50 years. The price these days is still less than $10 per person. Steak is more expensive, but steak is not the point here. Chicken even turns up in the desserts—a special chocolate ice-cream chicken dessert was recently added to the menu—and in the spacious bar, where paintings and other chicken memorabilia amuse diners as they wait for a table. Rhode Island's industrial history will remind you at every turn that you are not a laborer—not in the back-breaking, 19th-century, superhuman sense. But you can remind yourself that "hungry" is a relative term, and perhaps even convince yourself that by ingesting an all-you-can-eat dinner you are honoring a great labor tradition. *84 Inman Road, off Route 102, Burrillville; 401-769-2856.*

West of Slatersville, the industrial revolution, although still detectable in the region's mill buildings and waterways, seems not to have taken a permanent hold. Here, you still pass through preindustrial landscapes and townscapes. In many of these towns, the clock seems to have stopped not in the 19th century but in the 18th.

Harrisville, a village within Burrillville, is a perfect example. No matter how you arrive, no matter how high-powered your vehicle or your ideas, you feel as if you have ambled into town—or more correctly, as if the town has ambled halfway out along the road to meet you. One minute you are driving south on modest Route 98, passing a small lake and fields, the next you are on Main Street, which seems empty and quiet. There are no mini-malls or chain drugstores, just local businesses housed in 19th- and early 20th-century buildings that don't appear to have changed in decades.

■ **BUCK HILL WILDLIFE MANAGEMENT AREA** *map page 183, A-1*
Things haven't changed much either in the Buck Hill Wildlife Management Area, which occupies the state's northwestern corner. Reached by going north on Route 96 from Harrisville and then west on Hill, Whipple, and East Wallum Lake Roads to Route 100, this area is a great place to collect tips about native animals whose ancestors have been chewing the scenery for centuries. Having found one of the area's best-kept secrets, you follow marked trails that surround a duck-filled marsh and old roads that ramble back and forth across both the Massachusetts and Connecticut state lines.

Bring binoculars and spend a few hours here on a spring or autumn day. You may see an owl, pheasants, and flocks of wild turkeys that put on an elegant burst of speed as you approach. Then they disappear without a trace into the surrounding woods. Deer and foxes are also plentiful, as are deer hunters during the late autumn and early winter. You should probably forego a visit altogether in hunting season, or at least wear a fluorescent orange vest and hat. *Main entrance, Buck Hill Road off Route 100.*

■ **CHEPACHET** *map page 183, A-1*
South of Buck Hill in Chepachet, where Routes 100 and 102 converge, things seem equally sleepy, and excess seems unimaginable. We must, therefore, take the 1937 *WPA Guide to Rhode Island* at its word when it records the following about the town: "In the late 19th century, visitors summered at the taverns of this village from as far west as Chicago and St. Louis." Things were even livelier in 1826 when

The Brown and Hopkins Country Store in Chepachet is thought to be the nation's oldest continuously operated country store.

a parade animal, Betty, the Learned Elephant, got loose and stampeded through town. "Diverse hands fired upon Betty," notes a plaque on the bridge over the Chepachet River, near where she was shot and buried. Gone but not forgotten, Betty is honored each year on Elephant Day, and you'll see her image on trash cans and in other places.

You can learn more about Betty at the former **Job Armstrong Store,** an early 19th-century dry goods and grocery store that is now home to the Glocester Heritage Society. *1181 Main Street (Putnam Pike).*

Chepachet is hardly the raucous saloon town of yore. The most decadent things in sight are few antique and vintage clothing shops clustered in the small town center. **Stone Mill Antiques** (1169 Main Street), near the bridge, occupies the town's 1814 mill building.

The **Brown and Hopkins Country Store** both sells antiques and is one. Opened as a hattery in 1799 and converted into a general store in 1809, this is said to be the oldest continuously operated country store in America. It is almost impossible to ignore the overwhelming array of crafts, collectibles, and gourmet coffees and candies (the sweets displayed in an old oak counter). But if you squint hard and contemplate the springy, sloping, wide-plank floor, the lofty ceiling, and the pot-bellied stove for a moment, you'll easily manage to commune with the spirit of the old establishment. *1179 Main Street; 401-568-4830.*

To appreciate the Chepachet River's soothing presence, stroll across the town bridge to the fire station and follow the unmarked path that leads along the river to a pretty lily pond, where you can sit and watch the water hurtling itself over a romantic old dam.

Chepachet is a Native American name that loosely translates as "Devil's bag," a mysterious designation until you learn that this region, according to Narragansett folklore, is pockmarked with Devil's footprints. Diabolical hoof marks were reportedly visible on rocks outside Middletown and Wickford, while the Indian Drum Rock at Apponaug allegedly bore the imprint of the Devil's heel.

European colonists imported their own colorful beliefs. When the children and grandchildren of English dissenters settled Chepachet in 1693, some called themselves Seekers, some Friends, some Separatists, and some New Lights. Prayer meetings were held in crude cabin homesteads in a rocky wilderness already populated by hundreds of Native American gods and demons. All these elements—English, indigenous and natural—combined over time to form Christian beliefs that could accommodate the existence of witches and spirits inhabiting this alien land.

Stone Mill Antiques operates inside and outside Chepachet's 1814 mill.

■ **FOSTERS EVERYWHERE** *map page 183, A-2*

Spooky mythology cannot detract from the sheer pleasure of driving—dawdling, really—along the remarkably empty, gently twisting byways that lead from Chepachet to Foster. Well, it's not quite that simple. There is Foster, Foster Center, North Foster, and South Foster (which is in fact north of Foster Center). Or rather, there may be. Today, some Fosters seem not to exist. Straying from Route 102, you wander around in a Foster triangle bounded by Route 101, Route 94, and U.S. 6 until you notice a small grouping of 18th- and 19th-century houses, their gardens overflowing with old-fashioned roses. You have found Foster Center.

To call a little more attention to their town, perhaps, Foster Center residents decided in the early 1990s to build a covered bridge. Arson destroyed their first attempt, but using volunteer labor and donated lumber cut from local forests, they finally completed the **Swamp Meadow Covered Bridge** in 1994. This replica of an early-19th-century bridge crosses the pretty Hemlock Brook. *Central Pike (a dirt road), ¼-mile west of Route 94.*

Foster's other attractions are more understated. A handwritten sign outside one house, for example, offers "Hypnosis, Massage," but you know that if you become any more relaxed you will stay here forever. Fend off these Brigadoon-ish reveries by driving or biking along the surrounding byroads. Leaving Foster Center, for example, you may follow Walker Road or Howard Hill Road, make a jog across Route 14 to Hall Road, and then turn left onto Waterman Hill Road. The **Foster Town House** (180 Howard Hill Road; 401-392-9200), one of the oldest such buildings in the nation—it dates from 1796—is still used for town council meetings and is a good excuse to stop for a rest or a tour.

From Waterman Hill Road you can rejoin Route 102, but you won't want to. Stick to the generously tree-shaded side roads, where traffic is almost nonexistent. (The road surface is poor, however, so watch out for potholes.) You pass neat 18th-century Cape Cod cottage-style houses, where daylilies bob over listing wooden fences, and past farms that look like the models you played with as a child.

You return, unfortunately, to one of the more commercialized stretches of Route 102, though it is bordered for a time on either side by gigantic nurseries. The area around Foster Center was once pitted by gravel banks that supplied material for the local roads. Moosup Valley even reportedly boasted a gold mine. Today, thanks largely to Rhode Island's relatively mild winters, industrial-scale garden centers and nurseries do business here.

■ JOHNSTON *map page 183, B-2*

Delay your return to civilization a few moments longer by looping back to Providence via the **Dame Farm,** east of Foster Center in Johnston. You're not far at all from Smithfield's Powder Mill Ledges, your first stop in rural northern Rhode Island. Established in the late 18th century and still operated by the Dame family, which acquired the land in the 1890s, it has been preserved as a rural educational center. Dame Farm is part of the ominously named Snake Den State Park, but no alarming reptiles lurk in these cornfields, so you can amble happily amid tomatoes, squash, peppers and other produce without fear of attack. In season, you can pick your own apples. The trails here also wind through impressive oak and hickory forests. *29 Brown Avenue, off U.S. 6, Johnston.*

Elephants in Providence's Roger Williams Park Zoo.

■ TRAVEL BASICS

Getting Around: Route 146 travels northwest from Providence into the heart of the Blackstone River Valley, running more or less parallel to the river until Rhode Island's border with Massachusetts. Route 114 heads north on the eastern side of the river from Providence, passing through Pawtucket before turning west to Woonsocket. U.S. 44 and U.S. 6 travel west from Providence to the Connecticut border, and Routes 100 and 102 slice south along northern Rhode Island's western edge.

Climate: Northern Rhode Island has a generally moderate climate, with summer temperatures around 80 degrees Fahrenheit and spring and autumn temperatures ranging from 50 to 70 degrees. In winter, the temperature can descend below freezing, and the northern parts of the state average a little less than 3 feet of snow each year. Rhode Island typically receives more than 40 inches of rain a year, but rainfall distribution remains fairly constant.

SOUTHERN RHODE ISLAND

From Sakonnet Point along Rhode Island's eastern coast to Watch Hill in the west, southern Rhode Island seems to have been selected as the laboratory for myriad saltwater experiments. Forming tidal ponds, tidal rivers, salt marshes, coves, and inlets, the Atlantic Ocean seems to influence nearly every scene and activity. Travel in these areas is a pleasantly circular business as you meander from Bristol to Prudence Island and back to the mainland, or from Portsmouth to Little Compton, before losing your way—in the happiest sense—on Block Island.

Rhode Islanders use the term "South County" to refer to the area from Jamestown west to the Connecticut border, and north from the coast to West Greenwich and East Greenwich. Almost every road within this magical region leads to glorious open spaces and pleasingly eccentric towns. As in Connecticut, the coast from Westerly to Point Judith faces south. Motels and malls blight this stretch, though it is also graced by antiquated summer resorts and fine beaches. The only thing that proceeds in a straight line in southern Rhode Island is I-95, which should be avoided whenever possible. Abandon your linear ambitions, and remember that Rhode Island is tiny and you do not need to make time.

■ COVENTRY CENTER *map page 205, A-1*

Leaving Providence, for example, it would make sense in a plodding, literal way to proceed directly south. But why not return to the Revolutionary War and rural eras by sliding west on Route 14 and then south on Route 116 to Coventry Center before meandering farther south to Westerly and the coast? Stock up on picnic provisions and dine while you recline in one of the region's prettiest landscapes.

East of Route 116 off Route 117, the **General Nathanael Greene Homestead** at Spell Hall is the 1770 estate of the Revolutionary War hero. Second in command to George Washington, Greene played a critical role in the war's most decisive clashes—the battles of Trenton, Yorktown, and the Carolinas. In the *History of the American Revolution,* published in 1789, David Ramsay observed that "History affords but few instances of commanders who have achieved so much, with equal means, as was done by General Greene, in the short space of a twelvemonth. He opened the campaign with gloomy prospects; but closed it with glory."

At his homestead, Greene entertained the Marquis de Lafayette, the Comte de Rochambeau, and other notables. Much of the furniture on display here belonged to the Greene family, and some of the artifacts belonged to the general and his wife, Catherine Littlefield Greene. Catherine raised four children while Nathanael was fighting in the Revolutionary War and converted their home into an infirmary where French soldiers injured in the Battle of Rhode Island were treated. After her husband died, she contributed to the industrial revolution by using her government pension to subsidize the development of Eli Whitney's cotton gin.

The family was known for its innovation as well as Greene's heroism. Nathanael's father and brother built one of America's first trip-hammer forges to produce ironware such as door hardware and common household tools. You can see the remains of the forge if you walk down the wooded path behind the house

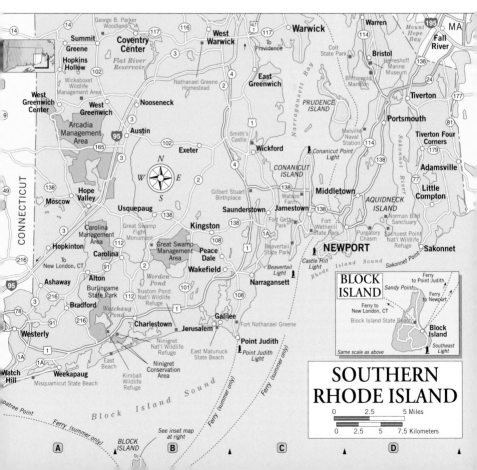

SOUTHERN RHODE ISLAND

Trees reflected in a Summit pond.

to the quiet banks of the Pawtuxet River. The cannon on the homestead's lawn is also thought to be their handiwork, though crafted at another forge. The family cemetery also on the grounds holds the remains of several generations of Greenes and their servants. *50 Taft Street (head south from Route 117 on Laurel Avenue and turn left on Greene Street); 401-821-8630.*

Fortified by this dose of history and inspired by the energy of the Greenes and their contemporaries, you could proceed south in efficient, military fashion down Route 3—or, even more ambitiously, along I-95—to the coast. But the whole point of visiting interior Rhode Island (and, one suspects, the secret agenda of interior Rhode Island itself) is to dawdle and digress. From the Greene homestead, for example, you might backtrack west on Route 117. After crossing Route 102, you notice a side street, Old Summit Road and follow it to the small village of **Summit,** once a stop on the New York, New Haven and Hartford Railroad line. The nearby farms and the 1862 **Summit Baptist Church** (12 Old Summit Road) evoke a more pastoral past, one that still bleeds through, if only partially, down the street at the **Summit General Store,** whose wares include hay and animal feed.

Nature without a price tag can be encountered a few miles northeast of Summit at the **George B. Parker Woodland,** a 600-acre forest in Coventry that has been preserved by the Audubon Society. Seven miles of well-maintained walking trails begin near the privately owned Isaac Bowen House, built between 1755 and 1795. Your forest walk through stands of hemlock and pine uncovers further evidence of a human presence. Cellar holes, chimney bricks, collapsed stone walls, and the remains of an 18th-century sawmill and charcoal kiln are scattered throughout the woods. Far more mysterious are the stone cairns that some archaeologists speculate may be the work of Native American tribes. *1670 Maple Valley Road east of Route 102; 401-295-8283.*

■ SOUTH COUNTY *map page 205, A-1/2*

The byroads to the west of Route 102—with appealing names like Skunk Hill Road and Molasses Hill Road—snake their way through large stretches of conservation land that is home to rabbits, deer, squirrels, raccoons, foxes, and many types of birds. You should do the same. The **Wickaboxet Wildlife Management Area** (off Plain Meeting House Road, West Greenwich) encompasses 722 acres of woodland, wetlands and hiking trails.

■ ARCADIA MANAGEMENT AREA *map page 205, A-1/2*

South of Wickaboxet and much larger at 14,000 acres, the Arcadia Management Area also contains woodland, wetlands, and numerous ponds and well-maintained hiking trails. If the sight of fresh water becomes too tempting on a hot summer afternoon, you may wade in at the Browning Mill Recreation Area (although swimming is not allowed), where a pretty beach borders the large pond and where children enjoy the miniature attractions of the adjacent stream-fed pool. Eighty percent of this West Greenwich region is wooded and the beech trees alone would make this a state treasure. But Arcadia also has the trout-filled Wood River and 40 miles of trails for riders, who may camp with their horses at Legrand G. Reynolds Horseman's Area. (Those seeking steeper thrills may wish to climb the daunting Rattlesnake Ledge to the north in Wickaboxet.)

The Ten Rod Road (Route 165) bisects the Arcadia area and was named for the thoroughfare's original width (10 rods equals 165 feet), which allowed farmers to drive herds of cattle to the seaport at Wickford. Hikers with a weakness for colorfully named paths should indulge their tastes on the Blitzkrieg Trail, which winds through the southeast corner of this dense forest until it comes to an end at Nooseneck Hill. A short drive north of Route 165 from Eschoeag brings you to one of the region's loveliest natural wonders, **Stepstone Falls.** The graceful cataract rushes over a series of rock ledges on which you may picnic or simply prostrate yourself. An adjacent nature trail passes the remains of an old gristmill and a derelict sawmill. To reach the falls from Route 165, head north on Eschoeag Hill Road and go right on Falls River Road, taking the bumpy half-mile drive to the Stepstone parking area. *Arcadia Management Area main entrance: Route 165, west of Route 3 and I-95; 401-539-2356.*

■ HOPKINTON *map page 205, A-2*
In this tiny corner of tiny Rhode Island, you have to smile when you come across hamlets named Moscow or Wyoming, the first communities you encounter outside the Arcadia forest. You also have to appreciate the sense of humor behind the creation of a Lilliputian world—the **Enchanted Forest**—inside the nation's smallest state. This imaginative children's amusement park occupies a couple of woodland acres and lures little people along fairy-tale trails to the Three Little Pigs house, the petting zoo, fairground rides, miniature golf, and other diversions. Picnic areas are scattered throughout and adult visitors will find themselves more charmed than bored. *Route 3 off I-95, Exit 2; 401-539-7711.*

To reach Westerly, you can follow Route 3 south or, in the meandering spirit, take Woodville Alton Road, which runs south from Route 3 between Hope Valley and Alton village. Stay your course as the byway turns into Alton Bradford Road, which crosses the Pawcatuck River before entering Bradford.

The more conventional route to Westerly also leads through **Bradford,** once called Shattuck's Weir, for a local Native American personage and for the famous weirs on which salmon and other fish were easily caught. The town later became known for its textile industry and granite quarries. Twenty-first-century Bradford has the soothing air of a place that has run out of energy but is not particularly perturbed by the fact.

■ WESTERLY *map page 205, A-3*
When the traveler and diarist Madam Knight stopped in Westerly in 1704, she was more than perturbed. She was appalled. "The family were the old man, his wife, and two children," she wrote of her visit to one habitation, "all and every part

On parade in downtown Westerly.

being the picture of poverty. . . . An Indian like animal came to the door on a creature very much like himselfe in mien and feature, as well as ragged clothing."
Dwellings and fortunes improved when this became a vigorous textile-producing
and granite-quarrying center in the 18th century. Greek Revival and Victorian
mansions still line many side streets.

Like so many Rhode Island towns, Westerly initially grew as an agricultural and
fishing settlement after the first English colonists established themselves here in
1648. The indigenous people—at various times, members of the Niantic, Pequot
and Narragansett tribes dominated—already appreciated the bountiful Pawcatuck
River. They named the banks extending for 7 miles on either side of the waterway
Misquamicut, which means "red salmon at this place."

When the first English settlers arrived in 1648, they encountered the Niantics
and their formidable leader Ninigret, who, between 1664 and 1665, repelled several
attacks from Connecticut by rival tribes and one invasion by English troops. The
settlers themselves had good relations with their Indian neighbors until a decade
later, when King Philip's War saw fierce fighting. Later, boundary disputes between

Massachusetts, Connecticut, and Rhode Island persisted until official lines were drawn in 1728. Nature, though, was not so easily ordered. Early attempts at sheep-raising were thwarted by packs of marauding wolves.

Shipbuilding along the Pawcatuck River fueled Westerly's growth from the 18th century well into the 19th century; several whaling ships were built, and vessels were outfitted for voyages to Newfoundland up until 1836. Where there are sailors there is grog, and during the late 18th century a section of Westerly along Main Street became known as Bungtown, thanks to the proliferation of waterfront gin and rum purveyors, whose cellars were littered with bungs that stopped the casks. On March 1, 1825, Charles Perry produced Westerly's first (albeit handwritten) newspaper, appropriately called the *Bungtown Patriot*. Westerly's first printed newspaper, published in 1851, bore the lofty but surely less accurate title *Literary Echo*. Westerly's granite quarries gained a national reputation in the mid-19th century, mostly because of the fine-grained quality of the stone, which was ideal for memorial monuments—a genre that 19th-century benefactors liked almost as much as they did literary echoes.

Petals line a pathway in glorious Wilcox Park.

The 18-acre heart of Westerly is **Wilcox Park.** Designed a century ago by Warren H. Manning, an associate of the famous landscape architect Frederick Law Olmsted, the green retreat is everything a park should be. Grassy slopes unfurl from a formal granite terrace like bolts of green velvet flung out by a professional draper with one experienced snap of the wrist. The Westerly Band, more than a century old, performs concerts in the bandstand, and on July evenings a free Shakespeare festival takes place. Mature native and exotic trees cast their welcome shadows, none more effectively than the gigantic weeping beech whose outer branches form an encircling cordon. Walk inside and you are under the tree's skirts in a copper-dappled cocoon, feeling like a small child who has stumbled on a magic hideout. The real children are nearby, whispering and squealing as they make their way in and out of a child-size weeping beech that competes for attention with a bronze sculpture, *The Runaway Bunny,* perfect for climbing. *Broad Street opposite Town Hall; 401-596-2877.*

Another of the town's great trees—a massive copper beech—stands outside one of Westerly's great houses, the Georgian-style **Babcock-Smith House.** Built around 1732 for Dr. Joshua Babcock—who was the town's first physician, its postmaster, the first Chief Justice of Rhode Island, and a friend of Benjamin Franklin—the gambrel-roof dwelling was later owned by Orlando Smith, who discovered granite on the site in 1846, thereby founding one of Westerly's major industries. The Smiths lived here until 1972, and many of the 18th- and 19th-century furnishings seen today belonged to the family. The well-proportioned doorway, flanked by carved pilasters and surmounted by a broken-scroll pediment, is particularly fine, as is the interior stair rail with twisted balusters. In many rooms, the wide-plank floors and heavy corner posts recall a pre-Georgian period of sturdy construction. Sadly, the street on which the Babcock-Smith House stands has altered greatly since Benjamin Franklin used to visit his old friend Joshua. Apart from the magnificent copper beech in the garden, Granite Street is now denuded of trees and much of it is pockmarked with mini-malls. *124 Granite Street (U.S. 1); 401-596-5704.*

Westerly has a decidedly mixed record when it comes to historic preservation, but several dozen downtown buildings, many of them on High, Canal, Elm, and Main Streets, are on the National Register of Historic Places. A great way to view them in summer is on the **Duck Land and Water Tour** (401-596-7761). Your means of conveyance, a "duck boat"—an amphibious landing vehicle from the World War II era—dips into water along the way.

■ WATCH HILL *map page 205, A-3*

If Newport's mansions to the east reek of new money, the Victorian seaside resort of Watch Hill, a village in Westerly—take Route 1A south and Watch Hill Road west—suggests the older, more discreet variety. On this western tip of Rhode Island, graceful rather than flamboyant houses perch on rolling hills, overlooking some of the state's most beautiful beaches. The fierce hurricane of 1938 that ravaged the Eastern Seaboard was so charmed with the summer cottages then dotting Napatree Point that it swept them away in one enthusiastic blast, bequeathing today's walkers a shoreline of unparalleled beauty.

A good place to watch the autumn hawk migration, Napatree Point is reachable only by taking a brisk, 1-mile walk; the spot also affords delightful views of the 1856 **Watch Hill Lighthouse** (Bluff and Larkin Roads) and an old military fort.

These straits were tempestuous long before 1938. The U.S. Coast Guard log for February 11, 1896, records the wrecking of the *Belle R. Huell,* which was carrying coal to Newport when she sprang a leak at 5 A.M. "The vessel badly strained by the heavy wind and mountainous seas. . . . At 7 A.M. a fearful squall from the S.S.W. accompanied by snow blew away the jib and foresail. The Captain's wife, Captain and crew, five all told, were safely landed to the beach by the use of Breeches-buoy. Ten minutes after the last man was landed on the beach, the mast of the vessel went down. . . ."

Built in 1868, the **Ocean House Hotel** has witnessed its share of storms, and today the wonderful Victorian leviathan herself shows signs of buffeting. The floors in the faded function rooms tilt as rakishly as the deck of a listing ocean liner, and the windows on the seaward wall subside against each other at odd angles, like charmingly crooked teeth. The effect is endearing rather than dispiriting, the enormous shady veranda is still magnificent, and the views are unparalleled. Watch Hill's private mansions are lovingly preserved and the surrounding beaches are some of the finest in New England. But the genteel decay of the Ocean House is also an essential part of the Watch Hill identity. There is nothing precious or slick about this old seaside resort, which is open seasonally. *2 Bluff Avenue; 401-348-8161.*

Bay Street in Watch Hill, looking out onto Little Narragansett Bay, is the village's sole commercial district, and the mostly local stores and restaurants are delightfully quirky and only open during the warmer months.

Watch Hill Lighthouse at sunset.

(top) Sip your tea—or your martini—indoors or outdoors at the Olympia Tea Room.
(bottom) The views are unparalleled from the Ocean House Hotel.

The **Olympia Tea Room** (74 Bay Street; 401-348-8211) for example, has been in business for almost 90 years, and it still serves some of the best seafood—and martinis—in the region. A few hundred feet away at the **Book and Tackle Shop** (7 Bay Street; 401-596-1770), you will be stopped in your tracks by racks of what may be the world's oddest postcards. How about a view from the top of a Westerly Fire Department ladder? Or a ghastly Foxwoods Casino buffet? Postcard aficionados will spend hours here, and those with childhood memories of seaside resorts will have an instant nostalgia attack.

Nostalgia notwithstanding, adults are barred from the **Flying Horse Carousel**, reputedly America's oldest carousel, built in 1867 and still turning at the end of Bay Street. But you can prolong your regression by watching those handsome chargers—each carved out of a single piece of wood—whirl their squealing riders around and around past the brass ring.

As you make your west-to-east run from Watch Hill to Narragansett, you will detect this modest, trend-resisting attitude not only in the tasteful scale of many seaside developments (although there are plenty of gray condominium developments), but also in the old-fashioned town centers and quiet side roads. U.S. 1, the main coastal thoroughfare, seems more bearable than its Connecticut equivalent, but you should wander along the back roads as they twist back and forth between ponds, ocean, and swamp to Narragansett. That unique maritime environment, by the way, makes the coast one of the finest bird-watching areas in the Northeast.

■ **NINIGRET NATIONAL WILDLIFE REFUGE** *map page 205, B-3*

For migrating humans, of course, the beach is the prime destination in summer, when southern Rhode Island's coastal rim teems with families and teenagers who exhibit their own colorful plumage and engage in courtship displays. Arrive in early spring or late autumn, however, and you may feel like the sole surveyor of beautiful shores like **Misquamicut State Beach** (Atlantic Avenue, east of Watch Hill) or **East Beach** (East Beach Road, Charlestown). Even during the summer, East Beach is spared overwhelming invasion by its limited parking facilities. Most visitors congregate at the parking-lot end of the beach. Walk east along the shoreline, wading in and out like a sandpiper as you go, and you may leave the crowd behind and be rewarded with views of Block Island hovering over the waves before you, and of Ninigret Pond and the dunes of the Ninigret Conservation Area at your back. *U.S. 1, Ninigret National Wildlife Refuge Exit; 401-364-9124.*

Inland, across U.S. 1, the expanse of the far larger **Burlingame State Park** (401-322-8910) attracts campers, hikers, canoeists, bicyclists, and a wide variety of waterfowl and woodland birds. The adjacent 29-acre **Kimball Wildlife Refuge** (401-874-6664), established by the Audubon Society in the 1920s on the southern shore of Watchaug Pond, provides beautifully landscaped nesting areas for birds and spying areas for birders.

■ CHARLESTOWN *map page 205, B-3*

If prolonged exposure to nature brings back memories of carefree youth, you should slip into your Laura Ashley floral-print smock and head over to the **Fantastic Umbrella Factory.** Here, the hazy spirit of the 1960s lives on in a series of converted barns in which you can buy crafts by the local townspeople. You can also shop for beaded accessories and organic snacks, and buy refrigerator magnets, Japanese paper lanterns, and much more. Here, as elsewhere in Rhode Island, slickness is not the goal. You bump along a dirt road on your right after the entrance to Ninigret Park and then proceed along narrow footpaths from one craft shop to the next, often threading your way through overgrown gardens and rusted junk cars. It's real. *4820 Old Post Road (Route 1A); 401-364-6616.*

Members of the Narragansett tribe still live in Charlestown, which was for centuries the burial ground of Narragansett sachems. The Royal Indian Burial Ground, on Narrow Lane off Route 2, is closed to visitors, but you may observe costumed dancing and ceremonial rituals at the annual Narragansett gathering in early August.

■ SOUTH KINGSTOWN BEACHES *map page 205, B/C-3*

From Charlestown, take the Old Post Road exit of U.S. 1 and follow the small Matunuck Schoolhouse Road, which hugs the coast. Make short detours to the right on Green Hill Beach Road and, a few miles later, on Moonstone Beach Road to stretch your legs on the area's small beaches.

A short drive farther east on Matunuck Schoolhouse Road brings you to Matunuck Beach Road, where the **Admiral Dewey Inn** has bedrooms that are not only lovely—high-poster or brass-trimmed iron beds, tasteful wallpaper and curtains—but free of televisions, telephones, and roaring air conditioners. (The town beach is but yards away, and there is usually a cooling breeze.) Most rooms have views of Block Island Sound. There's a wraparound porch with rocking chairs, and a parlor area with comfortable, overstuffed furniture that seems to say "sit in me."

The folks at the National Register of Historic Places declared the Dewey, which dates from 1898, "the best restoration of a beach boardinghouse on the Rhode Island shore." *668 Matunuck Beach Road, South Kingstown; 401-783-2090.*

A bit east off U.S. 1 in Jerusalem, ignore the young crowd making for the white sand of **East Matunuck State Beach** and, if calm weather and waters prevail, explore the rocky reef that extends out from the beach, where crabs, mussels, and starfish live happily in tidal pools untroubled by the fact that you may have just eaten some of their relations. *950 Succotash Road, off U.S. 1.*

■ GALILEE AND POINT JUDITH *map page 205, B/C-3*

Jerusalem and Galilee are busy fishing ports whose unpretentious restaurants serve some of the freshest seafood imaginable. What these towns and the nearby Port Judith lack in picturesque charm—fiberglass cruisers far outnumber wooden boats—they make up for in rough-and-ready vitality, the energetic sense you get in any true fishing town that the population, at a moment's notice, could cast off in pursuit of a school of tuna or bluefish.

A shorefront beach house along East Matunuck State Beach.

All summer long, the busy port hums with anticipation as fishermen set sail hoping for a record-breaking catch and holidaymakers board the Block Island Ferry dreaming of tranquility. If this energy proves infectious, contact the **Frances Fleet,** which operates day and overnight fishing trips. If you are content simply to observe leviathans, the *Lady Frances* herself will take you on whale-watching cruises. Nobody who spots the black fin of an 80-foot-long humpback whale slicing through the water can remain silent. You shout or gasp, and grab the arm of the stranger next to you, and when the giant tail rises, you perform a little hopping dance that you have not done since you were three years old. Humpback, finback, minke, and even right whales feed off Block Island, but you may also see sharks, giant sunfish, giant turtles, and menacing Portuguese man-o-wars. Be advised that these are rolling waters, and queasy would-be sailors should consider taking seasickness medication before setting sail. *33 State Street; 401-783-4988.*

If you return to Galilee with digestion undisturbed, pay a visit to **George's,** which has specialized since 1948 in the baked, stuffed quahogs (clams) known affectionately as "stuffies." *250 Sand Hill Cove Road; 401-783-2306.*

Fishing boats still operate out of Jerusalem (pictured), Galilee, and Point Judith.

In the spirit of fair comparison, you should drive a mile or so east on Sand Hill Cove Road and sample the chowder and clams at **Aunt Carrie's.** This seasonal no-frills establishment has been serving seafood for more than 80 years, and it understands hunger. If the summer queue is too long, you may order from Carrie's takeout window and eat on the grounds of the nearby lighthouse. *1240 Ocean Road, 0.3 mile north of Route 108, Point Judith; 401-783-7930.*

Its hook permanently baited with the alluring **Point Judith Lighthouse,** Point Judith juts into Block Island Sound, attracting fishing and ferryboats that churn up these waters. In a region with breathtaking vistas, the ones here never fail to enchant. Placards near the lighthouse tell the tales of ships lost at sea in the area. *1460 Ocean Road.*

■ **NARRAGANSETT** *map page 205, C-2/3*

The long strip of land known as Narragansett, extending north from Point Judith to Narragansett town, is bounded on one side by the ocean and lengthy beaches, and on the other side by Point Judith Pond. Once the rich fishing grounds of the Narragansett tribe, this region was subsequently farmed by a comparatively small number of landowners who owned large estates. In colonial Narragansett, farms of 10 square miles were common. An affluent farmer might have cultivated up to 5,000 acres and owned up to 100 slaves. In this respect, social conditions resembled those of the Virginia plantations rather than a Puritan settlement.

Driving here from Point Judith along Ocean Road, you pass most of the mansions built during Narragansett's golden age To see how you might have fit in, you may treat yourself to an expensive but memorable stay at **Stone Lea,** a B&B off Ocean Road. The elegant shingled house looks out across Narragansett Bay to Newport, Jamestown, Tiverton, and Block Island. Choose the Block Island room, and you will immediately wish you had packed a floor-length silk evening gown—it's that soigné. Fashion shows, though, are best attempted on the first night of your stay, because after Stone Lea's substantial breakfasts you may have trouble fitting into anything smaller than your car. *40 Newton Avenue; 401-783-9546.*

In the late 19th century, the railroad linked Narragansett to New York and Boston, and the town became a summer playground. The Narragansett Pier Casino, designed by Stanford White of McKim, Mead & White, was one of the Northeast's most prestigious vacation spots, but its heyday was short-lived. The building burned to the ground in a dramatic fire in 1900.

The Towers, made of granite and connected by an arch that spans Ocean Road, are all that remain. The Towers look incongruous in today's brash surroundings, like large Victorian ladies dressed in full-length bombazine gowns who have stumbled into a beach party whose dress code is thong. Stylish resorts like Narragansett are familiar with fashion outrages. Writing in 1891 of the two-piece wool bathing suits then worn by male bathers, a contributor to *Demerset's Monthly Magazine* painted a pathetic picture. "Barefoot as a mendicant, the stripes of your clothes strongly suggestive of Sing-Sing, your appearance a caricature of human kind, you wander up and down the beach a creature that the land is evidently trying to shake off and the sea is unwilling to take." The visitors center here has brochures and other information about southern Rhode Island. *36 Ocean Road; 401-782-2597.*

Fire may have swallowed McKim, Mead & White's casino, but the glamorous firm's stone **Coast Guard House** (40 Ocean Road; 401-789-0700), built in 1888 as a life-saving station, survives as a restaurant. Lunch, dinner, and stupendous Sunday buffets provide sustenance these days, to the accompaniment of grand ocean views. *40 Ocean Road; 401-789-0700.*

The Towers—all that remains of the Narragansett Pier Casino.

Narragansett in 1900. (Library of Congress)

The **South County Museum** is on a 175-acre nature preserve on the former estate of Rhode Island's Civil War–era governor, William Sprague, and his wife, Kate Chase—the daughter of Salmon P. Chase, the Secretary of the Treasury under Abraham Lincoln. The couple's home burned in 1909, but the museum's six buildings include a smithy with a working forge, a carpentry shop, a one-room schoolhouse, an early transportation building, and a letterpress printing shop. The Americana collection here illustrates life as it was lived on the farm, in the village, and on the sea, and it is certainly not the museum's fault if the working antique shops, along with the fine antique carriage collection, look far prettier today than they did when hard physical labor was the lifelong fate of most ordinary people. The museum site also contains a re-creation of a working farm from the 18th- and 19th-centuries. *Strathmore Street off Kingstown Road; 401-783-5400.*

■ **Peace Dale** *map page 205, B-2*

Back on the mainland, Peace Dale, one of Rhode Island's most picturesque historic villages, also recalls a time when stamina was a necessity for survival, not a fitness concept. East of U.S. 1 off Route 108, Peace Dale became a mill town in the early 1800s, when the Hazard family built textile factories and housing for workers beside the Saugatucket River. *The Weaver,* an impressive bronze relief outside the South Kingstown Public Library (1057 Kingstown Road) by Daniel Chester French, commemorates the local millworkers; French's works include the statue of Abraham Lincoln at the Lincoln Memorial in Washington, D.C. According to factory contracts, weavers were paid by the yard and received no more than one-sixth of their wages in cash, the rest coming as goods from the company store.

Small, quiet companies now occupy mill buildings that once produced clothing for slaves on southern plantations, shawls and cashmere items for the upper crust, blankets for the Union army, and khaki for World War I uniforms, but if you walk around the courtyard and contemplate the intact mill raceways, you can imagine Peace Dale at its most vibrant and ambitious.

You can pick up walking-tour maps at the library or across the street at the **Museum of Primitive Art and Culture,** on the second floor in a three-story stone building that originally contained the Hazard company store, the post office, and a boardinghouse. On exhibit at the museum are ethnological tools, baskets, pottery, blankets, apparel, and weapons from indigenous cultures of Africa, the South Seas, and North America. *1058 Kingstown Road; 401-783-5711.*

■ THE GREAT SWAMP *map page 205, B-2*
The obelisk off Route 2 in West Kingston is a troubling reminder of an extinct—or, to be precise, erased—culture. This plain monument marks the site of the Great Swamp Fight in 1675 during King Philip's War. It was here that militias from Massachusetts, Connecticut, and Rhode Island attacked the Narragansett tribe's winter encampment, killing hundreds of men, women, and children and prompting futile revenge attacks.

These days, the **Great Swamp Management Area,** a 3,300-acre wetland that borders the 1,000-acre Worden Pond, is one of Rhode Island's many natural jewels. Accessible by dirt roads and dikes, the swamp is intoxicating when the dogwoods bloom in spring and when the maples and tupelos blaze in autumn. Don't be surprised to see nesting ospreys—the state's largest colony—glaring down at you from their untidy households. *Liberty Lane off Route 2 or Route 138; 401-222-1267.*

■ KINGSTON *map page 205, B-2*
Kingston displays its enviable elegance most conspicuously on Kingston Road, where 18th- and early-19th-century houses predominate and where even the **Old Washington County Jail** (2636 Kingstown Road; 401-783-1328) is gracious enough to welcome innocent visitors into its cells. The granite structure, erected in 1861, replaced a wooden building from 1792 and served as a jail until 1956. Since 1961, it has housed the Pettaquamscutt Historical Society, which hosts exhibitions about the jail and area history.

■ **USQUEPAUG AND SAUNDERSTOWN** *map page 205, B/C-2*
A minor side trip west on Route 138 to Usquepaug, on the Queen's River, brings you to the **Kenyon Grist Mill,** built in 1750, where cornmeal for johnnycakes—a Rhode Island culinary specialty, along with quahogs (clams) and greening apples—is still ground on massive granite wheels. This is a fine place to learn about how a gristmill operates—and what the term "keep your nose to the grindstone" literally means—but it's wise to call ahead for an appointment. *21 Glen Rock Road; off Route 138; 401-783-4054.*

Another working water-powered mill can be viewed northeast of Kingston at the **Gilbert Stuart Birthplace,** which summons the artistic and bucolic past with works by New England's famous 18th-century painter (best known for the portrait of George Washington used on the U.S. one-dollar bill) and restored buildings, a pond, and landscaped gardens. Stuart, born in 1755, lived his first seven years in the red gambrel-roof family home. The wooden structure served double duty as the snuff mill of Stuart's father. *815 Gilbert Stuart Road, off Route 138/U.S. 1 or Route 1A, Saunderstown; 401-294-3001.*

The artist Gilbert Stuart lived the first seven years of his life in the red house on the left.

■ **WICKFORD** *map page 205, C-1*

Small, picturesque Wickford, off U.S. 1 north of Saunderstown, is home to some of the finest 18th- and 19th-century houses in the state. It is also where you will find **Wickford Gourmet Foods** (21 West Main Street; 401-295-8190), an emporium that displays its heavenly lunch specials alongside pastries, cheeses, jams and jellies, salsas and dips, caviar and pâtés, and other tempting comestibles. Eat on the small terrace or take your sustenance down to the pretty Municipal Wharf.

Suitably fortified, you should stroll down Wickford's main thoroughfare, a pleasing composition of old storefronts and 18th-century houses, and stray onto its leafy side streets. The Episcopal **Old Narragansett Church,** built in 1707 and where Gilbert Stuart was baptized, was moved from the outskirts of town to its present location in 1800. The structure, which houses the oldest church organ in North America—the instrument dates from 1680—is also noteworthy for its wineglass pulpit and slave gallery. *Church Lane, off Main Street; 401-294-4357.*

Farther north on U.S. 1 is **Smith's Castle.** As you approach, you enter a hushed retreat on a shimmering estuary where kingfishers flash between the reeds, ducks sun themselves, and a gigantic white mulberry tree offers shade. The original trading post here became a garrison during King Philip's War. It was burned during that conflict, and a tablet on the grounds marks the grave of 40 men who died in the Great Swamp Fight. A residence built in 1678 was enlarged into a plantation house in 1740. The structure was believed to have been fortified, hence the "castle" moniker, though it does not conform to modern notions of one. During its plantation era, 19 slaves raised hay, grains, and horses here, and the estate was among the largest plantations in Rhode Island. *55 Richard Smith Drive, off U.S. 1; 401-294-3521.*

■ **CONANICUT ISLAND** *map page 205, C-2*

Conanicut Island, also known as Jamestown Island, appears on the map as a mere stepping-stone to the mainland. But its rare delights should make you linger. A favorite summer ground of the Narragansett tribe, the island was named after their sachem, Conanicus, when it was settled by Quakers in the 1650s.

The **Jamestown Windmill** was built in 1787, continued grinding through the 19th century, and today has cattle for company as it contemplates the Newport Bridge, soaring across the bay to fabled Newport. *North Road at Weeden Lane.*

Old storefronts and 18th-century houses line Wickford's main thoroughfare.

The Newport Bridge arches behind the Jamestown Marina.

To get a powerful sense of how the island looked during the early years of its development, visit the 280-acre **Watson Farm,** owned by the Society for the Preservation of New England Antiquities. When border collies greet you in the Watson barnyard, you fear they may be costumed interpreters. But this is not that kind of farm. Don and Heather Minto, the enthusiastic managers for the last 20 years, will start you off on your self-guided farm hike (the farmhouse is off-limits to the public) as they attend to everything from neurotic guinea fowl to complacent eggplants. The brochure explains the agrarian history of the island and the farmland you are crossing. Reading becomes difficult, though, when you are distracted by the stunning views of Narragansett Bay, the beauty of the land dotted by sheep, and the antics of the collies, who take turns herding you and ambushing unsuspecting sticks. *455 North Road, 0.3 miles north of the windmill; 401-423-0005.*

Shoreside pleasures on Conanicut Island's southern tip include **Fort Wetherill State Park,** which provides spectacular views of Narragansett Bay and Newport Harbor. The underwater vistas—a sheltered cove that faces south is a popular scuba-diving spot—include flounder, squid, and other creatures swimming amid the sea lettuce. The park has hiking trails, and you can poke around the ruins of the fort, which was built in the late 1800s, or enjoy a picnic on a grassy lawn ringed by rock bluffs. *Fort Wetherill Road off Walcott Avenue; 401-423-1771.*

Rhode Island's first lighthouse, a wooden structure, was built in 1749 in nearby **Beavertail State Park.** This lighthouse went up in flames, but the current one, made of granite and erected in 1856, has stood the test of time and is open for touring during warm months. You can reach the rocky shoreline here by hiking through low brush or taking the stone stairs. *Beavertail Road; 401-423-9941 in summer, 401-884-2010 year-round.*

Fort Getty Park is the site of a fortification that guarded the east passage to Narragansett Bay during World Wars I and II. The beach here has restrooms and shower facilities. The Fox Hill Salt Marsh, a low-lying wildlife refuge of marshland that you can enter only with the permission of the Audubon Society of Rhode Island (401-949-5454), is at the entrance to Fort Getty Park. *Fort Getty Road off Beavertail Road; 401-423-7211.*

Beavertail Light, on Conanicut Island.

■ **NEWPORT** *map page 205, C-2/3, and page 229*

Between late May and September each year, the city of Newport's population about quadruples from its usual 30,000, and visitors drawn to its mansions and upscale shopping precincts swamp the small seaport town. There is much more to Newport than either of those attractions, though, and to explore this fascinating place in comfort you should arrive in spring or in autumn. Roses bloom into late November, after all, and the housemaid's welcome at the Astors' Beechwood mansion is warm even in April.

You can park all day for less than $15 (a half-hour for free) at the **Newport Visitors Center** (23 America's Cup Avenue; 800-326-6030), which has rest rooms and information about tours, accommodations, restaurants, and harbor cruises, and you can purchase single tickets or discount passes to the Gilded Age mansions.

Before heading up the hill from the visitors center into Newport's colonial heart, take a quick spin through the blocks of restored houses, inns, and taverns that abut

Newport, ca. 1878, just as mansion-building was kicking into high gear. (Library of Congress)

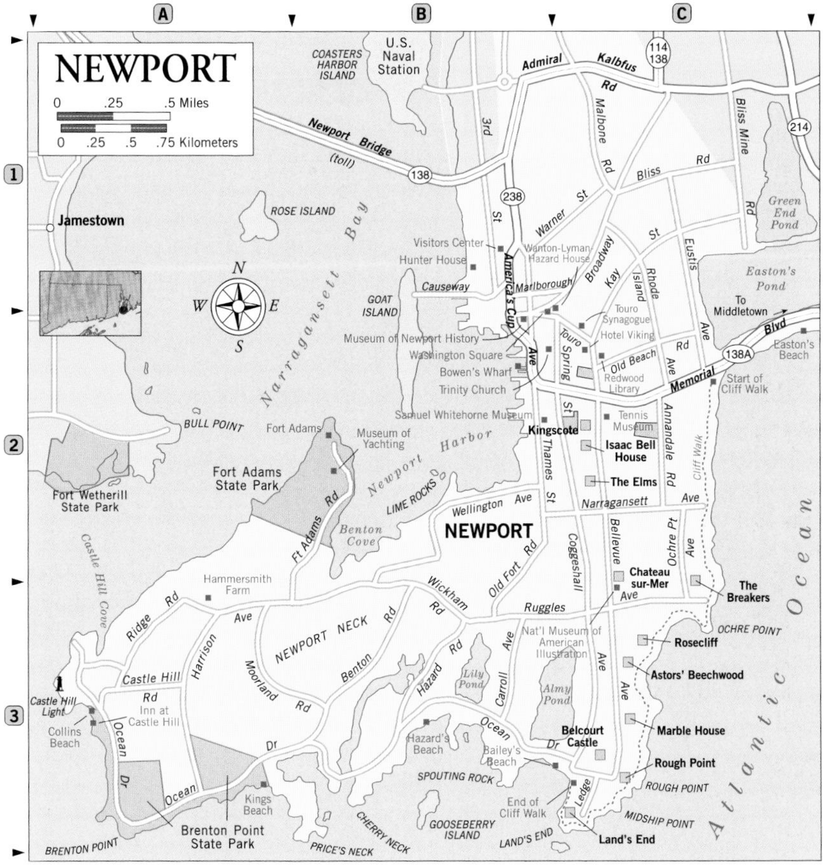

NEWPORT

0   .25   .5 Miles

0   .25   .5   .75 Kilometers

the center's parking lot. A walk toward the water on Bridge Street will land you at **Hunter House,** whose styling and tasteful landscaping underscore the refinement of 18th-century Newport. The Georgian Colonial house's north side was built between 1748 and 1754 by merchant Jonathan Nichols Jr. After his death in 1756, the house was sold to Col. Joseph Wanton, a merchant and deputy governor of Rhode Island, who built the south wing and a second chimney. A loyalist, Wanton fled Newport during the Revolution, and the house became the headquarters of French Admiral de Ternay, the commander of France's fleet when that country's forces occupied Newport in 1780. The grunts emanating from the basketball court at adjacent Storer Park may momentarily break the colonial spell, but nothing can diminish the restrained elegance of the Hunter House or the playful eccentricity of the carved pineapple over the doorway. This popular symbol of hospitality originated when colonial sea captains signaled their return by placing a fresh pineapple outside to declare an open house (and, say some, to serve as a warning to the captain's wife's lover that her husband was home). Hunter House contains many fine examples of 18th-century arts and crafts, including furniture by the distinguished craftsmen of Newport's Townsend and Goddard families and paintings by Gilbert Stuart and Samuel King. *54 Washington Street; 401-847-1000.*

■ **DOWNTOWN NEWPORT** *map page 229*

The **Museum of Newport History,** in the 1772 Brick House, is a good next stop—not only because of its exhibits of decorative arts, everyday artifacts, ship models, colonial silver, and historic illustrations and photographs, but also because of the voices that resonate throughout the building, bringing Newport's history to life. The audio program allows you to listen to Doctor Ezra Stiles and Mary Gould Almy reacting passionately in their diaries to the Revolutionary War siege that lasted from 1776 to 1780. While examining a land deed signed by William and Mary Dyer in 1644, hear the way Roger Williams described Narragansett customs or Anne Hutchinson questioned religious authorities. You may then board a reproduction of an 1890s omnibus for a video tour of Bellevue Avenue and its palaces. *127 Thames Street, at Washington Square; 401-841-8770.*

The Newport Historical Society, which operates the Museum of Newport History, also owns or manages the Wanton-Lyman-Hazard House, the Great Friends Meeting House, Seventh Day Baptist Meeting House, and the Newport Colony House. All of these colonial buildings are stops on the society's guided walking tours, but armed with the society's self-guiding maps, you can choose a theme—colonial Newport, seafaring, religion—and head out on your own, only to be distracted at every turn by overlapping history and humorous incongruity.

Head up Marlborough Street from the museum, for example, and you'll notice that the **Great Friends Meeting House** has Ruby's tattoo parlor as a neighbor. Newport's oldest religious building, the meeting house dates from 1699 and is a reminder not only of the town's religious tolerance but also of the Quakers' status as the dominant religious group during the colony's first century. *Farewell and Marlborough Streets; 401-846-0813.*

Diagonally across from the meeting house grounds, tiny **Liberty Tree Park** may look like an ordinary patch of green, but historic events have taken place here. In

One of Newport's oldest buildings, the White Horse Tavern first opened its doors in 1673. (following pages) Shops and eateries along busy Thames Street.

the mid-18th century, Newport slaves were permitted to hold elections for a black governor, and they did so at the park. *Thames and Farewell Streets.*

Opposite the park is the **White Horse Tavern,** which opened its doors to the thirsty public in 1673 and remains one of the oldest surviving taverns in the United States. Its dark, creaky interior still has a delightfully insulating effect. The restaurant has not stayed in business by responding to every new fad. It has moved with the culinary times in the most intelligent way and presents superb food cooked using classic French methods supplemented by only the most judicious dash of American flair. At the top of narrow stairs, you enter what every restaurant should be: a cocoon. A pleasingly plump waiter glides around your table with graceful efficiency and a decorous manner that suggests that he is glad you are here. Jackets are appropriate in the evening. After cocktails, choose the signature dish, beef Wellington, or the New Zealand rack of lamb, fresh seafood specials, or orange-cognac glazed duck, among other entrées. Vegetarian dishes are also prepared. Check out the crème brûlée, the dessert wine, the cheeseboard, and the port, and you will float out onto the street after dinner. *26 Marlborough Street; 401-849-3600.*

On your postprandial walk, you can see the nearby **Wanton-Lyman-Hazard House.** Built circa 1670 and the oldest surviving house in Newport, it started out with two rooms straddling a central chimney. Over the years a lean-to kitchen was added, and in the late 18th century, when the Lymans lived here, a two-story addition to the rear of the house was erected to accommodate the family's 13 children. When the house was restored by the Newport Historical Society, that addition was removed. *17 Broadway.*

Follow Broadway from the Wanton-Lyman-Hazard House to **Washington Square,** Newport's center today, as it was in the colonial era. The **Newport Colony House** still dominates Washington Square from all angles. Completed in 1739 and one of Rhode Island's rotating state capitols from 1790 to 1900, this exquisite brick building is where Newport citizens celebrated the repeal of the Stamp Act in 1766 and, 10 years later, listened to a reading of the Declaration of Independence. (More recent drama involved the shooting of scenes from Steven Spielberg's film *Amistad.*) After many years of restoration work, the house has been opened to the public for tours. *Washington Square near start of Broadway.*

The colonials might feel right at home in the square, stopping in for a superb pint of Guinness in **Aidans** (1 Broadway; 401-845-9311), an authentic Irish pub in a 300-year-old building, or tasting the blueberry muffins at **Ocean Coffee Roasters** (22 Washington Square; 401-846-6060).

Much of the square, previously known as the Parade, would also be familiar to Oliver Hazard Perry, a naval hero of the War of 1812 whose feats are commemorated with a statue across from his mansion. The handsome neoclassical structure, known these days as the **Buliod-Perry House,** was built circa 1750 for a French Huguenot named Peter Buliod; Perry purchased it in 1818. As with many buildings of this era, most notably the Redwood Library, the wood exterior was fashioned to appear as though it were made of stone. *29 Touro Street.*

No such deception was employed in the creation of the large wooden building across Touro Court from the mansion. The structure has settled so comfortably on its 18th-century foundations that its facade now balloons exuberantly out onto the street and its windows seem ready to pop.

The first Spanish and Portuguese Jews arrived in Newport in the 1650s, some of them believed to be from the West Indies. At first, they worshiped in private homes,

The Newport waterfront.

but in 1763 the community built the **Touro Synagogue,** the oldest synagogue in North America and one where Sephardic Orthodox ritual is still followed. When George Washington addressed the newly enfranchised congregation here in 1790, he pledged that the United States "gives to bigotry no sanction, to persecution no assistance." The Revolution, though, had ruined the fortunes of shipping magnates like Aaron Lopez, and many Jewish families left Newport during the turmoil. Closed in the early 19th century, the synagogue reopened in the 1880s, when industrial expansion attracted new Jewish immigrants. *72 Touro Street; 401-847-4794.*

Intersecting at odd angles and rambling down toward the water, the tangle of streets above the waterfront seems to hoard the afternoon light, particularly in late autumn when the spire of **Trinity Church** appears illuminated by a spotlight. Built by Richard Munday in 1726 and in continuous use ever since, the Episcopal house of worship is one of the nation's most striking colonial churches. Trinity was modeled on Boston's Old North Church, and its triple-decker, center-aisle, wineglass pulpit is one of the few remaining in America from that period. *Spring Street at Queen Anne Square; 401-846-0660.*

During the summer, traffic often clogs these narrow side streets and hot summer nights are typically filled with the percussion of drums and the twang of bass guitars emanating from waterfront nightclubs. But on a spring, autumn, or even winter night, an evening stroll along Spring Street reveals another Newport. The town's gas streetlights—Newport introduced the country's first in 1803—illuminate the brick pavements with a warm, flickering glow, and the only sounds are the echo of your footsteps and the rustle of small nocturnal animals in the blown leaves.

Populated today with specialty stores and restaurants, **Thames Street,** parallel to Spring, nevertheless retains its archaic waterfront character. Home first to colonial artisans, the neighborhood soon attracted sea captains. The **Francis Malbone House** (392 Thames Street; 401-846-0392), built around 1758 and a fine example of a merchant town house, is now a bed-and-breakfast inn.

The Federal-style mansion of Samuel Whitehorne, one of Newport's last merchant kings, is now the **Samuel Whitehorne Museum.** Whitehorne, who made a fortune in banking, shipping, rum distilling, and probably slave trading, built the mansion in 1811, intending it to be the ultimate symbol of his success. Sadly for him, he never saw the house completed. Two of his ships were lost at sea, leaving him bankrupt; his house was turned into first a boardinghouse, then apartments, and, at its nadir, a laundry.

Slated for demolition in the late 1960s, the house was bought by the tobacco and electric-power heiress Doris Duke and restored with subtle good taste under her vigilant supervision by the Newport Restoration Foundation. Duke founded the organization in 1968, and today it maintains and rents 81 historic properties that might otherwise have been razed.

On the tour, you'll see photographs of the house at various stages of decay. The operators of the shoestring businesses that occupied this site may not have appreciated their environment, but they can be thanked for covering the walls and floors with temporary materials rather than ripping them out. The restorers found not only intact paneling and floorboards but also wallpaper fragments. Duke believed that the furniture produced by Newport craftsmen was best displayed in Newport houses, and the museum, which exhibits a portion Duke's collection of Newport and Rhode Island furniture, gloriously benefits from this enlightened philosophy. The dining room contains particularly fine Townsend and Goddard furniture, but each room in the house reveals its own unique treasures. *416 Thames Street; 401-849-7300.*

Trinity Church stands in the center of old Newport.

Chopped up for firewood during the Revolutionary War siege, Newport's rebuilt, crowded wharves resemble malls on stilts these days. But there are genuinely nautical things happening at the **International Yacht Restoration School** (458 Thames Street; 401-848-5777), which welcomes visitors. Part of the school occupies the Steam Mill Building, a textile mill built in 1831. You can sample genuinely good seafood in oilcloth-and-ketchup-bottle style at nearby **Salas's Restaurant** (345 Thames Street; 401-846-8772), and on Bowen's Wharf, at the **Aquidneck Lobster Company,** you catch a literal whiff of the old days as lobstermen unload the day's catch. Should you want to head out to the sea yourself, boats leave from this wharf and nearby Bannister's Wharf.

■ BELLEVUE AVENUE *map page 229, C-2/3*

Fortunately for Newport, the new rich who arrived here during the 19th century's Gilded Age had little interest in the old town, which was consequently spared their improving zeal. They preferred to indulge their tastes on Bellevue and Harrison Avenues and Ocean Drive, where several existing buildings represent their aristocratic fantasies come to life.

In the spring of 1926, few of America's wealthy imagined the rough times ahead, let alone the economic collapse of 1929. Lavish parties were the norm, and several of Newport's wealthiest residents built the **Hotel Viking,** at a cost of more than a half-million dollars, to accommodate the overflow of guests from the Newport mansions. The name was selected as a nod to the earlier and somewhat cruder visitors who reportedly landed in Newport around A.D. 1,000. No proof of such an incursion exists, though Viking zealots insisted for years that the curious stone tower in Touro Park is a Viking remnant. Variously known as the Old Stone Mill, Viking

The Hotel Viking in the 1930s. (Hotel Viking)

Tower, or simply Mystery Tower, the lumpy structure is now thought to date from around the mid-17th century. The Hotel Viking retains its elegance despite the fact that many of the guests milling around the foyer these days are dressed in casual sports gear that would have made the 1920s patrons blanch. On a breezy summer afternoon, lunch under the trees on the outside terrace is a delight, and a stay here feels like an indulgence in the great tradition. *1 Bellevue Avenue; 401-847-3300.*

A superb resource with an uninterrupted chain of service, the **Redwood Library,** established in 1747, is one of the nation's oldest lending libraries, sure to delight bibliophiles who resent the encroachment of computer banks, videos, and gourmet coffees onto bookshelves nationwide. There are no videotapes in the Redwood. There are, however, outstanding special collections that include the library's original volumes, purchased used in 1749, along with world-renowned books about 18th-century furniture and decorative arts and a Venetian Bible from 1487. Six Gilbert Stuart paintings, one a self-portrait, are among the 18th- and 19th-century portraits lining the walls.

Despite its impressive holdings and equally distinguished membership—which included the writers Henry James, Edith Wharton, Washington Irving, and Julia Ward Howe—the ambience here is friendly, not rarefied. Understanding staff smile reassuringly as you attempt to hug the card catalog. They beam when you are struck dumb by the intricate beauty of the Claggett clock, which was manufactured in 1728 and marks not only the time but also days of the week, phases of the moon, high tides, and other influences. (Ask about the clock's clever repeater chord, which chimes the nearest hour so its listeners can tell time in the dark.) Cool off in the library's charming gardens and contemplate what is surely one of the nation's finest colonial exteriors. This Palladian building, which Thomas Jefferson saw before he built Monticello, served as the prototype for many Federal-era buildings. *50 Bellevue Avenue; 401-847-0292.*

The Spanish tennis champion Arantxa Sanchez-Vicario once opined that "grass is for cows." But the green heart of the **Newport Casino** was planted for sporting rather than agricultural purposes. American tournament tennis was born on these grass courts in 1881, and impeccably clad Lawn Tennis Club members and visitors still pound the turf. In July, the Miller Lite Tournament stops here as part of the men's tennis tour, right after Wimbledon. For Newport's fashion leaders, the Casino was an elegant way of farming out social duties that had, by the late 19th century, become dizzying. As Lena Lancek and Gideon Bosker observe in *The*

Beach: The History of Paradise on Earth, "So energetically had the summer colony expanded by the late 1870's that hostesses were hard-pressed to keep up with the demands of social obligations—lawn parties, luncheons, tennis matches, dinner dances, and theatricals—much less orchestrate their own."

The art critic Mariana Griswold van Rensselaer judged the Newport Casino in its heyday as a "mere summer-house for 'society's' amusement." (The word "casino" comes from the Italian *cascina,* or "little house.") That may be, but architect Stanford White's country club is unpretentious and pleasingly airy, the beneficiary of a late-19th-century architectural fashion in which shingles and colonial motifs were used as a deliberate attempt to create an image based on indigenous precedents. McKim, Mead & White, responsible for some of Rhode Island's finest structures, was the torchbearer of this style. The Casino complex originally included a riding ring and a theater, where Oscar Wilde and Basil Rathbone appeared. Today the Casino houses the very fine **International Tennis Hall of Fame and Museum,** whose high- and low-tech exhibits chronicle the sport's growth and honor early heroes such as Bill Tilden and Althea Gibson, along with more recent inductees like Ivan Lendl and Pam Shriver. *194 Bellevue Avenue; 401-849-3990.*

The James family lived in Newport briefly when Henry, the 16-year-old budding novelist, was forming his literary opinions. He also served as a volunteer fireman and suffered what he referred to as an "obscure hurt" on duty, an injury that has preoccupied certain psychologists ever since. Though he was convinced that "Saratoga is a hotel, Newport is a realm," James, who first saw promise in Newport's architecture, later dismissed the proliferating mansions as "white elephants . . . queer and conscious and lumpish . . . really grotesque."

You don't have to be Jamesian to notice, as you proceed down Bellevue Avenue, that there is something out of scale about the creations in this palatial subdivision, where a French-style hunting lodge sits next door to an Italianate villa on land that seems to have shrunk around its occupants. Testaments not only to the wealth but to the competitive instincts of their owners, Newport's mansions—like the interminable movements of a Bruckner symphony—became increasingly elaborate as they built up to that great architectural crescendo, the Breakers, the New York

(top) Casino ground, Newport, ca. 1902 (Library of Congress); (middle) tennis on the grass, ca. 1891 (International Tennis Hall of Fame & Museum); (bottom) the Casino today.

The indomitable Alva Vanderbilt, in a pre-1900 photograph. (New-York Historical Society)

The Pleasures of Newport

I have sometimes wondered, in rational moods, why it is that Newport is so much appreciated by the votaries of idleness and pleasure. Its resources are few in number. It is extremely circumscribed. It has few drives, few walks, little variety of scenery. . . . Last evening, it seemed to me as I drove along the Avenue, that I guessed the answer to the riddle. The atmospheric tone, the careful selection of ingredients, your pleasant sense of a certain climatic ripeness—these are the real charm of Newport, and the secret of her supremacy. . . .

The villas and "cottages," the beautiful idle women, the beautiful idle men, the brilliant pleasure-fraught days and evenings, impart, perhaps, to Newport life a faintly European expression, in so far as they suggest the somewhat alien presence of leisure—"fine old Leisure," as George Eliot calls it. Nothing, it seems to me, can take place in America without straightaway seeming very American; and, after a week in Newport you begin to fancy that to live for amusement simply, beyond the noise of commerce or of care, is a distinctively national trait. . . . Individuals here, of course, have private cares and burdens . . . but collective society conspires to forget everything that worries. . . .

Behind the line of villas runs the Avenue, with more villas yet—of which there is nothing at all to say but that those built recently are a hundred times prettier than those built fifteen years ago, and give one some hope of a revival of the architectural art.

—Henry James, *Portraits of Places,* 1883

Vanderbilts' summer "cottage." The **Preservation Society of Newport County** (401-847-1000) provides information about the Breakers and, unless otherwise noted, maintains the mansions listed below. At any of the society's houses, you can buy a discount pass good for admission to several of them.

Kingscote and the Isaac Bell House *map page 229, C-2*
To put Newport's infectious excess in context, start with Kingscote (Bowery Street off Bellevue Avenue)—a relatively modest 1841 Gothic-style home designed by Richard Upjohn for the Savannah planter George Noble Jones. The wooden structure, with its distinctive towers and eaves and Tiffany windows, was the first summer residence to be built on Bellevue Avenue. The Isaac Bell House (Bellevue Avenue and Perry Street), erected in 1883, is a sterling example of shingle-style architecture. The restoration of the Bell House, which was designed by McKim,

The garden facade of the Elms. (Preservation Society of Newport County)

Mead & White, is ongoing, and tours provide a sense of the work that goes into bringing an architectural gem back to life.

The Elms   *map page 229, C-2*
Perhaps the most elegant of the great mansions, the Elms was built in 1901 for the coal magnate Edward Julius Berwind. The Philadelphia architect Horace Trumbauer designed the house, drawing his inspiration from the 18th-century Chateau d'Asnieres outside Paris. The furniture on display here is exceptionally fine, and the surrounding grounds, terminating in a beautiful sunken garden, bestow an expansive air that many neighboring mansions lack. Another reason to consider a visit to the Elms is the informative self-guided audio tour. *Bellevue Avenue and Perry Street.*

Chateau-sur-Mer   *map page 229, C-3*
Chateau-sur-Mer (Castle on the Sea), a gigantic granite block, threw down the gauntlet of style in 1852, when it proclaimed how profitable the China trade had been for William Shepard Wetmore. Its occupants also set the standard for entertaining, throwing an elaborate picnic for more than 3,000 people in 1857. Richard

Morris Hunt redesigned the house in the French Second Empire style in 1870, adding as a visual centerpiece a 45-foot-tall entrance hall illuminated by a stained-glass skylight. The house was featured in the PBS miniseries of Edith Wharton's novel *The Buccaneers,* based on the story of Consuelo Vanderbilt, whose mother, Alva Vanderbilt, engineered her daughter's marriage to the British Duke of Marlborough. In real life, Consuelo summered down the street at Marble House, and some of the festivities to celebrate her ill-fated marriage took place there. *Bellevue and Shepard Avenues.*

The Breakers *map page 229, C-2/3*
Cornelius Vanderbilt II used his railroad fortune to finance this 70-room Renaissance-style palace, designed by Richard Morris Hunt. The mansion, built between 1893 and 1895, dominates the headland at Ochre Point Avenue and even today allows its humble visitors the illusion of commanding the ocean that continually pummels the cliff below. A monument to opulence, the Breakers makes breathtaking use of alabaster, marble, gold leaf, antique woodwork, and mosaics, and contains furnishings from around the world. What's odd, though, is the comparative plainness—even dullness—of the Vanderbilt bedrooms. Clearly what mattered was making an impression downstairs. *Bellevue and Ochre Point Avenues.*

National Museum of American Illustration *map page 229, C-2/3*
Vernon Court, a French-influenced gem by Carrère and Hastings, the firm responsible for the New York Public Library and many of Manhattan's most noteworthy mansions, was opened to the public in the late 1990s as a museum dedicated to American illustration. Among the stars here are original oil paintings by N. C. Wyeth, Maxfield Parrish, Howard Chandler Christy, and Norman Rockwell, many of them used in books and magazines of the late 19th and early 20th centuries. The pièce de résistance of the tour is the Rose Garden Loggia, where most of the panels from

Miss Liberty *(1943), by Norman Rockwell.*

Parrish's *A Florentine Fete* (1911), commissioned for the ladies' dining room at the Curtis Publishing Company of Philadelphia, are installed. You must apply in advance to visit the museum. *492 Bellevue Avenue; 401-851-8949, ext. 16.*

Rosecliff *map page 229, C-3*

Newport's mansions are undeniably wonder-filled. Rosecliff, built in 1902 for the silver heiress Theresa Fair Oelrichs—her father was one of the three partners in Nevada's Comstock Silver Lode—was modeled by architect Stanford White on the Grand Trianon at Versailles. The mansion's noteworthy interior elements include its heart-shaped staircase and Newport's largest ballroom. Hollywood loves the perfectly proportioned Rosecliff: scenes from *High Society, The Great Gatsby, True Lies, Amistad,* and other films have been shot here. *Bellevue and Marine Avenues.*

Astors' Beechwood *map page 229, C-3*

An incurable Anglophile, Caroline Webster Schermerhorn Astor mimicked Queen Victoria and even crowned herself the "Queen of American Society." For most of the late 1800s, she reigned over the elite circle known as "the 400," whose membership supposedly comprised the number of socially acceptable people who could fit comfortably into her ballroom on New York City's Fifth Avenue (where the

The fountain and entrance of the perfectly proportioned Rosecliff.

Empire State Building now stands). Visiting the Astors' Beechwood mansion today, you become one of the 400, as actors from the Beechwood Theater Company portraying the family's staff and guests guide you through the house and even smuggle you into the servants' quarters. The year is 1891, twittery Miss Drexler describes one of Mrs. Astor's dinners, and you leave laughing—but resolving to dress more appropriately for your next visit. A pretty Victorian sprig muslin, perhaps. Beechwood also stages murder-mystery tours, Christmas feasts, and the Astor Ball. Astors' Beechwood is not maintained by the Preservation Society. *580 Bellevue Avenue; 401-846-3772.*

Marble House   *map page 229, C-3*
The Marble House cost William K. Vanderbilt, Cornelius Vanderbilt II's brother, $2 million to build and $9 million to furnish in 1892—the local press reported at the time that the marble alone cost $7 million. A harmonious concoction of Versailles-inspired salons, Siena marble hallways, and gilded everything, the house, designed by William H. Hunt, was a birthday gift from Vanderbilt to his wife Alva, but shortly after its completion she divorced him. Alva retained the house as part of the settlement, but shuttered it in 1896 when she married Oliver Hazard Perry Belmont, who lived down the road at Belcourt Castle. Upon Belmont's death, she reopened Marble House and added the sublime Chinese teahouse that overlooks the water. *Bellevue Avenue and Ruggles Street.*

Belcourt Castle   *map page 229, C-3*
Belcourt, designed by Richard Morris Hunt and completed in 1892, is now crammed with antiques that its current owners, the Tinney family, have collected. But Alva's mark endures. When Alva learned that most old English libraries have warped floors, for instance, she ordered that Belcourt's library floor be appropriately distorted. The deliberate hump remains. Her gargantuan dining room table from Marble House—marble, of course—and her bedroom set are also here, the flaking lace overhanging her bed seemingly held together by spider webs. For his part, Mr. Belmont installed Newport's first shower, insisted that his horses dress for dinner, and supplied them with embroidered bed linen. Hunt's gloomy hunting-château architecture and the Tinneys' obvious cash-flow problems—legal fees from a highly publicized contested-will case set them back a bundle—have contributed to the mansion's slightly spooky ambience of faded glory. *657 Bellevue Avenue; 401-846-0669.*

Rough Point *map page 229, C-3*

Touring Newport's mansions can be exhausting and somewhat numbing. Try to fit them all in and you end up with one big mess of mansion in your mind. Rough Point, however, stands out from the rest. The former home of Doris Duke, this beautiful granite and sandstone house stands on a dramatic, rocky peninsula on Bellevue Avenue and has been preserved—inside and out—to look as it did when Doris Duke lived here. (When she died in 1993, she bequeathed the house and its contents to the Newport Restoration Foundation.) Tour groups are ferried to the estate in a shuttle bus that departs from the Newport Visitors Center, near the waterfront. Tickets are relatively expensive ($25), and the tour size is kept deliberately small. Consequently, you feel like a visitor, not part of a herd, as you approach a house that could have been the model for Manderley in Daphne du Maurier's novel *Rebecca*. Duke's taste informs every item—from paintings by Renoir, Van Dyck, and Gainsborough to 16th-century Belgian tapestries, from the matching Ming urns to the clunky telephone and television—as surely as Rebecca de Winter's did in du Maurier's novel.

In 1887, Frederick William Vanderbilt, a grandson of Cornelius Vanderbilt I, bought the southeastern tip of Bellevue Avenue, long known as Rough Point, demolished the existing wooden dwellings, and commissioned an English Manorial–style mansion that was completed in 1889. One of the more private Vanderbilts, Frederick probably dreaded invitations to family bashes at the Breakers and breathed a sigh of relief whenever he returned to the Victorian gloom of Rough Point. When James B. Duke, one of the nation's wealthiest businessmen, bought the house for $200,000 in 1922, he engaged Horace Trumbauer to add new wings and generally lighten the interior. When James died in 1925, his estate passed to his only child, 13-year-old Doris, who was immediately known as "the richest girl in the world." Doris's mother, Natalie, presided over Rough Point until her death in 1962 while her daughter traveled abroad. But after 1962, Doris spent each year in Newport, often from May to September, adding to her art collection and involving herself in preservation projects. (A tall, distinctive woman who vainly attempted to conceal her identity behind dark glasses, she was a familiar figure at local auctions and loved poking around in downtown antique stores.)

(opposite) Corinthian columns front Marble House, Alva Vanderbilt's birthday gift.
(following pages) Doris Duke's Rough Point estate. (Newport Restoration Foundation)

Duke's private life fueled gossip and sold newspapers. But the sublime paintings, furnishings, and artifacts she collected and arranged so adroitly at Rough Point reveal a private life that was precisely that. Dinner parties were intimate, often casual affairs. Doris, an accomplished pianist, played for her guests. When Martha Graham came to stay, the two women spent hours walking backwards up the stairs to stretch their calf muscles. An arresting yet poignant portrait of Duke hangs on the stairway, and estate manager Philip Mello, who worked here for more than 30 years, recalls her telling him that sitting for the portrait ruined her entire summer, except for one day when the artist, John de Tosta, put the wrong end of the brush in his mouth. These and many other stories are related by your guide as you contemplate, among other wonders, the Flemish and English oak tables, the dozen 18th-century French chairs with original gilt and upholstery, the 16th-century German triptych, and the Ritz crackers on the rickety table in a sun room that looks out onto one of the loveliest views imaginable. Contact the Newport Restoration Foundation (401-849-7300) or the Newport Visitors Center (23 America's Cup Avenue; 800-326-6030) for ticket information. *Bellevue Avenue and Ocean Drive.*

Land's End   *map page 229, C-3*

Writing in the early 1870s, Julia Ward Howe advised that "some effort should be made to develop an intellectual side to the Newport season, which threatens to evaporate into mere gaiety." Cerebral endeavors remained a low priority, however. Between 1890 and 1914, the summer season at Newport was an exercise in excess. A single ball might cost more than $100,000, and flaunting was mandatory until the introduction of income tax, among other economic changes, signaled the end of the Gilded Age. Few writers portrayed that age as acutely as novelist Edith Wharton, who bought Land's End as a summer house in 1893. *The House of Mirth, The Age of Innocence,* and other Wharton novels dramatize the dangers of varying from a set social pattern, and some of her observations are drawn from her experiences at Newport. (Wharton's childhood neighbors in Newport called her "Lily," the name she gave the tragic Lily Bart of *The House of Mirth.*)

At Land's End, Wharton began collaborating with the Boston architect Osgood Codman Jr. on a house interior and garden design that would lead to their book *The Decoration of Houses.* Published in 1897, the book was a major influence on 20th-century decoration. During her time at Land's End, though, Wharton became disaffected with Newport society. Wrote her biographer R. W. B. Lewis of this period:

She had been perfecting her role of hostess and had at dinner a procession of Astors and Van Alens, Belmonts and Goelets; but she was becoming more depressed than ever by her Newport neighbors. They seemed to her, in her own phrase, hermetically sealed off from those cultural movements which in Europe, as she understood, touched and affected even the socially frivolous.

Wharton later decamped to the Mount, in Lenox, Massachusetts. Still a private residence, Land's End may be viewed from the shore when you travel past the mansions to the southern end of Bellevue Avenue and take Ledge Road to the left.

■ **THE CLIFF WALK AND OTHER DIVERSIONS** *map page 229, C-3*
One of the most remarkable trails on any American coast, the Cliff Walk starts at Easton's Beach and stops just beyond Land's End at Bailey's Beach. Ocean winds bully you from one side and mansions glower at you from the other. In between, cloudbanks of wild roses reassure you with their sweetness. Originally a fisherman's trail, the walk was barricaded by mansion owners but later restored to the public when fishermen's shore rights overruled money in court. In warm, clear weather, a stroll on Cliff Walk can make for a breathtaking afternoon.

Glowing with virtue and windburn, you should reward yourself by motoring along Ocean Drive, which provides continuous sea drama and passes by **Brenton Point State Park** (Ocean Drive west of Harrison Avenue) and the **Inn at Castle Hill** (590 Ocean Drive; 401-849-3800). One of Newport's best hostelries, the inn lays out an impressive Sunday brunch. Park in the lot here and walk down the lawn to the Castle Hill Lighthouse; the vistas include Jamestown, the Newport Bridge, and Newport Harbor. On a sunny day you can drink in this atmosphere from an Adirondack chair, sipping a cocktail or other beverage.

From Castle Hill, Ocean Drive curls back toward town, its name changing to Ridge Road, which eventually intersects with Harrison Avenue. Near the intersection is **Hammersmith Farm,** a 28-room mansion on Harrison Avenue built in 1887 by John W. Auchincloss. As a young girl, Jacqueline Kennedy Onassis, whose stepfather was an Auchincloss, vacationed here—and even helped tend the chickens. On harbor cruises you can see the replica of the windmill that was her summer playhouse as a youngster. John F. Kennedy and Jacqueline Bouvier's 1953 marriage at Saint Mary's Church, on Spring Street, was followed by a reception at Hammersmith Farm, which the Kennedys visited often during his presidency.

The Cliff Walk, with the Breakers in the background.

On a fine autumn afternoon, a picnic at **Fort Adams State Park** can seem nearly as elegant. Fort Adams hosts the Apple and Eve Newport Folk Festival and the JVC Jazz Festival each August. At other times, visitors bask in the salt-water bathing facilities and pursue sports such as fishing, boating, soccer, and rugby. Also at Fort Adams is the **Museum of Yachting** (401-847-1018), where the *Gilded Age of Yachting* exhibit chronicles the nautical exploits of the rich and famous. If you don't feel up to circumnavigating the globe afterwards, you can slip over to the other side of Newport Harbor and the Goat Island Marina to board the *Aurora,* Newport's largest schooner, for a harbor cruise. *Fort Adams Road off Harrison Avenue.*

■ **MIDDLETOWN AREA** *map page 205, C-2*

Middletown, to the north of Newport, has long been a transcendent place. Bishop George Berkeley, one of the fathers of modern metaphysical philosophy, lived here from 1729 to 1731, and the **Whitehall Museum House** evokes not only his life but also the turbulent Revolutionary days when Whitehall served as a tavern and billet for British soldiers. The house, which is open during the summer and occasionally the rest of the year, contains 18th-century antiques, and the adjacent garden is styled to that period as well. *311 Berkeley Avenue; 401-846-3116.*

To awaken your own metaphysical insights, explore the astonishing watery terrain of three open spaces in the Middletown area. The 450-acre **Norman Bird Sanctuary** (583 Third Beach Road; 401-846-2577), laced with easy-to-walk trails and an absolute stunner in autumn, encircles tiny ponds and jabs the ocean with its rocky fingers. The peninsula that contains the **Sachuest Point National Wildlife Refuge** (off Route 138; 401-364-9124) juts defiantly into Rhode Island Sound, and the 150-foot-deep **Purgatory Chasm** (Purgatory Road; 401-846-2119) is a narrow cleft on the east side of Easton Point. Fleets of migrating waterfowl crowd the bird sanctuary and refuge in spring and autumn, and Purgatory Chasm to the west attracts daring humans who enjoy watching the ocean's perpetual assault on this narrow gorge.

Route 138 between Newport and Middletown is a wasteland of strip malls and fast-food outlets. **Tommy's Diner** (159 East Main Road; 401-847-9834), a fetching example of its exuberant species, is the only redeeming feature. To taste local wines, head over to the **Newport Vineyards and Winery** (909 East Main Road; 401-848-5161), which you can also tour.

■ PORTSMOUTH *map page 205, D-1*

Banished from the Massachusetts Bay Colony in 1637 for "the troublesomeness of her spirit," Anne Hutchinson reached Portsmouth in 1638, accompanied by her husband, 16 children, and numerous followers. Established the previous year by John Clarke and William Coddington, the settlement pledged that no inhabitant would be found "a delinquent for doctrine" and began a sleepy existence. The idyll was interrupted by the Battle of Rhode Island in 1778. Historical markers indicate battle sites and the earliest encampment at Founder's Brook, near the intersection of Boyd's Lane and Route 24.

Portsmouth retains its soothing aspect. You can enter into the spirit of the place by visiting **Greenvale Vineyards,** where a few dozen acres along the Sakonnet River are devoted to grape cultivation and where the Victorian family farm is listed on the National Register of Historic Places. Tastings are offered in a stable, but you are not encouraged to snooze in the straw afterward. *582 Wapping Road (take Braman's Lane off Route 138); 401-847-3777.*

Inland, East Main Street passes through acres of farms and nurseries and plowed fields that slope down to the sea. **Glen Farm** gives you a sense of an 18th-century Rhode Island plantation. Now a public sports ground complete with polo field and equestrian center, the estate retains the tree-lined avenues and broad, level fields that characterized the colonial landscape. This is a great spot to have a picnic, go for a stroll, or simply enjoy the view. *Linden Lane off Route 138.*

For contrast, visit the **Green Animals Topiary Garden,** where the elephants, giraffes, dinosaurs, and other creatures are sculpted out of California privet, yew, and English boxwood hedges. There is a formal rose garden here, and you can tour the 19th-century estate house, which contains an enchanting collection of Victorian-era toys. *380 Cory's Lane, off Route 114; 401-847-1000.*

At the northernmost tip of the Portsmouth peninsula, you'll have to decide whether to head across the Sakonnet Bridge to Tiverton and Little Compton or hop on the Prudence Vehicle Ferry and ride north to Prudence Island. But as this is Rhode Island, it's easy to do both.

■ TIVERTON, LITTLE COMPTON, AND ADAMSVILLE
map page 205, D-1/2

There should be a flashing sign on the Sakonnet Bridge warning travelers of the beauty that lies ahead in Tiverton and Little Compton, on the east side of the Sakonnet River. From across the bridge, the region looks like a bland cutlet of land terminating in the bony tip of Sakonnet Point, but this is actually Rhode Island's most bewitching mainland secret. You start to suspect as much when you are halfway across the bridge. Below you, swans glide through the reeds, yachts bob on still water, and tree-fringed meadows roll their way into neighboring Massachusetts.

In spring and autumn, this quiet corner has the vaguely confused look of a farming community that would rather be fishing. As you follow Route 77 south along the coast from Tiverton, you notice upturned boats lying alongside dairy cattle in the fields or sunbathing on grassy hillocks. Few traces of the once-thriving textile industry remain. It is equally hard to imagine the charming fishing village of Tiverton in tumult. During the Revolutionary War, however, this was a mustering point for Colonial soldiers and the site of Maj. Silas Talbot's daring capture of the *Pigot,* a 200-ton British galley humiliated by Talbot's small sloop.

Antiques and housewares shops inhabit centuries-old structures in **Tiverton Four Corners.** On summer Sundays you can poke through the **Chase-Cory House** (3908 Main Road; 401-624-8881), an early-18th-century domicile whose exhibits provide clues about the hardscrabble ways of whaling captains and their families. The adjacent **Gray's Ice Cream** (16 East Road; 401-624-4500), a long-time area favorite for "cabinets," the local term for milkshakes, evokes no such tribulations. If you're feeling adventurous, forgo vanilla or strawberry and try a blueberry-ginger-flavored one instead.

Tiverton and Little Compton are perfect cycling country. To sample one of the best routes, head west on Neck Road at Tiverton Four Corners, circle Nonquit Pond, and branch out to beautiful Fogland Point (take Foghorn Road to High Hill Road) before returning to Route 77 on Pond Bridge Road. You can bicycle the 25 miles from Tiverton to Little Compton in about four hours without suffering. Afterward, reward yourself with a glass of **Sakonnet Vineyard** estate wine. New England's largest winery offers generous tastings, informative tours, cooking classes, and even bed-and-breakfast accommodations. *162 West Main Road, Little Compton; 401-635-8486.*

Tiverton Four Corners.

Fishing boats in Sakonnet Harbor.

The road from Sakonnet Vineyard to Sakonnet Point passes 18th-century houses and modest farms before reaching Little Compton, a town with a graveyard at its center. Note the gravestone whose inscription reads "Elizabeth, who should have been the wife of Simeon Palmer," a caustic reference by her husband to the fact that Elizabeth confined herself to housekeeping. The grave of the renowned Indian fighter Benjamin Church recalls the important role played by this region in King Philip's War, first when "squaw-sachem" Awashonks signed a peace compact with the British in 1675, and later when Church led the small group of soldiers who captured Metacom.

A very different encounter with Little Compton inhabitants occurred in 1936 when George Hibbett, a member of the Little Compton Historical Society and a professor of English at Columbia University, set out to obtain phonographic recordings of the speech mannerisms and accents of the town's oldest residents. Little Compton's relative isolation at that time made the group something of a cultural rarity in the region. Old-timers were invited to a story-swapping party and encouraged to exchange tales and reminiscences. They duly obliged. Subsequent analysis revealed the regional speech to be clipped and sharply staccato, with few or no traces of the northern New England accent. Examples of Little Compton's vernacular were "helpkeeper" for housekeeper, "showa" for shore, "hahly" for hardly, "krass-ligged" for cross-legged, and "lodge" for large. The records survive as part of the *Linguistic Atlas of the United States and Canada.*

Fishing boats and modest summerhouses huddle around Sakonnet Harbor, and beyond it the wind-whipped outcrop of Sakonnet Point holds its own against the encroaching ocean. When you turn inland toward Adamsville, the water seems to follow you, creating marshes and ponds visible through the trees. Pay your respects to the state bird, the Rhode Island Red hen, first imported from China and developed in Little Compton in the 1850s. It is now commemorated with a bronze plaque in the center of Adamsville.

Amble down the road a block to peruse the wares at **Gray's Store,** said to be the nation's oldest general store. Built in 1788 by Samuel Church, this is the sort of place where few items are ever discarded: Gray's still displays an ancient soda fountain, tobacco cases, and ice chest. The cheddar on sale is also aged, though not quite as much. *4 Main Street; 401-635-4566.*

■ **EAST BAY** *map page 205, D-1*

Head back toward Portsmouth on Route 24 but watch for signs to Mount Hope Bridge, which leads north across Narragansett Bay to Bristol and the East Bay region. The 14-mile East Bay Bike Path, along Narragansett Bay from Bristol to Providence, offers a relatively undemanding gradient and superb views. In Warren, north of Bristol, the smaller Warren Bike Path runs to the Massachusetts border.

■ **BRISTOL** *map page 205, D-1*
Genteel Bristol, a lively sailing town at the tip of the East Bay has an abundance of coffee shops and waterfront pubs. Along Hope, High, and Thames Streets are many fine 18th-century mansions, most of them built with profits from the slave trade. According to some estimates, more than 20 percent of all slaves crossed the Atlantic to colonial America in Rhode Island vessels, and Bristol slavers carried the largest percentage of that cargo. James DeWolf, the owner of a Cuban sugar plantation, was reputed to be the second-richest man in the United States at the end of his life. The house at 56 High Street (still a private residence) was built in 1793 to proclaim his wealth.

If thoughts of the DeWolfs and their associates sully your view of Narragansett Bay and Prudence Island, venture down the wooded path at **Blithewold Mansion, Gardens, and Arboretum,** whose notable attributes include a Japanese water garden, the largest redwood tree east of the Rockies, and a 45-room stone and stucco English-style mansion with period furnishings and treasures from the family's travels. From a small wooden landing at Blithewold you can observe the ocean dousing the setting sun and watch cormorants hurrying home from a day's gluttony. *101 Ferry Road; 401-253-2707.*

The story at the **Herreshoff Marine Museum** is also uplifting. John Brown Herreshoff, blind in one eye at birth, lost sight in his other eye during his teen years but went on to establish one of the nation's most important boat-building enterprises. By 1878, J. B., as he was known, had been involved in shipbuilding for nearly two decades, but that year he teamed up with his brother Nathanael to form the Herreshoff Manufacturing Co. Early products included the *Lightning* (1876), which was the first U.S. navy torpedo boat, and the *Gloriana,* considered by many the first modern yacht. Nathanael, who designed the *Gloriana,* went on to create six of the company's seven America's Cup–winning vessels and was renowned for his lightweight hulls and many other innovations. Dozens of vintage photographs document the company's accomplishments, and the Hall of Boats contains several dozen classic sailing and power vessels built between 1859 and 1947. *1 Burnside Street; 401-253-5000.*

To continue the nautical theme, take the short ferry ride to **Prudence Island,** a glorious conundrum, a beautiful, relatively undeveloped place in the middle of Narragansett Bay. Home to about 200 year-round residents and many deer, the roughly 6-mile-long, 2-mile-wide island has no hotels or restaurants and only two small stores. Bring lots to eat and drink and head north from the ferry to the pretty beach at Pine Hill Point. Follow the cart path to Providence Point, the island's northernmost tip. If this seems too ambitious, walk south from the Bristol Ferry landing to the Sandy Point Lighthouse, which overlooks a small beach, then a half-mile farther to reach a nature trail that brings you to the Heritage Foundation of Rhode Island Park, which forms the island's middle. *Ferry boarding: Church Street Wharf, near Thames Street, Bristol; 401-253-9808.*

You can stay on land and walk though **Colt State Park,** or pedal its paved 3-mile bike path. Off Route 114 on the north side of town, the park occupies the estate of Samuel Pomeroy Colt. The nephew of the famous gun maker from Hartford, Colt made his money in rubber and used some of it to create a farm here.

Still farther north is the **Audubon Society of Rhode Island Environmental Education Center,** a large interactive natural history museum whose exhibits include a life-size walk-through model of a whale that would put any greedy cormorant in his place. *1401 Hope Street (Route 114); 401-245-7500.*

■ **WARREN** *map page 205, D-1*
Route 114 continues north to Warren, worth a stop for its historic district, which includes the orange brick **Warren Town Hall** (Main and Croade Streets), built in the 1890s, and, across Croade Street, the **George Hail Library** (530 Main Street; 401-245-7686). Try to time your visit for a Wednesday afternoon, the only time the **Charles Whipple Greene Museum,** on the library's second floor, is officially open (though you can call for an appointment to visit at other times). The eclectic collection here includes colonial clothing, navigational and other tools, scrimshaw and china, and World War I helmets.

Warren is also known for institutions like the **Delekta Pharmacy and Soda Fountain** (496 Main Street; 401-245-6767), where the Delekta family has been brewing coffee cabinets since the 1940s. The pharmacy building itself has been standing since 1858 and still has its original ceramic-tile floor, pressed tin ceiling, and mahogany and marble soda fountain.

■ **BLOCK ISLAND** *map page 205, B-3*

A dollop of land measuring just 11 square miles, nibbled at and occasionally chewed by the Atlantic Ocean, Block Island, 12 miles off the Rhode Island coast, is one of New England's greatest wonders. You can see everything in a day, particularly in spring or autumn, when the summer crowds have retreated. But be prepared to stay forever. It is not simply the sound of the wind on an October night that will make you want to move here, or the complete darkness that swallows the road ahead and sharpens your hearing. It's the island's apparently infinite store of surprises that will draw you back time and time again.

Block Island has a turbulent history. Named *Manisses* ("Manitou's little island") by the Narragansetts, the island saw its first English settlement in 1661, was besieged during the French and Indian Wars, and was terrorized by deserters during the Revolutionary War. None of this is imaginable, however, as you stand on what feels like the edge of the world and look back on the beautiful landscape.

(following page) Mohegan Bluffs Natural Scenic Area.

More than 20 percent of Block Island is part of the Greenway trail network, preserved by the Nature Conservancy and cooperating island residents, and at least 40 rare species of bird and animal life thrive here. Hike through Rodman's Hollow, or across the Lewis-Dickens Farm Nature Preserve, both on Cooneymous Road. Harbor seals sunbathe in Cow Cove (near Settler's Rock) and loons giggle on Chaqum Pond. Walking the Clay Head Trail (off Corn Neck Road), you proceed along a honeysuckle-scented lane toward the distant artillery barrage of surf and suddenly emerge on a rock-strewn cove bounded by red cliffs. Admiring the 150-foot-high Mohegan Bluffs from Southeast Lighthouse, which has the most powerful beam on the eastern seaboard, you are startled by the resonant hiccup of an American bittern camouflaged in the reeds below. Even the wide, sandy strip of Crescent Beach, on the island's eastern shore, astonishes with its variety of sandpipers nervously avoiding the waves.

Another way to appreciate the island's interior is to rent a kayak at **Oceans & Ponds,** the kayak center at the Orvis store. The staff will give you a short lesson and then drive you to the dock in New Harbor, where you can glide off into the waters of Trims Pond, Harbor Pond, or the far bigger and windier Great Salt Pond. In the smaller ponds, you can bob alongside curious ducks and geese. More intimidating craft roar through Great Salt Pond, but Skipper's Island and Cormorant Point Cove are quiet havens. Nervous sailors may confine their explorations to Sachem's Pond, which allows only the tiniest ripple to disturb its smooth waters and sandy little beach. If you'd prefer not to wear yourself out paddling, take a two-hour scenic ocean cruise aboard *Ruling Passion,* a 45-foot trimaran. *Ocean and Connecticut Avenues; 401-466-5131.*

Block Island provides social pleasures to go with the natural ones. From May through September, the island's restaurants and lodgings are all open, and only pretentiousness is in short supply. The tiny **Bethany's Airport Diner** (Block Island State Airport; 401-466-3100) is a good place to enjoy off-season banter as you relish a fine breakfast. And as they put the magnificently ramshackle **Spring House Hotel** (52 Spring Street; 401-466-5844) to bed for the winter, the staff of this 1852 Victorian giant will happily fill you in on local history or gossip. Whether you are toying with a local seafood special with vegetables from the garden at the **Hotel Manisses** (401 Spring Street; 401-466-2421) or disappearing into the fisherman's platter at **Finn's Seafood Restaurant** (212 Water Street; 401-466-2473), overlooking the harbor on Water Street, you will be happy.

A wooden dory rests on the quiet Block Island waterfront, in front of hotels along Water Street.

■ TRAVEL BASICS

Getting Around: Interstate 95 runs diagonally across the middle of southern Rhode Island from Connecticut nearly to the coast before shooting north to Providence. Except when you're in a hurry, it should be avoided at all costs. The frequently more scenic Route 138 travels east–west across the middle of the region, crossing two islands (Conanicut and Aquidneck) as it passes through Jamestown, Newport, Middletown, and Portsmouth. U.S. 1 hugs the coastline from Westerly all the way up to Warwick. The **Block Island Ferry** (401-783-4613) serves Block Island year-round from Point Judith and during the summer from Providence, Newport, and New London, Connecticut.

Climate: Excepting stormy days along the coast, the climate in southern Rhode Island is only slightly milder than that in northern Rhode Island. Expect temperatures of 80 degree Fahrenheit in July and August and ones from the mid-50s to 70 degrees in the late spring and early fall. Winter temperatures can go below freezing, and severe storms occasionally overwhelm Block Island.

P R A C T I C A L
I N F O R M A T I O N

■ AREA CODES AND TIME ZONE

Connecticut's area codes are 203, from Greenwich to Waterbury; 860 in Hartford and areas west; and 959 in areas east of Hartford. The area code in all of Rhode Island is 401. Both states are in the Eastern time zone.

■ METRIC CONVERSIONS

1 foot = .305 meters   1 mile = 1.6 kilometers   1 pound = .45 kilograms
Centigrade = Fahrenheit temperature minus 32, divided by 1.8

■ CLIMATE/WHEN TO GO

Summers in Connecticut and Rhode Island can be hot and humid, with highs usualy around 80 degrees Fahrenheit along the coast and in the 90s inland. Spring can be rainy and windy and autumn is typically mild, with temperatures in the 60s and 70s. Winters can be cold, often dipping below freezing from December into March.

Many attractions in Connecticut and Rhode Island are open seasonally or, if open year-round, only for a few days or hours a week. So it's wise to call ahead before heading off for a visit. Some attractions are open only during the warmer months, usually from April or May to October or November, though ones on college or university campuses may be closed during the summer. Some of the historic houses and other buildings mentioned this book can only be visited on guided tours; you can save yourself time by calling ahead to find out when tours are being conducted.

■ GETTING THERE AND AROUND

■ BY AIR

Bradley International Airport (BDL), 12 miles north of Hartford, is Connecticut's main airport. *Schoephoster Road off I-91, Exit 40, Windsor Locks; 860-292-2000; www.bradleyairport.com.*

T. F. Green State Airport (PVD), 10 miles south of Providence, receives flights from international and domestic carriers. There are regional airports in Westerly, Newport, and Block Island. *U.S. 1, Warwick; 401-737-4000; www.pvdairport.com.*

New York City's **John F. Kennedy International Airport** (JFK; 718-244-4444) and **LaGuardia Airport** (LGA; 718-533-3400) are within a drive of an hour or two of many destinations in Connecticut. The Web address for both airports is www.panynj.gov/aviation.html. Boston's **Logan International Airport** (BOS; I-93 North, Exit 24; 617-561-1800; www.massport.com/logan), less than an hour's drive north of Rhode Island, receives flights from many domestic and some international carriers and is often a less expensive alternative to T. F. Green.

■ By Car

The principal driving routes through Connecticut are I-84, running diagonally northeast to southeast, and I-95, which follows the coast from Greenwich to Providence and then proceeds inland to Norwood. Interstate 91 runs north-south in the west, and I-395 runs north-south in the east. Route 9 runs from Hartford through the Connecticut River Valley to Old Saybrook. Scenic Route 169 winds through the northeast's tranquil Quiet Corner.

Interstate 95 provides the fastest route through Connecticut to Rhode Island (and through that state itself). Within Rhode Island, I-295 loops to the northwest of Providence and is a convenient route to the Blackstone Valley (exit north on Route 146) from southern Rhode Island. U.S. 1 travels more or less parallel to I-95 through the region.

■ By Bus

Bonanza Bus Lines has scheduled service to Hartford, Farmington, and Providence from Boston and New York. *800-556-3815; www.bonanzabus.com.*

Greyhound provides service to Connecticut and Rhode Island from many cities. *800-231-2222; www.greyhound.com.*

Peter Pan Lines serves major destinations along the eastern seaboard. *800-237-8747; www.peterpanbus.com.*

Rhode Island Public Transit Authority has bus routes throughout the state in addition to ferry service. *401-781-9400; www.ripta.com.*

■ **By Train**

Amtrak has service from New York to Boston, with Connecticut stops at Stamford, Bridgeport, New Haven, Mystic, New London, and Hartford. In Rhode Island, Amtrak serves Providence and Kingston, which is 18 miles from Newport. *800-872-7245; www.amtrak.com.*

Metro-North Railroad has service form New York to Greenwich, New Haven, New Canaan, Waterbury, and many other towns. There is no service to Rhode Island. *800-638-7646; www.mta.info.*

■ **By Bicycle**

For information about cycling around Connecticut, contact the Connecticut Bicycle Coalition. *1 Union Place, Hartford; 860-527-5200; www.ctbike.org.*

For information about Rhode Island cycling, visit the tourism division's Web site. *www.visitrhodeisland.com/recreation/biking.html.*

Bicycling through Wickford.

■ FOOD

Connecticut's most sophisticated restaurants (and correspondingly steep prices) are found in shore towns like Greenwich and Westport, in the Litchfield Hills, and, in a more casual form, in smaller towns like Guilford and Stonington. Longtime New England dishes such as pot roast have surrendered the field to nouvelle cuisine and California light, but no-frills diners and rickety seafood restaurants serving less fancy cuisine survive alongside their more fashionable neighbors.

Providence is renowned for its Italian restaurants, Newport for culinary landmarks like the White Horse Tavern. But Rhode Island as a whole provides a superb choice of seafood and ethnic and plain old Yankee cuisine, in quirky establishments that range from the clam shacks of Galilee to Gourmet Foods of Wickford. Regional specialties include johnnycakes—griddle-cooked corn cakes originally known as "journey cakes" because of their portability—and the indigenous clam, or quahog, which may be fried, stuffed, eaten raw, or served in a chowder.

Connecticut and Rhode Island also have well-established wineries, many of which also serve excellent food. In recent years, many brew pubs have opened.

■ LODGING

Connecticut offers everything from luxury spas and sumptuous inns to monolithic hotels and drab motels. Generally speaking, the closer you are to New York City the more you will pay and the more frills you can expect. Historic inns in towns like Greenwich and Westport, for example, and wealthy enclaves like the Litchfield Hills have elevated pampering to an art form. Hartford, New Haven, Bridgeport, and other cities have the usual large hotels and chain motels; modest bed and breakfasts and casual inns are more common in the smaller coastal towns like Madison and in the rural villages of the northeastern corner.

Rhode Island's tourist accommodations are concentrated mostly along the coast. Splendid, if faded, old resort hotels survive, particularly around Watch Hill and on Block Island, where bed-and-breakfast accommodations can still mean a room in somebody's house. Tiny motels and holiday cabins are also common along the coast to Narragansett. Providence has chain hotels and more intimate inns in the city's historic district, and Newport has every form of accommodation imaginable, from grand hotels to affordable motels and inns. Some of the fanciest lodgings are former Gilded Age mansions.

■ RESERVATIONS SERVICES
B&B Ltd. *203-469-3260.*
Newport Reservations. *800-842-0102.*
Nutmeg B&B Agency. *860-236-6698; www.bnb-link.com.*

■ HOTEL AND MOTEL CHAINS
Best Western. *800-528-1234; www.bestwestern.com.*
Choice Hotels. *800-424-6423; www.choicehotels.com*
Crowne Plaza. *800-227-6963; www.crowneplaza.com*
Days Inn. *800-325-2525; www.daysinn.com.*
Doubletree. *800-222-8733; www.doubletree.com.*
Hampton Inn. *800-426-7866; www.hamptoninn.com*
Hilton Hotels. *800-445-8667; www.hilton.com.*
Holiday Inn. *800-465-4329; www.6c.com.*
Hyatt Hotels. *800-233-1234; www.hyatt.com.*
Marriott Hotels. *800-228-9290; www.marriott.com.*
Radisson. *800-333-3333; www.radisson.com.*
Ramada Inns. *800-272-6232; www.ramada.com.*
Sheraton. *800-325-3535; www.sheraton.com.*
Westin Hotels. *800-228-3000; www.westin.com.*

■ CAMPING

Most campgrounds in Connecticut and Rhode Island have showers, toilet facilities, and picnic shelters adjacent to campsites. Many campsites are located within or near parks with hiking trails, lakes, and bird-watching areas.

Campground Owners Association. *860-521-4704; www.campconn.org.*
Connecticut Camping Association. *860-456-1032; www.ctcamps.org.*
Connecticut State Parks Division of Parks and Forests. *860-424-3200; dep.state.ct.us/stateparks.*
National Recreation Reservation Service. (For sites managed by the U.S. Forest Service and the Army Corps of Engineers.) *877-444-6777; www.reserveusa.com.*
Recreational Service. (For sites managed by the Bureau of Land Management.) *www.recreation.gov.*

■ OFFICIAL TOURISM INFORMATION

Connecticut. *800-282-6863; www.ctbound.org.*
Rhode Island. *401-222-2601; www.visitrhodeisland.com.*

Blackstone Valley. *401-724-2200; www.tourblackstone.com.*
Central Connecticut. *860-225-3901; www.centralct.org.*
Coastal Fairfield County. *203-899-2799; www.coastalct.com.*
Connecticut River Valley. *860-347-0028; www.cttourism.org.*
Hartford. *860-244-8181; www.enjoyhartford.com.*
Housatonic Valley. *203-743-0546; www.housatonic.org.*
Litchfield Hills. *860-567-4506; www.litchfieldhills.com.*
Mystic Coast and County. *800-692-6278; www.mycoast.com.*
New Haven. *203-777-8550; www.newhavencvb.org.*
Northeast Connecticut. *860-779-6383; www.ctquietcorner.org.*
Northern Rhode Island. *401-334-1000; www.nrichamber.com.*
Providence. *401-274-1636; www.providencecvb.com.*
Waterbury. *203-597-9527; www.waterburyregion.com.*

■ USEFUL WEB SITES

Connecticut Ornithological Society. Rare-bird alerts. *www.ctbirding.org.*
Connecticut Post. The state's biggest daily newspaper. *www.connpost.com.*
Department of Transportation. Road conditions, traffic cams. *www.dot.state.ct.us.*
Freedom Trail. Historic sites of the American Revolution. *www.ctfreedomtrail.com.*
New Haven Advocate. Regional weekly. *www.newhavenadvocate.com.*
Newport Daily News. Rhode Island daily. *www.newportdailynews.com.*
Preservation Society of Newport County. Maintains a dozen of Newport's famed "cottages." *www.newportmansions.org.*
Providence Journal. News from the city's biggest daily. *www.projo.com.*
Providence Preservation Society. All about the city's art and architecture. *www.providencepreservation.org.*
Visit New England. What to see and do in the region. *www.visitnewengland.com.*
Wine Trail. Winery itineraries and other info. *www.ctwine.com.*
Yankee Publishing. New England history, lore, and lifestyles. Tips and resources. *www.newengland.com.*

■ Festivals and Events

■ February

Newport Winter Festival. Food, music, games, ice sculpting, and a children's fair. *401-847-7666; www.newportevents.com.*

■ March

Kinsale Festival of Fine Food, Newport. Chefs from Newport's sister city, Kinsale, Ireland, show off their cuisine. *800-976-5122; www.gonewport.com.*

■ June

International Festival of Arts and Ideas, New Haven. This festival brings together artists and thinkers from around the world for art shows, performances, lectures, and other events. *888-278-4332; www.artidea.org*

Great Chowder Cook-Off, Newport. Top chefs from across the nation compete. *401-846-1600; www.newportfestivals.com.*

Rose and Garden Weekend, Hartford. Elizabeth Park Rose Garden displays, plus garden tours at area mansions. *860-244-8181.*

■ July

New England Arts and Crafts Festival, Milford. New England artisans sell their handmade goods on the town green, and there's food, music, and entertainment. *203-878-6647; www.milfordarts.org.*

■ August

JVC Jazz Festival, Newport. Long-running fest attracts musicians from around the world. *401-847-3700; www.festivalproductions.net/jvc/newport.*

Milford Oyster Festival. Great craft fair on town green; entertainment near the harbor; oysters and seafood for sale. *203-878-5363; www.milfordoysterfestival.org.*

Mystic Outdoor Art Festival. Sidewalk art show has more than 300 artists selling their work, plus food and entertainment. *860-572-5098.*

New Haven Train Show. Connecticut's biggest train show, with more than 300 displays. *203-239-1346; www.afstrains.com/show.htm*

Newport Folk Festival. Trendsetters and traditionalists perform at this renowned music fest. *401-847-3700; www.newportfolk.com.*

Woodstock Fair. Arts and crafts, food, entertainment, rides, games, and cattle and dairy shows. *860-928-3246.*

■ **SEPTEMBER**

Housatonic Dulcimer Celebration, New Milford. Musicians from around the world converge on the town. *860-669-5618.*

Newport International Boat Show. Yachts, powerboats, sailboats, nautical products. *401-846-1115; www.newportexhibition.com.*

Woodbridge Arts & Crafts Fair. Handmade items, fine art. *203-483-8562.*

■ **OCTOBER**

Haunted Newport. Halloween haunted-house tours and graveyard walks. *www.hauntednewport.com.*

Octoberfest, Newport. Bavarian music, food, biergarten, crafts. *401-846-1600; www.newportfestivals.com.*

■ **DECEMBER**

Christmas in Newport. Tree-lighting parties, crafts, candlelight house tours, and other events. *401-849-6454; www.christmasinnewport.org.*

Festival of Trees and Traditions, Hartford. Yuletide tree-cutting at the Wadsworth Atheneum. *860-278-2670.*

INDEX

COMPASS AMERICAN GUIDES

Alaska	Las Vegas	Pennsylvania
American Southwest	Maine	San Francisco
Arizona	Manhattan	Santa Fe
Boston	Massachusetts	South Carolina
Chicago	Michigan	South Dakota
Coastal California	Minnesota	Tennessee
Colorado	Montana	Texas
Florida	Nevada	Utah
Georgia	New Hampshire	Vermont
Gulf South: Louisiana, Alabama, Mississippi	New Mexico	Virginia
	New Orleans	Wine Country
Hawaii	North Carolina	Wisconsin
Idaho	Oregon	Wyoming
Kentucky	Pacific Northwest	

ACKNOWLEDGMENTS

■ FROM THE AUTHOR

I am grateful to Kit Duane, the lead editor of Compass Southern New England, from which this book derived, for her patience, precision, and sense of humor; to photographer Jim Marshall for being an inspired and inspiring co-conspirator; to Jim Aaron, Daniel Aaron, Katherine A. Powers, and Julie Graham for advice and assistance; to Annabel Davis-Goff for encouragement; to Trisha Howells for technical and moral support.

Thanks to the staff of the following libraries and research institutions: Connecticut Historical Society, Hartford; Mystic Seaport, Mystic; Redwood Library, Newport; Rhode Island Historical Society, Newport; Providence Athenaeum, Providence; and the Society for the Preservation of New England Antiquities, Boston. Thanks also to Nina Stack at Block Island Tourism and Evan Smith and Kathyrn Farrington at Newport County Convention & Visitors Bureau.

■ FROM THE PUBLISHER

Compass American Guides would also like to thank Connecticut resident Susan Volanth for her editorial contributions, Rachel Elson for copyediting the manuscript, and Ellen Klages for proofreading it.

All photographs are by James Marshall unless otherwise credited below.

Alfred A. Knopf, Inc., p. 39; Bettman/Corbis, p. 32 (BE023014); Buttolph-Williams House, p. 116; Mark G. Cappitella, p. 133; Coastal Fairfield County Convention & Visitor Bureau, p. 65; Connecticut Historical Commission, p. 36; Connecticut Historical Society, p. 46; Foxwoods Resort Casino, p. 143; Carol Glover, p. 213; Hempsted Houses, p. 90; Rob Heyl, p. 124; Hill-Stead Museum, p. 122 (photo by Ray Hope, Meyers Studio); Robert Holmes, p. 136; Hotel Viking, p. 238; International Tennis Hall of Fame & Museum, Newport, Rhode Island, p. 241; John Carter Brown Library, Brown University, p. 18; John Hay Library, p. 39; Library of Congress, p. 228; Library of Congress, Cabinet of American Illustration, p. 221 (LC-USZ62-24268); Library of Congress, Daguerrotype Collection, p. 64 (LC-USZ62-109908); Library of Congress, General Collections, p. 30; Library of Congress, Historic American Buildings Survey, p. 29; Library of Congress, Prints and Photographs Division, pp. 24 (LC-USZ62-15057), 70 (LC-USZ262-92126), 194 (LC-USZ62-105999),

Critics, booksellers, and travelers all agree: you're lost without a Compass.

"This splendid series provides exactly the sort of historical and cultural detail about North American destinations that curious-minded travelers need."
—*Washington Post*

"This is a series that constantly stuns us...no guide with photos this good should have writing this good. But it does." —*New York Daily News*

"Magnificent photography. First rate."—*Money*

"Written by longtime residents of each destination...these handsome and literate guides are strong on history and culture, and illustrated with gorgeous photos."
—*San Francisco Chronicle*

"History, geography, and wanderlust converge in these well-conceived books."
—*Raleigh News & Observer*

■ ABOUT THE AUTHOR

Anna Mundow has lived and traveled in New England since 1983. A native of Ireland, she is a correspondent for the *Irish Times* and a book critic for the *Boston Globe.* She is a regular contributor to *Newsday* and has provided commentary on BBC Radio, Monitor Radio, and WGBH television. The author of *Compass Southern New England,* Mundow has also written for the *Los Angeles Times, Mirabella, Boston Magazine,* the *Manchester Guardian,* and many other publications.

■ ABOUT THE PHOTOGRAPHER

James Marshall began making photographs as a teenager in his basement darkroom. Since 1978 he has traveled extensively throughout Asia, North America, and Europe, covering events and documenting cultures. Along the way, he produced and edited *Hong Kong: Here Be Dragons; A Day in the Life of Thailand;* and *Planet Vegas: A Portrait of Las Vegas.* After nearly 20 years in New York and Connecticut, in 1997 he moved to the coast of Maine, where he especially enjoys the fish chowder.